See what other readers had to say about
Chicken Soup for the Soul:
Christmas Cheer!

Chicken Soup for the Soul has another winner with this book full of
Christmas cheer! A great read for children of all ages,
from 90 days to 90 years.
~*Mr. Santa Claus*

We heartily endorse *Chicken Soup for the Soul: Christmas
Cheer* for its heartwarming, humorous, and joyous stories
of the holiday season.
~*The North Pole News Times*

While we normally prefer to eat carrots,
this chicken soup made my whole family glow.
~*Rudy Olph*

What a fabulous collection of stories from real people, celebrating
everything about Christmas, from family traditions, to the joy of
giving, to a reminder of what Christmas is really about. What a
great Christmas present for the whole family.
~*Elf Ladies Auxiliary Committee*

I confess that I liked it.
~*E. Scrooge*

Chicken Soup for the Soul
for the Soul®
Christmas Cheer

Our **101** BEST STORIES

With love, to

Jill

From

Santa

Date

Dec 25 - '08

Chicken Soup for the Soul® Our 101 Best Stories:
Christmas Cheer; Stories about the Love, Inspiration, and Joy of Christmas
by Jack Canfield, Mark Victor Hansen & Amy Newmark
Published by Chicken Soup for the Soul Publishing, LLC   www.chickensoup.com

The publisher gratefully acknowledges the many publishers and individuals who
granted Chicken Soup for the Soul permission to reprint the cited material.

Cover illustration and interior illustration of Santa Claus courtesy of ShutterStock.com/©
Victorian Traditions. Background cover illustration courtesy of iStockPhoto.com/mstay.
Back cover photo courtesty of Jupiter Images/Photos.com. Interior background illustration
courtesy of iStockPhoto.com/maljuk

Cover and Interior Design & Layout by Pneuma Books, LLC
For more info on Pneuma Books, visit www.pneumabooks.com

Distributed to the booktrade by Simon & Schuster. SAN: 200-2442

Publisher's Cataloging-in-Publication Data
(Prepared by The Donohue Group)

Chicken soup for the soul. Selections.

   Chicken soup for the soul : Christmas cheer : stories about the love,
inspiration, and joy of Christmas / [compiled by] Jack Canfield [and] Mark
Victor Hansen ; [edited by] Amy Newmark.

   p. ; cm. -- (Our 101 best stories)

   ISBN-13: 978-1-935096-15-3
   ISBN-10: 1-935096-15-X

1. Christmas--Literary collections. 2. Christmas--Anecdotes. I. Canfield, Jack,
1944- II. Hansen, Mark Victor. III. Newmark, Amy. IV. Title. V. Title: Christmas
cheer

PN6071.C6 C5 2008
808.8/033   2008935338

PRINTED IN THE UNITED STATES OF AMERICA
on acid∞free paper
16 15 14 13 12 10 09 08   01 02 03 04 05 06 07 08

Chicken Soup for the Soul

Christmas Cheer

Our **101** BEST STORIES

Stories about the
Love, Inspiration, and
Joy of Christmas

Jack Canfield
Mark Victor Hansen
Amy Newmark

CSS

Chicken Soup for the Soul Publishing, LLC
Cos Cob, CT

Chicken Soup for the Soul

Contents

❶

~The True Meaning of Christmas~

❷

~Christmas through the Eyes of Children~

3
~The Spirit of Giving~

4
~Holiday Humor~

❺
~Special Holiday Memories~

❻
~Holiday Traditions~

❼
~The Santa Files~

❽
~Lessons from Christmas Past~

❾
~The Love of Family~

Chicken Soup for the Soul

A Special Foreword

by Jack and Mark

*F*or us, 101 has always been a magical number. It was the number of stories in the first *Chicken Soup for the Soul* book, and it is the number of stories and poems we have always aimed for in our books. We love the number 101 because it signifies a beginning, not an end. After 100, we start anew with 101.

We hope that when you finish reading one of our books, it is only a beginning for you too – a new outlook on life, a renewed sense of purpose, a strengthened resolve to deal with an issue that has been bothering you. Perhaps you will pick up the phone and share one of the stories with a friend or a loved one. Perhaps you will turn to your keyboard and express yourself by writing a Chicken Soup story of your own, to share with other readers who are just like you.

This volume contains our 101 best stories and poems about Christmas and that wonderful time of year. We share this with you at a very special time for us, the fifteenth anniversary of our *Chicken Soup for the Soul* series. When we published our first book in 1993, we never dreamed that we had started what became a publishing phenomenon, one of the best-selling series of books in history.

We did not set out to sell more than one hundred million books, or to publish more than 150 titles. We set out to touch the heart of one person at a time, hoping that person would in turn touch another person, and so on down the line. Fifteen years later, we know that it has worked. Your letters and stories have poured in by the hundreds of thousands, affirming our life's work, and inspiring us to continue to continue to make a difference in your lives.

On our fifteenth anniversary, we have new energy, new resolve, and new dreams. We have recommitted to our goal of 101 stories or poems per book, we have refreshed our cover designs and our interior layout, and we have grown the Chicken Soup for the Soul team, with new friends and partners across the country in New England.

We are not alone in loving the Christmas holiday season. We love reuniting scattered family members, watching the wonder on the face of a child, seeing the look of joy on the face of a gift giver. The rituals of the holiday season give a rhythm to the years and create a foundation for our family lives. We love the chance to gather with our communities at church, at school, and even at the mall, to share the special spirit of the season, brightening those long winter days.

In this new volume, we have selected our 101 best stories and poems about Christmas and the holiday season. We hope you will laugh and cry and marvel as much as we did while reading them, and that will share them with your families and friends. We have identified the 41 *Chicken Soup for the Soul* books in which the stories originally appeared, in case you would like to read more stories about families, faith, parenting, and the other seasons of our lives. We hope you will also enjoy the additional books in "Our 101 Best Stories" series.

With our love, our thanks, and our respect,
~*Jack Canfield and Mark Victor Hansen*

Chapter 1

The True Meaning of Christmas

Christmas — that magic blanket that wraps itself about us,
something so intangible it is like a fragrance.
It may weave a spell of nostalgia.
Christmas may be a day of feasting, or of prayer,
but always it will be a day of remembrance —
a day in which we think of everything we have ever loved.

~Augusta E. Rundel

Double Angels

Be an angel to someone else whenever you can,
as a way of thanking God for the help that another angel has given you.
~The Angels' Little Instruction Book
by Eileen Elias Freeman

Waking up to the sound of my alarm, I smiled at the joy of only having to wait one more day. I got out of bed and threw some clothes on. Digging around the kitchen for some breakfast, I settled on a bowl of Cheerios and some leftover pizza from the night before. After watching cartoons, playing some video games and chatting on-line with some friends, it suddenly hit me that I hadn't bought a present for my mom. It was Christmas Eve, and the stores were going to be closing pretty soon. So I threw some shoes on, grabbed my skateboard and set off to the mall.

I swung open the heavy glass door into the mall only to see an incredible sight. People were running and panicking everywhere, trying to find the perfect gift for their loved ones. It was total madness. I decided to begin trying to make my way through the crowds when a guy in a black coat came up to me and told me with desperation in his voice that he had lost his brown leather wallet. Before I could say a word, he shoved his gray business card into my hand.

"Please call me at the number on the card if you happen to find it," he said. I looked at him, shrugged my shoulders and replied, "Yeah, no problem. I'll do that."

He turned to stop another person, and I continued to make my way through the unending stream of shoppers to look for a gift for my mom. I searched everywhere, up and down the mall in every store, with no luck. Finally, toward the very end of the mall, I spotted a small antique and glass-art store. It looked like it might have some interesting stuff—not the same as I'd seen in every other store. I figured I had nothing to lose so I went in.

Papers and boxes had been thrown everywhere from all the greedy Christmas shoppers digging around for the perfect gifts. It was pretty bad. It looked like a dirty bedroom with smelly clothes scattered around in it. As I tried to make my way through the pile of stuff, I tripped over a box in the aisle and fell flat on my face. I was so frustrated and worn out from shopping that I stood up, screamed and kicked the box. It flew through the air and hit a big, high-priced clay statue, almost knocking it over. My anger had gotten the best of me, but luckily no harm was done.

As I picked up the box to put it back on the shelf, I noticed a flat, green box hidden under some wrapping paper. I opened it up to find an amazing glass plate with a Nativity scene on it. There it was, the perfect gift, just lying in some trash waiting for me to find it. It felt like one of those moments when you hear angels singing hallelujah and beams of light stream down right over the place where you're standing. I smiled broadly, gathered it up and headed for the cash register. As the cashier was ringing up my purchase, I reached into my pocket to get my money. But my pocket was empty! I began to scramble around searching every pocket when I realized I had left my wallet at home. This was my last chance to get my mom a gift since the mall would be closing in ten minutes and it was Christmas Eve. It would take me twenty minutes to skate home and back. That's when I started to panic. Now what do I do? I silently asked myself.

So I did the only thing I could think of at that moment: I ran outside the store and started to beg people for money. Some looked at me like I was crazy; others just ignored me. Finally, giving up, I slumped down on a cold bench feeling totally defeated. I really had no idea what to do next. With my head hanging down, I noticed that one of my shoes was untied. Great, I thought. All I'd need now is to trip over my shoelace and break my neck. That'd be the perfect ending to this useless trip.

I reached down to tie my shoe when I spotted a brown wallet lying next to the front leg of the bench. I wondered if it could be the wallet that the man in the black coat had lost. I opened it and read the name on the driver's license inside. Yep. It was his. Then my mouth dropped in awe when I discovered three hundred dollars inside.

I never even questioned what I should do. I knew that I had to do the right thing, so I found a nearby pay phone and made a collect call to the number on the gray business card. The man answered and said that he was still in the mall. He sounded really happy and relieved. He asked me if I would meet him at the shoe store, which happened to be right next to the antique and glass store. When I got there, the man was so excited that he thanked me over and over while he checked to see if his money and credit cards were still there.

I turned to drag myself out of the mall and back home when I felt the man grab my shoulder. Turning to face him, I let him know that I hadn't taken anything. "I can see that," he replied. "I don't think I've ever met a kid like you who would return all that money when he could have taken it without anybody knowing." Then he opened up the wallet and handed me four twenty-dollar bills, thanking me again.

In great excitement, I leaped into the air and shouted, "Yes!" I thanked him this time and told him I had to hurry and go get my mom a present before the mall closed. I made it to the store just as they were getting ready to lock up. The lady was really nice about it and let me in.

I bought the glass plate and started skating home, grateful that everything had worked out. I found myself whistling Christmas carols as I replayed the evening over in my head. Suddenly, it hit me. I realized that I had been sort of a Christmas angel for the man who had lost his wallet, and that he had been the same for me when I'd forgotten mine. Double angels! I thought. It was another one of those moments when choirs of angels begin to sing and beams of light shine down on you. I knew that I'd never forget this Christmas Eve for as long as I lived.

The next morning, my mom opened my "miracle present." The look on her face assured me that she really loved it. Then I told her all about what happened when I was trying to get her gift. The story made the plate even more special to her.

Still, to this day, she keeps that green glass plate on our main shelf as a centerpiece. It reminds her of me, of course, but it continues to remind me that amazing things can happen when you least expect them. Especially during that magical time called Christmas.

~David Scott
Chicken Soup for the Soul Christmas Treasury for Kids

An Elf's Tale

One can pay back the loan of gold,
but one dies forever in debt to those who are kind.
~Malayan Proverb

It was six o'clock at the mall, and I was as exhausted as an elf on Christmas Eve. In fact, I was an elf and it was Christmas Eve. That December of my sixteenth year, I'd been working two jobs to help my parents with my school tuition and to make a little extra holiday money. My second job was as an elf for Santa to help with kids' photos. Between my two jobs, I'd worked twelve hours straight the day before; on Christmas Eve, things were so busy at Santaland that I hadn't even had a coffee break all day. But this was it—only minutes more, and I'd have survived!

I looked over at Shelly, our manager, and she gave me an encouraging smile. She was the reason I'd made it through. She'd been thrown in as manager halfway through the season, and she'd made all the difference in the world. My job had changed from stress-filled to challenging. Instead of yelling at her workers to keep us in line, she encouraged us and stood behind us. She made us pull together as a team. Especially when things were their craziest, she always had a smile and an encouraging word. Under her leadership, we'd achieved the highest number of mall photo sales in California.

I knew it was a difficult holiday season for her—she'd recently suffered a miscarriage. I hoped she knew how great she was and what a difference she'd made to all her workers, and to all the little children who'd come to have their pictures taken.

Our booth was open until seven; at six, things started to slow down and I finally took a break. Although I didn't have much money, I really wanted to buy a little gift for Shelly so that she'd know we appreciated her. I got to a store that sold soap and lotion just as they put the grate down. "Sorry, we're closed!" barked the clerk, who looked as tired as I was and didn't sound sorry at all.

I looked around and, to my dismay, found that all the stores had closed. I'd been so tired I hadn't noticed.

I was really bummed. I had been working all day and had missed buying her a present by one minute.

On my way back to the Santa booth, I saw that Nordstrom was still open. Fearful that they, too, would close at any moment, I hurried inside and followed the signs toward the Gift Gallery. As I rushed through the store, I began to feel very conspicuous. It seemed the other shoppers were all very well-dressed and wealthy—and here I was a broke teenager in an elf costume. How could I even think I'd find something in such a posh store for under fifteen dollars?

I self-consciously jingled my way into the Gift Gallery. A woman sales associate, who also looked as if she'd just stepped off a fashion runway, came over and asked if she could help me. As she did, everyone in the department turned and stared.

As quietly as possible, I said, "No, that's okay. Just help somebody else."

She looked right at me and smiled. "No," she said. "I want to help you."

I told the woman who I was buying for and why, then I sheepishly admitted I only had fifteen dollars to spend. She looked as pleased and thoughtful as if I'd just asked to spend $1500. By now, the department had emptied, but she carefully went around, selecting a few things that would make a nice basket. The total came to $14.09.

The store was closing; as she rang up the purchase, the lights were turned off.

I was thinking that if I could take them home and wrap them, I could make them really pretty but I didn't have time.

As if reading my mind, the saleslady asked, "Do you need this wrapped?"

"Yes," I said.

By now the store was closed. Over the intercom, a voice asked if there were still customers in the store. I knew this woman was probably as eager to get home on Christmas Eve as everybody else, and here she was stuck waiting on some kid with a measly purchase.

But she was gone in the back room a long time. When she returned, she brought out the most beautiful basket I'd ever seen. It was all wrapped up in silver and gold, and looked as if I'd spent fifty dollars on it—at least. I couldn't believe it. I was so happy!

When I thanked her, she said, "You elves are out in the mall spreading joy to so many people, I just wanted to bring a little joy to you."

"Merry Christmas, Shelly," I said back at the booth. My manager gasped when she saw the present; she was so touched and happy that she started crying. I hoped it gave a happy start to her Christmas.

All through the holidays, I couldn't stop thinking about the kindness and effort of the saleswoman, and how much joy she had brought to me, and in turn to my manager. I thought the least I could do was to write a letter to the store and let them know about it. About a week later, I got a reply from the store, thanking me for writing.

I thought that was the end of it, until mid-January.

That's when I got a call from Stephanie, the sales associate. She wanted to take me to lunch. Me, a fifteen-dollar, sixteen-year-old customer.

When we met, Stephanie gave me a hug, and a present, and told me this story.

She had walked into a recent employee meeting to find herself on the list of nominees to be named the Nordstrom All-Star. She was confused but excited, as she had never before been nominated. At the point in the meeting when the winner was announced, they called Stephanie—she'd won! When she went up front to accept the award, her manager read my letter out loud. Everyone gave her a huge round of applause.

Winning meant that her picture was put up in the store lobby, she got new business cards with Nordstrom All-Star written on them, a 14-karat gold pin, a 100-dollar award, and was invited to represent her department at the regional meeting.

At the regional meeting, they read my letter and everyone gave Stephanie a standing ovation. "This is what we want all of our employees to be like!" said the manager who read the letter. She got to meet three of the Nordstrom brothers, who were each very complimentary.

I was already a little overwhelmed when Stephanie took my hand. "But that's not the best part, Tyree," she said. "The day of that first store meeting, I took a list of the nominees, and put your letter behind it, with the 100-dollar bill behind that. I took it home and gave it to my father. He read everything and looked at me and said, "When do you find out who won?"

"I said, 'I won, Dad.'"

"He looked me right in the eye and said, 'Stephanie, I'm really proud of you.'"

Quietly, she said, "My dad has never said he was proud of me."

I think I'll remember that moment all my life. That was when I realized what a powerful gift appreciation can be. Shelly's appreciation of her workers had set into motion a chain of events—Stephanie's beautiful basket, my letter, Nordstrom's award—that had changed at least three lives.

Though I'd heard it all my life, it was the Christmas when I was an elf—and a broke teenager—that I truly came to understand that the littlest things can make the biggest difference.

~Tyree Dillingham
A 5th Portion of Chicken Soup for the Soul

Christmas Magic

Blessed is the season
which engages the whole world in a conspiracy of love!
~Hamilton Wright Mabie

I wish I could tell you that the whole thing happened because I'm caring and unselfish, but that wouldn't be true. I had just moved back to Wisconsin from Colorado because I missed my family and Denver wages were terrible. I took a job at a hospice in Milwaukee and found my niche working with the patients and families. As the season changed into fall, the schedule for the holidays was posted:

DECEMBER 24: 3-11 Barbara
DECEMBER 25: 3-11 Barbara

I was devastated. Newly engaged, it was my first Christmas back home with my family after many years. But with no seniority, I had little clout to get Christmas off while my dedicated colleagues worked.

While lamenting my predicament, I came up with an idea. Since I couldn't be with my family, I would bring my family to the hospice. With the patients and their families struggling through their last Christmases together, maybe this gathering would lend support. My family thought it was a wonderful plan, and so did the staff. Several invited their relatives to participate, too.

As we brainstormed ideas for a hospice Christmas, we remembered the annual 11:00 P.M. Christmas Eve service scheduled in the hospital chapel.

"Why don't we take the patients to church?" I suggested.

"Yes," replied another staff nurse. "It's a beautiful candlelight service with music. I bet the patients would love it."

"Great. And we can have a little party afterwards, with punch, cookies and small gifts," I added.

Our enthusiasm increased as we planned the details of our hospice Christmas celebration.

Now, it never occurred to me that all these great ideas might not float so well with the administration. It never occurred to me that we might have to get permission for each of these activities—until the director called me into her office.

"Uh, Barb, I'm hearing rumors of a Christmas Eve celebration here at the hospice."

"Well, yes," I replied. Eagerly, I outlined all the plans and ideas the staff had developed. Fortunately for my career, she thought involving our families with the unit activities was a wonderful idea, too.

"But," she said, "certainly you are not serious about taking the patients to church. It has never been done."

"Yes, I'm serious. It would mean a lot to the patients and families."

"Very seldom do you see any patients at this service, and if they do go, they are ambulatory and dressed." She shook her head. "Our patients are too sick to go."

"But a number of them have indicated an interest," I argued.

"I cannot authorize the additional staff needed."

"The family members can help."

"What about the liability?"

Now I felt like saying, "What could be the worst thing that could happen—someone dies in church?" But I didn't. I just kept convincing her, until she begrudgingly gave approval.

Christmas Eve arrived. Family members gathered in the lounge and decorated a small tree, complete with wrapped packages. Then we implemented our plan for the staff and families to transport the patients to the chapel. While most of the patients had family members with them, one young girl had no one. At just nineteen, Sandy had terminal liver cancer. Her mother had died of cancer three years previously, and her father stopped coming long ago. Perhaps he couldn't sit by the bedside of another loved one dying so young. So my family "took charge" of Sandy. My sister combed her hair while my mother applied just a hint of lipstick. They laughed and joked like three old friends as my fiancé helped her move to a gurney.

Meanwhile, other nurses hung IVs on poles, put IVACs on battery support and gave last-minute pain meds. Then, with patients in wheelchairs and on gurneys, we paraded our group into the chapel just as they were finishing "Joy to the World," with the organ and bells ringing out in perfect harmony. Silence descended on the congregation as we rolled slowly down the aisle. The minister just stood there with his mouth open, staring. Everyone turned around to look at us. We faltered in our steps, each movement echoing in the large, crowded chapel.

Then the magic began.

One by one, people stood up, filed into the aisle and began to help us. They handed patients hymnals and distributed programs. They wheeled patients to the front so they could see well. They handed out candles to be lit for the closing hymn. One woman adjusted Sandy's pillow and stroked her hair. Throughout the service, the congregation catered to our patients, guiding them through the worship.

The beautiful service closed with a candlelight recessional to "Silent Night." Voices rang in disjointed harmony as the congregation assisted us in exiting the chapel and returning our charges to the unit. Many stayed to share punch and cookies and stories.

As I got Sandy ready for bed that late night, she whispered, "This was one of the nicest Christmases I ever had."

When I shared her comments with my family later, we realized the magic that evening was on many levels. The unit had a special climate we'd never experienced before. Sandy had one of the best

Christmases she'd ever known. The congregation had shared in a special, caring way. But we also realized that this evening impacted our family as well. We felt closer, bonded in purpose and spirit.

Since that Christmas, my family has been blessed with many Christmases together—but I think that one was the best. Like the author Bill Shore, I, too, believe that when you give to others and give to the community, you create something within yourself that is important and lasting. He calls it the "Cathedral Within."

Our family cathedral is a little stronger for the privilege of giving that Christmas.

~Barbara Bartlein
Chicken Soup for the Nurse's Soul

The Christmas Rose

God gave us memories that we might have roses in December.
~J.M. Barrie, Courage

A light snow was falling as she turned the key to open Rose's Flower Shop. The name didn't take much imagination, but then it was better than "Rosie's Posies" as Clint had suggested when she had first begun the business.

"Going to the Towers again this year?" asked Cass Gunther, who was opening the European deli next door.

Rose nodded. It was what they did every year. Supper and drinks at the club and Christmas Eve at the posh Park Towers. Swimming. The hot tub. Maybe take in a show. It was a tradition.

She turned on the lights, feeling bone-tired. As usual, people waited until the last minute to place their Christmas orders. Why did she do this every year? It wasn't the money, though business had gone well. It filled her days, and there was something soothing about working with flowers.

"I'll be home for Christmas..." the sentimental lyric wafted from the radio under the counter. Home was four extravagantly-decorated walls, which she welcomed at the end of the day, but when it came down to it, what was really there for her? Perhaps if they'd been able to have children. They'd had a reasonably good marriage, the best house on Carriage Drive, money in the bank and enough friends to keep them from feeling lonely. And goodness knows they were too busy to think about whether or not they were happy. Bills for the mortgage, the car and boat, and a half dozen credit cards never stopped.

Rose sighed. A hollowness plagued her. Even anticipating Clint's surprise when he received the Pendleton sport coat she'd bought held little joy. His gift to her would be something beautiful, expensive... but she couldn't remember last year's gift or when they had taken time to really talk to each other.

She felt suddenly at odds, cross. Perhaps if they'd kept up with the family. But family meant Clint's two aunts in Virginia and her stepfather in Wyoming, none of whom seemed famished for their company. Hungry, that was it. She'd forgotten to eat breakfast.

The bell over the door announced a customer, but she kept her back to the counter, consulting the order book.

"Excuse me, Miss," an elderly voice called from behind her.

I haven't been a Miss in fourteen years, thank you. She swallowed the caustic retort and turned slowly to find an old man smiling at her.

He had all his teeth, a look of kind apology and a full head of wavy white hair. He held a plaid cap across his chest and gave her a quaint little bow like an aging Sir Galahad. "I'm looking for some flowers—for my wife."

At those words, something luminous lit him from within. She wondered if Clint ever looked that way when he spoke about her. "I see," she said slowly, waiting.

He tapped gnarled fingers over his cap in meditation and with warm authority in his raspy voice said, "Not just any flowers. It must be Christmas roses."

"Well, we have roses. American beauty, reds, pink, tea and yellow...."

"Oh, no," he said, shifting his weight from one foot to the other. "Christmas roses—white as snow—with some of that feathery fern tucked in. And I'd like a big red bow, too."

"It's Christmas Eve, sir, and I'm afraid we're fresh out...."

"My wife loves white roses," he continued, looking at something she couldn't see. "They remind her of the Babe of Christmas and the purity of his heart. She hasn't seen any roses for such a long time. And now that..."

The old man's shoulders drooped ever so slightly, then straightened again. Rose heard the faint tremor and was touched by something beautiful in the old face that made her think of alabaster. No, alabaster was too cold.

"She's ill now...." He paused and tucked his cap under his arm. "We served at a medical clinic in West Africa for more than thirty years. But we've had to return home. Nell has Alzheimer's. We're living at Country Gardens...."

"Oh, I'm sorry," Rose breathed.

The man rushed on without a trace of bitterness. "I have a little room on the floor just below the nursing wing where Nell is. We share meals together—and we have our memories. God has been good to us."

Rose returned his smile, uncomprehending, but unable to deny the man's sincerity. White roses on Christmas Eve? She might be able to get them from Warrensville, but it would be a stretch.

"We'll be spending Christmas Eve in my room—just the two of us—a celebration," he was saying. "Christmas roses for Nell would make it perfect."

"I may be able to get them sent over from Warrensville...." Rose bit her lip. Was she crazy? It would take a miracle. Then there was the price. "How much do you want to spend?"

The man set his cap on the counter and dug out a faded wallet from his trousers that had seen several winters. He pushed four five-dollar bills toward her with childlike eagerness, then seeing her dismay, hesitated. "I hope it's enough."

"I could give you a nice spray of red roses in a bud vase," Rose began. White rose centerpieces would start at thirty-five dollars. Then the delivery charge would run another twenty, especially on Christmas Eve. If she could get them!

"I had hoped for a real special bouquet..." he broke off, and she read his profound disappointment.

"Leave it to me. I'll do my best to get you something nice," she began, astounded by her own words.

"Bless you!" the old man said, reaching across the counter and grasping her hands. "Can they be delivered around four or five? It will be such a surprise! I can't thank you enough." Nearly dancing, he replaced his cap and began backing toward the door. "Arnold Herriman—Room 7! Merry Christmas! God bless you! God bless you!"

What had a tired old man with a sick wife have to be so happy about? She puzzled over that through the next few orders, then placed a call to a supplier in Warrensville. They could get her a dozen white roses at $42.50—but it would be four o'clock before they could be relayed to her shop.

"Okay," she said wearily, realizing that she herself would have to deliver the Christmas roses to Mr. Herriman. No matter. Clint would likely be delayed by a promising client.

The flowers arrived at ten minutes to four, and Rose quickly arranged them in a silver bowl, tucking in the feathery greens and sprigs of baby's breath and holly. She secured a lacy red bow into the base and balanced it in one hand while locking the door with the other.

Country Gardens hardly resembled its name. Surely a couple who'd spent a lifetime healing the sick in an obscure village deserved better in the sunset of their years.

She found the residential wing and tentatively approached Room 7. Arnold Herriman, in the same old trousers and shirt, with a crimson tie, beamed at her. She entered a room with a few pieces of old furniture and walls bursting with pictures and certificates. On the hall table was a crèche. The Babe of Christmas and the purity of his heart, Herriman had said.

A diminutive woman sat on the sofa with hands folded over a patchwork quilt on her lap. She had a translucent complexion and vacant blue eyes above two brightly rouged cheeks. A bit of red ribbon had been tucked into her white hair. Her eyes widened, then spilled with tears when she saw the flowers.

"Nell, darling. It's your surprise — Christmas roses," Arnold said, placing an arm around the woman's fragile shoulders.

"Oh, how lovely!" Nell stretched out her arms, her face transformed in radiance. She rubbed one wrinkled cheek against the delicate petals, then turned a watery gaze on Rose. "Do I know you, dear?"

"This is the nice lady from the flower shop who made your bouquet," Arnold said.

"Can you stay for a while, dear?" she asked. "We'll be finished with our patients soon, and we'll take you to our house for tea."

"Oh, no..." stammered Rose.

Arnold touched his wife's shoulder. "The patients are all gone, dear. We're home, and it's Christmas Eve."

Rose's throat ached with unshed tears and the sense that something beautiful lived here from which she was excluded. Could it be that in living their lives for others, these two old people who had nothing but each other and a bouquet of white roses had everything that was important?

Suddenly, Nell plucked one of the long-stemmed white roses from the elegant bouquet and held it out to Rose. "Please, I have so many. You must take one for yourself!"

"Yes," Arnold said, taking the stem from his wife and pressing it toward her, "thank you for all your trouble. God bless you."

She wanted to say that he already had, that bringing them the Christmas roses had made her happier than she could remember in a long time, that on this Christmas Eve she had learned something about the meaning of the holiday she had missed until now.

~Lt. Col. Marlene Chase
Chicken Soup for the Soul Christmas Treasury

My Best Christmas

It is Christmas in the heart that puts Christmas in the air.
~W.T. Ellis

The holidays are heading my way this year with the usual frenetic rush. There's so much to celebrate that I can't help pausing every now and then and pinching myself to make sure it's all real.

I've been promoted in my job at a Portland, Oregon, apartment complex. My twin daughters, Deirdre and Caitlin, both have happy memories and challenging careers. And Caitlin and her husband, Matt, have settled close to my home, which is a joy. Combine this with the recent arrival of my first grandchild, and it's going to be an especially blissful Christmas.

Yet no matter how wonderful our holiday is, there's no way it can possibly top my best Christmas ever. Paradoxically, that came during the worst year of my life—a year that taught me some profound lessons about giving and receiving and realizing what I already had.

It happened when I was struggling through the financial and emotional morass that follows a very difficult divorce. I had the girls, thank goodness. But I also had a car that wouldn't run, a house that was in danger of being repossessed, and a marginal job that wasn't keeping up with the bills. Because of the house and the car and my job, I was told I was ineligible for food stamps. We were in serious trouble.

By December, we didn't have much money left, and the power company was threatening to shut off service. I had nothing to spend on the girls for the holidays. I do have a flair for handcrafting things, so I made a few whimsical gifts from scraps we had around the house. But there would be no new clothes or bicycles or any of the popular toys my children had seen advertised on TV appearing under our tree. There would certainly be no special treats, no holiday feast with all the trimmings. I found myself staring at the worst Christmas of our lives.

My large extended family had helped a little—and could have helped a lot more, if they'd known the extent of our plight. But the divorce had left me feeling like a failure, and I was too humiliated to let anyone know just how desperate things had become.

Soon, my bank account and credit completely dried up. With no food and no money, I swallowed my pride and asked the girls' elementary school principal for help. The kindly woman put Deirdre and Caitlin, then ten years old and in fourth grade, on the government-subsidized lunch program. She even arranged it so the children could go to the school's office each day to pick up their lunch tickets, which looked just like everyone else's. My daughters never knew.

I thought things couldn't get any worse, but about a week before Christmas, my employer, a painting contractor, stunned me by shutting down operations for the holidays and telling me I was laid off. The girls left for school, and I stayed home to battle my despair in the private gloom of a dark, snowy day.

That afternoon, a car pulled into the driveway. It was the school principal—the same woman who had helped me put Deirdre and Caitlin on the lunch program. In the car, she had a giant foil-wrapped gift box for us. She was so respectful of my feelings. "Now, Jill, I want you to know that every person who signs up for the lunch program automatically gets one of these around the holidays," she said. "It's just something the school district does."

As soon as she left, I set the box on my dining room table and discovered that it contained all we needed for a fine holiday meal.

There were also two bright pink boxes, each containing a Barbie doll.

I was hiding the dolls in a closet when Deirdre and Caitlin came home from school. Through the window, they saw the big box on the table and came racing in the door squealing gleefully and jumping up and down.

Together, the excited girls went through the box, admiring everything. There was fresh fruit, canned vegetables, candies, nuts, cookies, chocolates, a large canned ham and much more. I felt so elated, as if all my burdens had been lifted—or at least the stress over how we were going to make it through the holidays had been. Then Deirdre asked where the box had come from.

As I gently explained that it had come from the school district, Deirdre's whole demeanor quickly changed. She stepped back and looked down. "Oh, Mom," she finally said after a prolonged silence. "This is so nice, but they've made a terrible mistake. They meant to give this to a poor family."

Rather awkwardly, I tried to tell her that the three of us, at least temporarily, were indeed poor. But Caitlin chimed in with Deirdre. "No, they must have meant this for someone who really needs it. Someone needy."

A sinking feeling swept over me as the girls began to ponder the dilemma of whom to give the box to. I didn't stand in their way, but a touch of despair came creeping back. Selfishly, I thought, what am I going to do? I have almost nothing to give them for Christmas.

The girls finally settled on giving the box to an elderly neighbor named Juanita, who worked in a nearby laundry and lived alone in a dilapidated old house down the street. Its wood-burning stove—her only source of heat—had broken down, and Juanita had been ill lately. Even her dog was sick.

Deirdre and Caitlin repacked the gift box and hefted it out to the garage. There, beside the broken-down Volvo, they put the cargo on Deirdre's red wagon.

I watched through the kitchen window as my two girls, clad in coats and scarves and smiles from earmuff to earmuff, pulled the heavy wagon toward Juanita's house. Suddenly, the snowy street began to sparkle, and a little sunlight broke through that dark sky. I stood there with goosebumps and began to realize the beauty and meaning of what was happening, and it changed everything.

I began to feel joy. Today, fifteen Christmases later, I still treasure the warm blessing the girls and I received in a note from Juanita. And now, as Deirdre and Caitlin—two college-educated, successful, grown women—start families of their own, I finally feel ready to share my story and tell them some things they didn't know about that year of the big gift box.

The truth is, it was a great Christmas. Thanks to them, it was the best of my life.

~Jill Roberts
Chicken Soup for the Christian Family Soul

The Gift of Grr-Face

It isn't the size of the gift that matters,
but the size of the heart that gives it.
~The Angels' Little Instruction Book
by Eileen Elias Freeman

The mother sat on the simulated-leather chair in the doctor's office, picking nervously at her fingernails.

Wrinkles of worry lined her forehead as she watched five-year-old Kenny sitting on the rug before her.

He is small for his age and a little too thin, she thought. His fine blond hair hung down smooth and straight to the top of his ears. White gauze bandages encircled his head, covering his eyes and pinning his ears back.

In his lap he bounced a beaten-up teddy bear. It was the pride of his life, yet one arm was gone and one eye was missing. Twice his mother had tried to throw the bear away to replace it with a new one, but he had fussed so much she had relented. She tipped her head slightly to the side and smiled at him. It's really about all he has, she sighed to herself.

A nurse appeared in the doorway. "Kenny Ellis," she announced, and the young mother scooped up the boy and followed the nurse toward the examination room. The hallway smelled of rubbing alcohol and bandages. Children's crayon drawings lined the walls.

"The doctor will be with you in a moment," the nurse said with an efficient smile. "Please be seated."

The mother placed Kenny on the examination table. "Be careful, honey, not to fall off."

"Am I up very high, Mother?"

"No dear, but be careful."

Kenny hugged his teddy bear tighter. "Don't want Grr-face to fall either."

The mother smiled. The smile twisted at the corners into a frown of concern. She brushed the hair out of the boy's face and caressed his cheek, soft as thistledown, with the back of her hand. As the office music drifted into a haunting version of "Silent Night," she remembered the accident for the thousandth time.

She had been cooking things on the back burners for years. But there it was, sitting right out in front, the water almost boiling for oatmeal.

The phone rang in the living room. It was another one of those "free offers" that cost so much. At the very moment she returned the phone to the table, Kenny screamed in the kitchen, the galvanizing cry of pain that frosts a mother's veins.

She winced again at the memory of it and brushed aside a warm tear slipping down her cheek. Six weeks they had waited for this day to come. "We'll be able to take the bandages off the week before Christmas," the doctor had said.

The door to the examination room swept open, and Dr. Harris came in. "Good morning, Mrs. Ellis," he said brightly. "How are you today?"

"Fine, thank you," she said. But she was too apprehensive for small talk.

Dr. Harris bent over the sink and washed his hands carefully. He was cautious with his patients but careless about himself. He could seldom find time to get a haircut, and his straight black hair hung a little long over his collar. His loosened tie allowed his collar to be open at the throat.

"Now then," he said, sitting down on a stool, "let's have a look."

Gently he snipped at the bandage with scissors and unwound it from Kenny's head. The bandage fell away, leaving two flat squares of gauze taped directly over Kenny's eyes. Dr. Harris lifted the edges of the tape slowly, trying not to hurt the boy's tender skin.

Kenny slowly opened his eyes, blinked several times as if the sudden light hurt. Then he looked at his mother and grinned. "Hi, Mom," he said.

Choking and speechless, the mother threw her arms around Kenny's neck. For several minutes, she could say nothing as she hugged the boy and wept in thankfulness. Finally she looked at Dr. Harris with tear-filled eyes. "I don't know how we'll ever be able to pay you," she said.

"We've been over all that before," the doctor interrupted with a wave of his hand. "I know how things are for you and Kenny. I'm glad I could help."

The mother dabbed at her eyes with a well-used handkerchief, stood up and took Kenny's hand. But just as she turned toward the door, Kenny pulled away and stood for a long moment, looking uncertainly at the doctor. Then he held his teddy bear up by its one arm to the doctor.

"Here," he said. "Take my Grr-face. He ought to be worth a lot of money."

Dr. Harris quietly took the broken bear in his two hands. "Thank you, Kenny. This will more than pay for my services."

The last few days before Christmas were especially good for Kenny and his mother. They sat together in the long evenings, watching the Christmas tree lights twinkle on and off. Bandages had covered Kenny's eyes for six weeks, so he seemed reluctant to close them in sleep. The fire dancing in the fireplace, the snowflakes sticking to his bedroom windows, the two small packages under the tree—all the lights and colors of the holiday fascinated him. And then, on Christmas Eve, Kenny's mother answered the doorbell. No one was there, but a large box was on the porch wrapped in shiny gold paper with a broad red ribbon and bow. A tag attached to the bow identified the box as intended for Kenny Ellis.

With a grin, Kenny tore the ribbon off the box, lifted the lid and pulled out a teddy bear—his beloved Grr-face. Only now it had a new arm of brown corduroy and two new button eyes that glittered in the soft Christmas light. Kenny didn't seem to mind that the new arm did not match the other one. He just hugged his teddy bear and laughed.

Among the tissue in the box, the mother found a card. "Dear Kenny," it read. "I can sometimes help put boys and girls back together, but Mrs. Harris had to help me repair Grr-face. She's a better bear doctor than I am. Merry Christmas! Dr. Harris."

"Look, Mother," Kenny smiled, pointing to the button eyes. "Grr-face can see again—just like me!"

~Gary Swanson
Chicken Soup for the Soul Christmas Treasury

Santa in Disguise

*You can't live a perfect day without
doing something for someone who will never be able to repay you.*

~John Wooden

I scratched my thumbnail across the thick white frost that covered the window. With my eye pressed against the cleared spot, I could see the outside thermometer hanging against the weather-beaten siding. It read a chilling twenty degrees below zero. Inside, it didn't feel much warmer. Frozen condensation creeping down the walls looked liked last night's leftover spaghetti noodles.

Because we couldn't yet afford a furnace, I had stuffed newspapers into the center of the old pot-bellied stove and piled them high with logs. The flick of the match was the beginning and also the end.

John gulped a half-cup of coffee, grabbed a slice of toast and hurried off to his job at the paper mill. Three-year-old Anne and two-year-old Michael sat huddled together, waiting patiently for a cup of hot cocoa.

I poked another log into the stove and felt the cozy warmth replace the cold that chilled every bone in my body. That's when I heard a strange noise. At first, it sounded like the rustling of crumbling newspapers, but it grew louder and began to roar.

I yanked open the door leading to the vacant upstairs and shrieked as I saw huge yellow and blue flames devouring the walls.

Everything blurred. I heard frantic voices and then someone crashed through the front door.

"Your house is on fire. We have to get you and the kids out of here."

A neighbor wrapped the children in blankets and carried them to her car. I snatched the phone and called my father.

Functioning on automatic pilot, I carried out a drawer containing important papers. Ignoring the danger, I charged back inside. With Christmas just five days away, I was determined to rescue the suit I'd purchased for John. It had taken me fifty weeks to pay for it. A stranger grabbed my arm and dragged me out of the house.

My dad notified the mill, and John returned home. In less than an hour, all that remained of our house was the chimney standing in the center of a pile of smoldering ashes.

The next few days were chaotic. We'd moved in temporarily with my parents. The phone and doorbell rang constantly. Everyone, friends and strangers alike, wanted to help. The donated clothes in one of the spare bedrooms eventually replenished the Red Cross inventory. My friends from the Home Bureau replaced my canned goods from their own shelves.

A day before Christmas, the owner of Carl's Auto Supply Store called, "I'd like to see you and your husband this afternoon at five o'clock. Can you come?"

I couldn't imagine what he wanted, but I told him we'd be there.

Mr. Carl was known around town as Mr. Scrooge. He sold auto parts for cash only. He sold seasonal items but never had a clearance sale at the end of the season. No credit and no deals. Rumors had it that he didn't believe in charity organizations and refused to donate to them. He wouldn't even buy Girl Scout cookies.

When we arrived, he acknowledged us with a nod and continued helping a customer. After everyone had left, he locked the door.

He then asked, "What ages are your children? Boy or girl?"

Without another word, he grabbed two large boxes and proceeded down the aisle. New toys of all descriptions were displayed on the shelves. He picked up two packages of building blocks and dropped one in each box. "Little girls like to build, too." His mouth almost smiled.

He stuffed the boxes. A dump truck in one, a baby doll in the other. When the boxes were nearly full, he topped them off with books to read and books to color.

Mr. Carl thrust the toy-filled boxes toward us. "Take these and give your children a nice Christmas." He looked directly at first one and then the other of us.

"There's one condition. You aren't to tell a soul. I don't want anyone else to know. Understood?"

Over the years, there's been another rumor circulating. A Santa-in-disguise has come to the rescue of many people in need.

We know for a fact that it's true.

~Jeanne Converse
Chicken Soup for the Christian Family Soul

The Santa Claus on I-40

*Christmas is not as much about opening our presents
as opening our hearts.*
~Janice Maeditere

*T*he wipers struggled to push the heavy, wet snowflakes off the windshield while they kept rhythm to Willie Nelson singing "On the Road Again."

Trint hit the eject button on the tape player. He'd heard that song four times in the last two hours and was sick of it. He shrugged his aching shoulders, trying to shake off the miles. It was still a long way to Memphis, a storm was blowing in and Interstate 40 was getting hazardous.

In the distance, Trint spotted the welcome glow of lights at a truck stop and decided to pull off the road and grab a bite to eat while he waited to see if the weather would break or turn into an icy blizzard that would shut down the roads until morning.

He eased his orange Freightliner and fifty-three-foot-long trailer into an empty spot and shut it down. He was hauling a heavy load of tires to Nashville, and after that he was picking up a load in Baltimore and heading to Chicago.

He reached for his jacket and hesitated when he saw the box on the passenger seat. His mother had been worried about him spending

Christmas on the road alone and had given him a box filled with presents. He smiled; his mom still treated him like he was a kid. He looked at his watch. It was nearly midnight on Christmas Eve, so he might as well open his gifts now.

Trint tore open the box and found a warm flannel shirt, probably blue. It was hard to tell in the dim light, but his mom knew his favorite color was blue. There were some heavy socks and leather gloves. Mom was always fussing over him and worrying her youngest son would get cold. There were homemade cookies and fudge and a red stocking with Santa Claus on it. He reached into the stocking and pulled out a toy tractor trailer that looked a lot like his rig and wondered how many stores his mother had to go to before she found such a close match.

His eyes stung. Next month he'd be twenty-five years old. He was a man. Men didn't cry over cookies and a toy truck or because they were a thousand miles away from home on Christmas.

He climbed out of his cab and a cold blast of air hit him in the chest like a fist. He pulled his collar up and ran across the parking lot to the all-night cafe. He was tall and thin and without much meat on his bones to protect him from the cold. Inside, it was warm and cozy. A dozen truckers were spread out at the counter and tables. A man and woman and small boy were huddled in a booth, and they looked tired and unhappy.

Trint felt sorry for the boy. He looked like he was around eight years old, and no kid should have to spend Christmas Eve in a truck stop. The parents were loading up on coffee and Trint guessed they'd been driving somewhere to spend the holidays with relatives, and the snow forced them to hole up here. They were drinking coffee, hoping to stay awake so they could finish their trip if the weather cleared up.

"It's so cold outside, I was spitting ice cubes," a fat trucker at the counter said, and the others laughed.

A cute waitress with blond hair offered Trint a menu.

"I'll have biscuits and gravy...." he said.

"And iced tea with lemon," she finished the order for him. "You're the only trucker around here who doesn't drink coffee." She smiled and didn't seem in a hurry to leave.

"I'm surprised you remember me." Trint returned her smile.

"How could I ever forget those beautiful brown eyes and your country accent?" she asked, hoping he would guess that she watched for him every time a truck pulled in.

"Well, I remember you, too," he grinned. "You want to be a schoolteacher. I think you said first or second grade, you're putting yourself through college by working here at night and your name is Melinda."

"You do remember!" she said, liking the soft way he said her name. Color flushed her cheeks and she hurried off into the kitchen.

Funny how truckers picked up bits and pieces of other people's lives. He looked across the room. Some of the truckers' faces looked familiar but he didn't know any of their names. He might see them again tomorrow at another truck stop, or never see them again. Sometimes the job seemed awfully lonely. Trint liked driving a truck, he liked seeing new places and he liked the good pay, but sometimes, like tonight, he felt lonesome and wondered if this was really the life for him.

He missed his family. His mom raised four kids by herself on a forty-acre farm in Missouri, but no matter how scarce money was, she'd always made sure they had a good Christmas. He thought about his box of gifts in the truck.

He looked at the kid again and knew what he had to do. He forced himself back into the bone-chilling cold outside to walk to his truck. He grabbed the Christmas stocking from the cab and hurried back to the warmth of the cafe.

He walked to the booth where the family sat in weary silence.

"I think Santa Claus left this for you," Trint said and handed the red stocking to the boy.

The boy looked at his mother. She hesitated just a second and nodded. The boy eagerly reached out and took the stocking and dug inside.

"Wow! Mom, look! A big rig just like the real ones outside!" His crooked grin lit up the whole room.

"Tell Santa... well, tell him thanks," the boy's father said and shook Trint's hand long and hard. The mother smiled gratefully.

Trint returned to the counter and ate his biscuits and gravy. He gave the waitress a twenty-dollar tip and told her Merry Christmas. She said the money was too much, but he told her to use it to buy some books for school, and she took it and slipped him a piece of paper.

"Take good care of yourself," she said. "And hurry back."

"I will... Melinda," he promised and noticed she had the bluest eyes he'd ever seen.

Trint walked outside. It had stopped snowing and a handful of stars sparkled through a break in the clouds.

There was a tap on the window behind him and he turned to look. It was the boy. He was holding up the truck and laughing. Trint waved goodbye, and the boy waved back.

Trint felt good. Somewhere along the road tomorrow he'd call home and talk to his brothers and kid sister. He'd tell his mom about giving the toy to the kid. She'd like that.

Trint reached his truck and stopped. Somebody had written "Merry X-mas," in the snow on his windshield and hung a candy cane on his side mirror. He wondered if it was Melinda or the boy or one of the truckers.

He started up his engine and felt the roar and power as he slowly pulled up to the road. Soon the snowplows would be out and clear the Interstate, but right now the road stretched out like a silver ribbon.

A quiet peace filled Trint's heart. He was a lucky guy. He had a job he loved, Melinda's phone number in his pocket, clear weather and miles of open road ahead.

He wasn't tired anymore, or lonely. He loved this life and he wouldn't change a thing.

~Linda Stafford
Chicken Soup for the Soul Christmas Treasury

Our
Matchbox Christmas

*I*t was a rainy California Christmas Eve. Our tree was lit up, and it shone through the large picture window of our home in military quarters at Port Hueneme. My husband would finally be spending Christmas with us. He had often missed the holidays due to deployments, leaving me and our three small children alone for Christmas. He had just returned home from Vietnam and would be home for six months. Then he would have to go back to fighting the war in Vietnam.

Our children, six, four and two years old, were anxiously waiting for their daddy to return from battalion headquarters. He had to "muster and make it." Their little noses had been pressed against the big frosty window almost all afternoon, waiting for him to come back home.

Their daddy was a Seabee, and we were all as proud of him as we could be, but we often struggled to make ends meet. Once a month, I would buy a month's worth of groceries, and this month, I had managed to squeeze in a large turkey and all the trimmings, to cook for our Christmas Eve meal, but money for presents was scarce. I had bought my husband a small gift, and he had bought me one. The children each had a handful of tiny department-store toys, all individually wrapped and waiting for the big day. There were no names on the small gifts; I could feel through the paper and tell what they were.

I saw my husband's car headlights cut through the dark winter mist that engulfed our home. I pushed back my hair and straightened my clothes. The children and I rushed to the door. This was our big night! It had been our tradition back home in Texas to eat our big meal on Christmas Eve night, and this year we were going to eat better than we usually did. Our little table was laden with all sorts of tasty-looking food. Each of the kids would get to open one present, and Santa Claus would be coming after they went to sleep.

To my surprise, when I opened the door to give my husband a big kiss, standing behind him were three burly Seabees. They hung their heads as they entered our home, as if to apologize for intruding on our family feast.

"Honey," my husband said, almost apologetically, "these are some of the guys who were with me in 'Nam. Their families are thousands of miles away. They were just sitting in the barracks, and I asked them if they wanted to come eat with us. Is it okay if they stay?"

I was thrilled to have Christmas company. We, too, were thousands of miles away from friends and family. It had been so long since we had "entertained." We gladly shared our small feast with those three huge Seabees. After dinner, we all sat down in the living room. The children started begging to open their gifts. I sat them down and walked over to the tree to get them each a tiny wrapped gift.

As I glanced up, I could see my husband's friends sitting there looking sad and distant. I realized how bittersweet it must feel to be here with us. I knew they must be thinking about their own children, wives and homes. They were staring down at the floor, lost in the loneliness of the season, trying to shake the horrible memories of the war they had just left — a war to which they would soon return.

Quickly, I scooped up six colorfully wrapped Matchbox cars. I called each of our children's names, and they quickly opened their presents. Soon, all three of them were rolling their cars on the floor.

I walked over to the men. "Well, what do you know?" I said. "Old Santa must have known you were going to be here!"

Those big old Seabees looked up in surprise. They opened their treasures: a Matchbox car for each of them. Within seconds after they opened the gifts, those men were grinning from ear to ear, down on the floor playing with their tiny cars.

I looked up at my husband. "How about me?" he asked. "Did Santa leave me anything?"

I reached under the tree and handed him a tiny present also. He joyfully joined our children and his friends. They must have played for hours. They ate, told funny stories and laughed while they rolled those race cars around on the floor.

I watched them there, filled with pride. These men had fought for us and kept us free. Free to have nights like this one, and others that were to come.

I didn't really know these men, but there they were, sitting on our floor. They would have given the world to be back home with their loved ones, but it wasn't possible. They had committed to defend our country. They were trying to make the best of an awful time in their lives.

Soon, the races were over, the food was almost all devoured, and each of the men said their goodbyes and left our home, their faces shining with new hope. In each of their hands, clutched tightly, was a tiny Matchbox car.

Years have passed since that Christmas Eve night. Two of the men returned from the war. One didn't.

We have seen them over the years, visited their homes, met their families. The men have swapped war stories while the women shared "left at home to do it all by ourselves" stories. Our children played together.

When we first met again, I was surprised to learn that every one of the men had kept their cars in their pockets when they were in 'Nam. When times got tough, and everything would get still, the men would quietly take out those little cars. They would give each other a grin, as if to promise that there would be another race and that they would see another day.

And they showed me how, high on a mantel, or proudly displayed in a shadow box, safely tucked away from harm, they still have their tiny Matchbox cars!

~Alice Smith
Chicken Soup for the Military Wife's Soul

One Cup at a Time

othing seems to bring people together like Christmas. The fact that I was now in prison made no difference. It didn't start that way at first.

The guards had placed a Christmas tree—roots and all—in each unit. The idea was for the men to make the decorations to go on it from whatever they could find. Creativity was to be our only limit, with the winning unit awarded soda and popcorn.

The tree sat in the corner for a whole week. It seemed to be a symbol of the stripped dignity we all felt, being incarcerated at this time of year. Remarks were made by the inmates passing by as to what the staff could do with their tree. I, too, fell victim to the overall gloom that seemed to match the gray-colored snow clouds outside my window. My longing for home and hearth made my spirits sink to an all-time low. I thought of the chain of events that put me here. I was feeling so depressed that I couldn't even muster up contempt for those responsible for sending me to prison. All the blame seemed to come back to one person—me.

I walked out into the open space of the unit and sat down on a chair to watch the others pass by—going nowhere. I sat away from some of the men who were seated at the other end of a long line of chairs. Straight ahead was the tree, its branches brittle from neglect. Pine needles lying on the floor told of its need for water and even I, foul mood and all, could not deny a tree a drink of water. I went to my cell, got my cup, filled it in the sink and walked back to the tree. I was almost afraid to move a branch for fear of it cracking. Its need for water was worse than I thought. After several trips of carrying water, one cup at a time, a lifer by the name of Buck came forward with a bigger cup full of water.

"All the water in the world ain't gonna help these roots," I thought. Just then a young man named Shorty handed another cup of water to me. Several dozen trips for water were needed before the roots showed evidence of being saturated. Shorty poured in another six or seven cups, filling the bottom of the tin tub that held the tree.

"Just in case it wants a drink of water later," he said.

As we stood around like medical interns who had just saved our first patient, it was Shorty who said what we were all thinking.

"It looks kinda naked, doesn't it?"

"I guess I could dig up somethin' ta put on it," Buck grumbled.

"I'll make the rounds and see who can help," said Shorty, taking off in a different direction than Buck.

I retreated to my cell with old memories of grade school running through my head, when glue and paper were crafted into wondrous masterpieces that Mom displayed with pride. My eyes shifted to a roll of toilet paper I had stashed away in a corner. Then I went on a hunt for a bottle of white glue that I had long since forgotten. After dumping my worldly belongings from the footlocker, I finally found the glue wedged next to some letters from my ex-lawyer. I like to take those letters out now and then. They were always good for a laugh — rereading the worthless promises of freeing me soon after a speedy retrial. To say the words were not worth the paper they were written on was truer than I ever imagined.

The letterhead was printed with big gold stripes that ran down each left-hand border. A spark of creativity connected some two remaining brain cells of mine that had been dormant for far too long. I mixed the white glue with warm water until I had a thin milky soup. Then I took the toilet paper and unrolled a handful. By dipping it into the mixture, I could squeeze it out and roll long skinny sticks. I bent them in the shape of candy canes and laid them on our heater to dry and harden. With childlike glee, I took my lawyer's letters and with a pair of rounded kiddie scissors, I trimmed off the gold edging from every page. My lawyer's letters are finally good for something, I thought, as the radiator baked my creations into the shape of candy canes. I took the gold strip of paper and twisted a gold stripe down one of the drying sticks. A fine job, I thought, even if I do say so myself. They looked good enough to eat — all twenty-four of them.

As I stepped out into the unit, I was surprised to see a crowd of people around the Christmas tree. Buck was coordinating the trimming with all the tact of the cruise director on the Titanic. Handmade paper chains and ornaments were being hung everywhere. Someone had taken cotton batting out of three pillows and had balled it up to make a snowman.

Someone else had shredded the tinfoil potato chip bags into long strips and was hanging them as tinsel. I was not disappointed in the least when my candy canes got lost amongst the other wonderful items. The tree looked beautiful after a few hours.

We were all standing back to admire our work when Shorty came out of his cell carrying something. In his hand he had an angel. He'd covered a plastic bottle with the white silk lining he had cut out of his bathrobe, giving the angel a robe of her own. The head was made from a tennis ball and covered with hair he cut from his own head. He had cut the face from a magazine and glued it onto the angel's head. The wings were made of real pigeon feathers that he must have collected from the yard. Our angel looked a little weird, but it was the thought that counted.

Buck pulled up a chair for Shorty to stand on, and he proudly placed his angel on top of the tree. Shorty turned to all of us with a smile that was accented by his clumps of missing hair, asking, "How's that?"

"It looks right purdy," said Buck, and everyone agreed.

Our unit won first prize, and we enjoyed the soda and popcorn. Our tree was planted in the yard for everyone to enjoy, with hopes it would survive the winter. It did. The following summer was a hot one. A drought was killing everything, everything but the little Christmas tree, which somehow stayed watered all summer. Men carried water to it, one cup at a time.

~Steven Dodrill
Chicken Soup for the Soul Christmas Treasury

What Goes Around Comes Around

For the spirit of Christmas fulfils
the greatest hunger of mankind.
~Loring A. Schuler

She was a special-duty nurse at a London hospital, and she had been assigned to care for a desperately ill German student from a nearby college. The young man had contracted pneumonia and was in critical condition. Staff physicians held out little hope for his survival. The student, aware of his perilous circumstances, pleaded with the nurse to keep him awake, saying, "If I go to sleep, I'll never wake up."

Throughout the long hours of the night, Gordon kept her patient from drifting off into sleep. With painstaking detail she told him the biblical Christmas story—the journey to Bethlehem, the birth in a stable, the adoration of the shepherds, the visit of the Magi, the flight into Egypt. When she had exhausted the story, she sang to him every Christmas carol she could recall from memory. And whenever her patient seemed on the verge of falling asleep, she gently shook him back to consciousness.

The dawn of that Christmas morning found the student still alive and able to celebrate the day. The crisis passed, and the young man gradually improved and was released from the hospital.

Several years passed. Britain and much of the rest of the world were engulfed in World War II. Gordon, now a medical doctor, had been conscripted into the service of her country. Because she was fluent in Norwegian and a skilled skier, she was placed undercover in Nazi-occupied Norway.

One morning, German occupation troops arrested her along with scores of Norwegian civilians. Someone had tipped off the Germans that one of that group was a British secret agent. Knowing that her true identity and mission would be discovered, Gordon prayed that death would come quickly and that she would not be subjected to torture.

Gordon was brutally shoved into a small room, where she faced her interrogator, a Nazi soldier. The man reached for his side arm. My prayer is answered, she thought. Then their eyes met, and there was surprise at the mutual recognition. The German student and the English nurse were face to face again. Replacing his gun in its holster, the soldier pointed to the back door and said: "Go. I give you back your Christmas."

~Victor Parachin
Chicken Soup for the Christian Family Soul

12

Good Instincts

Dogs are miracles with paws.
~Attributed to Susan Ariel Rainbow Kennedy

*T*he wind whistled round the corner of the house, thunder rolled and rain slashed against the windows — not a night to be outside but rather to sit by the fire, thankful for the solid walls and roof overhead. I could imagine Dr. Frankenstein's creation being abroad on such a night. I was alone, my husband away and the nearest neighbor a quarter mile down the road. Alone, that is, except for Lassie, a shaggy, black-and-white border collie, who sat with her head in my lap, her intelligent, brown eyes gazing up at me as if to say, don't worry, we'll be all right.

Lassie had arrived at our front door four years earlier by her design, not ours. Throughout the eighteen years she was with us, she proved time and time again to be a superb judge of character. We never knew if it was as a result of her sense of smell or sound — or some sixth sense — but, whatever it was, she definitely possessed a talent we humans lacked. On first meeting she would either wag the tip of her tail a couple of times to indicate that the visitor was acceptable, or slightly curl her top lip, which told you to be wary. Always accurate, her gift was never more apparent than on this night.

The doorbell rang. I decided not to answer it. It rang again, more insistently this time. Whoever was there was not going away. Still I hesitated. On the fourth ring, with Lassie by my side, I finally answered the call. My stomach lurched and my mouth went dry, for there, silhouetted by the porch light, stood the monster himself. Not as big as I imagined but equally menacing. A twisted body under a heavy overcoat, one shoulder hunched higher than the other, and his head leaning slightly forward and to one side. Gnarled fingers at the end of a withered arm touched his cap.

"May I use your phone?" The voice came from somewhere back in his throat and, although the request was polite, his tone was rough.

I shrank back as he rummaged in his pocket and produced a piece of paper. Shuffling forward he handed it to me. I refused to take it. Believing he might try and force his way in, I looked at Lassie to see if she was ready to defend the homestead. Surprisingly, she sat by my side, the tip of her tail wagging.

You're out of your mind, Lassie, I thought. But there was no denying the sign and, based on past experience, I trusted her instincts.

Reluctantly, I beckoned the stranger into the hallway and pointed to the phone. He thanked me as he picked up the instrument. Unashamed, I stood and listened to the conversation. From his comments, I learned his van had broken down and he needed someone to repair it. Lassie always shadowed anyone she mistrusted until they left the house. Tonight she paid no attention to our visitor. Instead, she trotted back into the living room and curled up by the fire.

Finishing his call, the man hitched up the collar of his overcoat and prepared to leave. As he turned to thank me, his lopsided shoulders seemed to sag and a touch of sympathy crept into my fear.

"Can I offer you a cup of tea?" The words were out before I could stop them.

His eyes lit up. "That would be nice."

We went through to the kitchen. He sat while I put the kettle on. Bent over on the stool, he looked less menacing, but I still kept a wary eye on him. By the time the tea had brewed, I felt safe enough to draw up another stool. We sat in silence, facing each other across the table, cups of steaming tea in front of us.

"Where are you from?" I finally asked, for the sake of conversation.

"Birmingham," he answered, then paused. "I'm sorry if I frightened you," he continued, "but you've no need to worry. I know I look strange, but there's a reason."

I said nothing, and we continued to sip in silence. I felt he would talk when he was ready, and he did.

"I wasn't always like this," he said. I sensed, rather than heard, the catch in his voice. "But some years ago I had polio."

"Oh," I said, not knowing what else to say.

"I was laid up for months. When I managed to walk again, I couldn't get a job. My crippled body put everyone off. Eventually, I was hired as a delivery driver, and as you know from my phone call, my van broke down outside your house." He smiled his crooked smile. "I really should be getting back so I'm there when the mechanic arrives."

"Look," I said. "There's no need to sit outside in this weather. Why not leave a note in your van telling them where you are?"

He smiled again. "I'll do that."

When he returned, we settled by the fire in the living room. "You know," I said, "if it hadn't been for Lassie here, I wouldn't have let you in."

"Oh," he said, bending forward to scratch her head. "Why?"

I went on to explain her uncanny ability to judge people, then added, "She sensed you for what you really are, while I only saw the outside."

"Lucky for me she was around," he said, laughing.

After two hours and several more cups of tea, the doorbell rang again. A man wearing overalls under a hooded raincoat announced the vehicle was repaired.

Thanking me profusely, the stranger headed out into the night, and a few minutes later, the taillights of his van disappeared down the road. I never expected to see him again.

But on the afternoon of Christmas Eve, I answered the door to find the rainy-night stranger standing there. "For you," he said, handing me a large box of chocolates, "for your kindness." Then he placed a packet of dog treats in my other hand. "And these are for Lassie, my friend with the good instincts. Merry Christmas to you both."

Every Christmas Eve, until we moved five years later, he arrived with his box of chocolates and packet of dog treats. And every year he got the same warm welcome from our wise Lassie.

~Gillian Westhead as told to Bill Westhead
Chicken Soup for the Dog Lover's Soul

Chapter 2

Christmas through the Eyes of Children

Our hearts grow tender with childhood memories and love of kindred,
and we are better throughout the year for having, in spirit,
become a child again at Christmas-time.

~Laura Ingalls Wilder

13

Seeing Love in the Eyes of Santa Claus

Our death is not an end if we can live on in our children.
~Albert Einstein

*T*he call came early in the afternoon. Anxiously awaiting and dreading it, we were still somewhat relieved when it finally came.

Our neighbor Mary's pain and suffering had ended, but now her family was experiencing grief that is known only by those who have lost a loved one. The children were especially touched by the event, even though both parents had prepared them.

Of the children, I knew that Christine would accept her mother's death more easily. The memory of her visit with Santa Claus would soften her pain. I knew this firsthand because I dressed up as Santa Claus the year she shared her precious secret.

My husband was initially going to put on the Santa suit and visit the neighbors, but at the last moment had qualms about the trip to Mary's house. Mary was then terminally ill, and the children were trying to understand. What would he say if the children asked him to make their mother well again? I had recently read an article about "proper" Santa responses. It explained how to ward off children's requests for live animals and what to say if they wanted their illness cured, etc. So I felt knowledgeable enough to pretend to be Santa, even though I was a woman.

The beard and wig hid everything except my eyes, and, of course, the oversized suit took care of the rest. After practicing a few hearty "Ho Ho Ho's," I was ready to go.

The younger child, Katey, opened the door. Her eyes grew wide, her smile was small and crooked. Her older sister, Christine, was solemn and uninterested, barely aware that I had arrived. I was invited into the living room, and I encouraged the girls to come over and talk. Katey soon warmed up to me and excitedly told me about all the presents that she expected to see under the tree.

Christine edged closer to me, but she still seemed unsure. When she finally looked at me, she suddenly became excited and a wide grin spread across her face. Not saying a word, she continued to stare at me, speechless. Everyone in the room kept asking her to tell Santa what she wanted for Christmas, but it was almost as if she didn't hear them, she just continued to stare at me and smile. Finally the adults drifted away.

"Christine," I said, "what do you want Santa to bring you?"

Her smile got smaller, and she said, "You know, Santa, my mom is really sick."

My stomach did a flip-flop, and I knew her next request would be to ask Santa to make her mommy well again.

"Well," Christine continued, "my mom told me that even though one day she would die, she would always be around for me. I told her I didn't understand that. So she told me a secret. She said whenever I wanted to know that she was near me, to look into faces of people who loved me, and I would be able to see her in their faces, and know she loved me.

"Santa, it didn't work! When I looked into my sister's face, I just saw my sister, and when I looked at my dad, I just saw my dad. And I was afraid to tell my mom that the secret wasn't working. I didn't want to make her sad.

"But, Santa, today it worked! When I looked into your eyes just now, they looked just like my mom's eyes, and now I know the secret will come true. My mom will never leave me, because I can find my mom in the faces of the people who love me."

-Loric McCrone
Chicken Soup for the Christian Family Soul

———————————————

The Friday Christmas Tree

"**M**ommy," six-year-old Brian cried, as he pulled on his pajamas, "the other kids said we're going to have a Christmas tree for the house! What's a Christmas tree?"

Snug in their small bedroom at this Christian shelter for women and children, Jenny Henderson held him and four-year-old Daniel close. "It's a beautiful tree that helps people be glad for Jesus," she said. "People decorate them at Christmas time. They buy each other presents and put them under the trees."

Daniel wrinkled his nose. "What's 'decorate' mean? What's Christmas?"

Their mother sighed. All the years she had lived with the boys' father, he refused to let them celebrate anything, no matter how much she pleaded. No birthdays. No holidays. And certainly no Christmas.

So the boys had never blown out birthday candles, watched TV, decorated a Christmas tree, hung up stockings, eaten a big Christmas dinner or opened any gifts.

When the Henderson home became so sad with all the arguing, controlling and bossing, Jenny and the boys moved to the shelter home. Now they were free to celebrate everything, including Christmas, with the other mothers and children there.

Jenny gave Daniel a hug. "I'll tuck you both under the covers and tell you a wonderful story about Jesus and Christmas."

She recounted the detailed story of the first Christmas night, then told them about decorating a Christmas tree, giving Christmas presents to each other, and telling God thank you for baby Jesus.

"Wow!" Brian cried. "I want to love baby Jesus, too. And I want to decorate a Christmas tree, too!"

"Me, too!" Daniel echoed. "Please, Mommy, please!"

Jenny laughed. "Mrs. Naples, the house manager, says we're going to have a big Christmas tree decorating party this Saturday. All the kids who live here will be able to help, including you two."

Brian and Daniel were so excited, they could hardly get to sleep. And the very first thing Daniel asked when he woke up the next morning was, "Is it Saturday yet? Can we decorate the tree yet?"

Finally, that Friday, they heard a great shout. "The tree's here!" All the children scrambled down the stairs. There at the front door were three men carrying the biggest, most beautiful, fragrant evergreen, so big it almost stuck in the doorway. The men set it up on a stand, and everyone gathered around. It almost reached the ceiling!

"Can we decorate it right now?" Daniel asked.

Mrs. Naples laughed. "No, remember it's still Friday, Daniel. We'll have our decorating party tomorrow."

Just then she got a phone call in the office. It was the boys' father. Since Mr. Henderson had never hurt the boys, he was allowed to come to the shelter and take them out on visits. He was coming the next day to take them out for a while—right at decorating time.

The boys loved their father, of course. But they did so want to decorate their very first Christmas tree. "Please, Mrs. Naples," Brian begged, "could we put just one pretty thing on the tree tonight? Just one small decoration?"

The house manager looked at the beautiful tree. She looked at the two boys and she looked at the other children. "Well, what do you think, children?" she asked. "Would that be fair? Let's take a vote."

"Yes!" they all shouted.

A short time later, all the children helped carry not just one little decoration, but whole boxes of them into the living room. They set them around the waiting tree.

"All right, boys," Mrs. Naples said to Brian and Daniel. "You have an hour. During that time you may decorate to your hearts' content. We won't plug anything in, but you take out anything in any of the boxes. Tomorrow while you're gone we'll take the decorations off so the other children can have their chance putting them on. But tonight is your night."

Then she shooed the other children away and left the two boys alone.

Brian and Daniel had never been so happy in their entire lives. They picked up each shiny ball, each shimmering garland, each handful of icicles, as carefully as if they had been made of diamonds, then placed them lovingly on the tree.

A little later, Mrs. Naples stopped by to see how they were doing. All around the bottom branches—as high as little boys' arms could reach—glittered joyful ornaments of blue, red, green, gold and silver, plus loop upon loop of garlands, and handfuls upon handfuls of icicles.

But instead of standing there admiring their work, the two boys were on their knees with their eyes closed tightly, praying.

"Thank you, dear Jesus," Brian began, "for getting bornded at Christmas time. And thank you for letting us decorate your Christmas tree. That's the bestest Christmas present I could ever get."

"Oh, and, Jesus," his little brother added, "when Daddy comes here tomorrow and sees our beautiful tree, please let him like it and not be mad. And help him want to love you, too."

Brian thought a moment. "You're right," he agreed. "That would be the bestest Christmas present of all."

~Bonnie Compton Hanson
Chicken Soup for the Christian Soul 2

Paul's Bike

I love the Christmas-tide, and yet,
I notice this, each year I live;
I always like the gifts I get,
But how I love the gifts I give!
~Carolyn Wells

Late one June evening, our oldest son, his dad and I discussed a newspaper route with a morning delivery manager. From the dining room I could hear the television where a younger son, Paul, watched his favorite program.

The man described two available routes. "And if you keep a route for at least a year, the bike we lend you becomes yours to keep."

"How old do you have to be to have a paper route?" Paul piped in.

I stared at Paul. How long had he been sitting at the other end of the table?

"How old are you, son?" asked the manager.

Paul stretched himself as tall as possible. "Ten."

"Well," answered the manager, "we like the boys to be at least eleven."

"But you have two routes in our area. I could do one," insisted Paul.

"Okay, if your parents agree that you can do it. Let me know tomorrow."

After the man left, I laid out some rules. "If you take these routes, they are yours, not mine. Don't expect me to drive you when the weather is bad or you get up late. I don't want to remind you to collect each month either."

The manager trained the boys for two days. On Saturday he presented each boy with a paper-route bike.

The bike was one-speed, large, fat, tired and ugly red. A basket rested over each side of the back fender to hold papers, and a large canvas bag hung from the handlebars.

I watched Paul's face. He smiled, rode the bike down the driveway, then parked it in the garage. After the first week of riding the bike to school, he chose to walk.

Each morning, Paul got up early on his own to deliver his papers. Even if I offered to drive him in the freezing cold, he refused. He finished his collections on time without my urging. Each month he cashed his checks at the local drugstore, paid his paper bill and hid his profits in a sock in his underwear drawer.

With Christmas a couple of months away, the boys and I made many trips to Target. Each boy went his own way. I'd find Paul in the bicycle department.

"Why are you always looking at bikes?" I asked him. "You have one that you seldom ride."

"Mom, the kids make fun of my clunky paper-route bike. I want one like everyone else has. By Christmas I'll have enough money to buy this one."

Every day after school, Paul counted his money. On each trip to various stores, his brother showed me Christmas gifts he'd purchased. Paul never bought anything. He spent the whole time sitting on new bikes. In December, he did his collections early.

On our final Christmas shopping trip, I again discovered Paul at the bicycle department. His shopping cart was empty. "Are you buying the bike?" I asked.

"I have enough money," he boasted.

"Well, hurry up. We'll wait for you at the front." We waited and waited. At last Paul came out carrying one little bag to the car.

Each boy took his turn in my bedroom, secretly wrapping his gifts. Paul didn't take long. He placed a few small packages under the tree.

That night I went to tuck the boys into bed as usual. When I entered Paul's room, he lay on his back, staring at the ceiling. His brown eyes sparkled. "I can hardly wait for Christmas," he said. He put his hands behind his head, and his face filled with a huge smile.

"Why, Paul?" I dreaded his answer. "Will your new bike arrive soon?"

"I didn't buy it, but I spent all my money!" He looked happier than I'd ever seen him. "Everyone's going to love what I got them for Christmas!"

~Linda L. Osmundson
Chicken Soup for the Mother and Son Soul

Christmas Is Coming!

Christmas is the season for kindling the fire
of hospitality and the genial flame of charity in the heart.
~Washington Irving

I sat on the floor near Jeremy, my three-year-old, and handed him assorted ornaments to put on the Christmas tree. He stood on a holiday popcorn can to reach the middle section of the tree, which was as high as he could reach. He giggled with a child's pure delight every time I said, "Christmas is coming!" Although I had tried many times to explain Christmas to him, Jeremy believed that Christmas was a person. "Christmas is coming!" he would giggle. "And all of these presents are for Christmas when she comes!"

I was sitting back, watching him smiling to himself as he carefully placed each ornament on the tree. Surely he can't know enough about Christmas to love it this much, I thought.

We lived in a small apartment in San Francisco. Although the weather was usually mild, this Christmas season it was chilly enough for us to need a fire. On Christmas Eve I threw in a starter log and watched my son sliding around the apartment, sock-footed on hardwood floors. He was anxiously awaiting Christmas. Soon he couldn't stand it any longer and began jumping up and down. "When will she be here, Mommy? I can't wait to give her all these presents!"

Again I tried to explain it to him. "You know, Jeremy, Christmas is a time of year, not a person, and it will be here sooner than you know. At twelve o'clock, Christmas will be here but you will probably be sleeping, so when you wake up in the morning it will be Christmas."

He laughed as if I was telling a silly joke. "Mommy," he said, "will Christmas eat breakfast with us?" He spread out his arms over the gifts under the tree. "All of these presents are for Christmas! All of them!"

I tickled his belly and laughed with him. "Yes," I said. "They are all for Christmas!"

He scampered about the apartment until fatigue slowed him down and he lay on the rug by the tree. I curled up next to him and when he finally fell asleep I carried him into his bed.

I decided on a hot chocolate before bed and as I drank it I sat near the window looking down on the decorated streets of San Francisco. It was a beautiful scene. But there was one thing that disturbed me. Directly outside our apartment, in the spot where I usually left the garbage, was what looked like a crumpled heap of old clothes. But I soon realized what the heap really was. It was an old homeless woman who usually hung out near the corner store down the street. She was a familiar sight in the neighborhood, and I had tossed a few coins into her bag a few times after shopping at the grocery. She never asked for money, but I think she got quite a few handouts from passersby because she looked so helpless.

As I looked out on this Christmas Eve, I wondered about this poor old woman. Who was she? What was her story? She should be with family, not sleeping in the cold street at this special time of year.

I felt a sinking feeling inside. Here I was, with a beautiful child sleeping in the next room. I had often felt sorry for myself as a single mom, but at least I wasn't alone and living on the streets. How hopeless and sad that would be for anyone, let alone a woman who must be about eighty years old.

I went to my front door and walked down the steps to the street. I asked the old woman if she would like to come inside. At first, she hardly acknowledged me. I tried to coax her; she said she didn't want my help. But when I said I could use a little company, she relented and agreed to spend Christmas with Jeremy and me.

I arranged for her to sleep in the living room on our foldout couch. The next morning, I was awakened by Jeremy yelling at the top of his lungs. "Christmas is here! Christmas is here, Mommy!"

I quickly pulled on my robe and hurried to the living room, where I found a very excited little boy presenting a very surprised "Christmas" with gifts from under the tree. "We've been waiting for you!" he shouted joyfully. He giggled and danced around as she opened the presents he had given her.

I don't think "Christmas" had known a Christmas like this for a very long time. And neither had I. I also knew that it would have taken more than just one special day to lift the burden from that old lady's weary heart, but I was thrilled when she promised to come back the following year. I hope she will. And Jeremy knows she will.

~Deb Gatlin Towney
Chicken Soup for the Single's Soul

The Giving Trees

Blessed is the season which engages
the whole world in a conspiracy of love!
~Hamilton Wright Mabie

I was a single parent of four small children, working at a minimum-wage job. Money was always tight, but we had a roof over our heads, food on the table, clothes on our backs and, if not a lot, always enough. My kids told me that in those days they didn't know we were poor. They just thought Mom was cheap. I've always been glad about that.

It was Christmas time, and although there wasn't money for a lot of gifts, we planned to celebrate with church and family, parties and friends, drives downtown to see the Christmas lights, special dinners, and by decorating our home.

But the big excitement for the kids was the fun of Christmas shopping at the mall. They talked and planned for weeks ahead of time, asking each other and their grandparents what they wanted for Christmas. I dreaded it. I had saved $120 for presents to be shared by all five of us.

The big day arrived and we started out early. I gave each of the four kids a twenty-dollar bill and reminded them to look for gifts that cost about four dollars each. Then everyone scattered. We had two hours to shop; then we would meet back at the "Santa's workshop" display.

Back in the car driving home, everyone was in high Christmas spirits, laughing and teasing each other with hints and clues about what they had bought. My younger daughter, Ginger, who was about eight years old, was unusually quiet. I noted she had only one small, flat bag with her after her shopping spree. I could see enough through the plastic bag to tell that she had bought candy bars—fifty-cent candy bars! I was so angry. What did you do with that twenty dollar bill I gave you? I wanted to yell at her, but I didn't say anything until we got home. I called her into my bedroom and closed the door, ready to be angry again when I asked her what she had done with the money. This is what she told me:

"I was looking around, thinking of what to buy, and I stopped to read the little cards on one of the Salvation Army's 'Giving Trees.' One of the cards was for a little girl, four years old, and all she wanted for Christmas was a doll with clothes and a hairbrush. So I took the card off the tree and bought the doll and the hairbrush for her and took it to the Salvation Army booth.

"I only had enough money left to buy candy bars for us," Ginger continued. "But we have so much and she doesn't have anything."

I never felt so rich as I did that day.

~Kathleen Dixon
A 5th Portion of Chicken Soup for the Soul

Owed to Joy

A daughter is a day brightener and a heart warmer.
~Author Unknown

*T*he year my youngest daughter, Shelly, was four, she received an unusual Christmas present from "Santa."

She was the perfect age for Christmas, able to understand the true meaning of the season, but still completely enchanted by the magic of it. Her innocent joyfulness was compelling and contagious and a great gift to parents, reminding us of what Christmas should represent no matter how old we are.

The most highly prized gift Shelly received on that Christmas Eve was a giant bubble-maker, a simple device of plastic and cloth the inventor promised would create huge billowing bubbles, larger than a wide-eyed four-year-old girl. Both Shelly and I were excited about trying it out, but it was dark outside so we'd have to wait until the next day.

That night, after all the gifts had been opened, I read the instruction booklet while Shelly played with some of her other new toys. The inventor of the bubble-maker had tried all types of soaps for formulating bubbles and found Joy dishwashing detergent created the best giant bubbles. I'd have to get some.

The next morning I was awakened very early by small stirrings in the house. Shelly was up. I knew in my sleepy mind that Christmas Day would be held back no longer, so I arose and made my way toward the kitchen to start the coffee. In the hallway I met my daughter, already wide awake, the bubble-maker clutched in her chubby little hand, the magic of Christmas morning embraced in her four-year-old heart. Her eyes were shining with excitement. She asked, "Daddy, can we make bubbles now?"

I sighed heavily. I rubbed my eyes. I looked toward the window, where the sky was only beginning to lighten with the dawn. I looked toward the kitchen, where the coffeepot had yet to start dripping its aromatic reward for early-rising Christmas dads.

"Shelly," I said, my voice almost pleading and perhaps a little annoyed, "it's too early. I haven't even had my coffee yet."

Her smile fell away. Immediately, I felt a father's remorse for bursting her bright Christmas bubble with what she must have seen as my own selfish problem, and my heart broke a little.

But I was a grown-up. I could fix this. In a flash of adult inspiration, I shifted the responsibility. Recalling the inventor's recommendation of a particular brand of bubble-making detergent—which I knew we did not have in the house—I laid the blame squarely on him, pointing out gently, "Besides, you have to have Joy."

I watched her eyes light back up. "Oh, Daddy," she beamed. "Oh, Daddy, I do."

I broke records getting to the store, and in no time at all we were out on the front lawn creating gigantic, billowing, gossamer orbs—each one conjured of purest Joy and sent forth shimmering in the Christmas sun.

~Ted A. Thompson
Chicken Soup for the Father & Daughter Soul

Christmas Derailed

Fairies are invisible and inaudible like angels.
But their magic sparkles in nature.
~Lynn Holland

oxes, ribbons and wrappings cluttered the entire room, evidence of a rowdy but generous Christmas morning for five-year-old Christopher and his three-year-old brother, David. But Christopher was far too withdrawn and quiet for a little boy who had just received his first electric train set. A bit concerned, I kept watch from the corner of my maternal eye while I scrambled eggs, maintained a running conversation with Grandma and periodically hauled Blossom, our bumbling sheepdog, away from the now listing tree.

What could be wrong? Tummy ache? Christopher wasn't complaining. Disappointment? Not likely, considering his ecstatic response when he saw the train set. Annoyed by the toddling interference of his little brother? No, David played across the room, chattering incessantly to his grandpa and daddy.

Yet I knew a mysterious, dark cloud hung over Christopher's mood this Christmas morning and carved a furrow of deep thought across his forehead. What in the world was making him so sad and dejected? Unable to find a moment alone with him in all the holiday chaos, I worried as he periodically retreated to his room, only to reappear with the same gloomy look.

When the breakfast dishes were finally put away, and the rest of the family had settled into the quiet hum of conversation and coffee, I took my cup of tea and slid to the floor next to Christopher, where he distractedly spun a wheel on one of his new trucks.

"Hey, honey," I whispered quietly in his ear, "I noticed that you seem a little sad this morning. What's wrong?"

"Well, Mommy," he said in a melancholy little voice, "remember that ring I got in the gumball machine? I gave it to the Tooth Fairy for Christmas."

Oh no, I groaned inwardly.

"How did you do that?" I asked, with a foreboding sense of what I was about to hear.

"Oh, I put it under my pillow where she always looks. But she didn't take it. I been checking all morning, and it's still there. And I really wanted to give her a present. How come she didn't want it?" he asked plaintively, looking up at me for an answer.

Rejected by the Tooth Fairy! How could she have been so thoughtless? And how could I explain without completely deflating the faith and kind heart of this little boy?

"Hmmm," I stalled. "Do you think she's busy collecting teeth this morning? Maybe she'll come later."

He considered the possibility thoughtfully, but shook his head. "No, I don't think so. She comes at night when kids are asleep."

I had to make this right. But how? Moments passed while I groped for another idea—any idea. Then, quite unexpectedly, Christopher's entire being erupted with eureka joy.

"Mommy, I bet I know why she didn't take it!" he blurted. "I bet she's Jewish!" And with that resolved, off he ran, smiling broadly, to engineer his new electric train.

~Armené Humber
Chicken Soup for the Soul The Book of Christmas Virtues

Chapter
3

The Spirit of Giving

You can give without loving,
but you can never love without giving.

~Author Unknown

Our *"Family"*

My daughter Gina was in Mrs. Melton's fourth grade class. After only a month in school, she began to come home on a regular basis asking for pencils, crayons, paper, etc. At first I just dutifully provided whatever she needed, never questioning her.

After ongoing requests for items that should have easily lasted a mere six weeks of fourth grade, I became concerned and asked her, "Gina, what are you doing with your school supplies?" She would always respond with an answer that satisfied me.

One day, after supplying the same thing only a week earlier, I became irritated with her pleading for more and sternly asked her once more, "Gina! what is going on with your school supplies?" Knowing her excuses would no longer work, she bent her head and began to cry. I lifted her tiny chin and looked into those big brown eyes, filled now with tears. "What?! What is wrong?" My mind was racing with all sorts of ideas. Had she been bullied by another child? Was she giving her supplies to him or her to keep from being hurt, or to gain their approval? I couldn't imagine what was going on, but I knew it was something serious for her to cry. I waited for what seemed like an eternity for her to answer.

"Mom," she began, "there is a boy in my class; he doesn't have any of the supplies he needs to do his work. The other kids make fun of him because his papers are messy and he only has two crayons to color with. I have been putting the new supplies you bought me in his desk before the others come in, so he doesn't know it's me. Please don't get mad at me, Mom. I didn't mean to tell you a lie, but I didn't want anyone to know it was me."

My heart sank as I stood there in disbelief. She had taken on the role of an adult and tried to hide it like a child. I knelt down and hugged her to me, not wanting her to see my own tears. When I pulled myself together, I stood up and said, "Gina, I would never get mad at you for wanting to help someone, but why didn't you just come and tell me?" I didn't have to wait for her to answer.

The next day, I visited Mrs. Melton. I told her what Gina had said. She knew John's situation all too well. The oldest of four boys, their parents had just moved here and when the school presented them with the school supply list for all four grades, they were overwhelmed. When the boys came to school the next week, they barely had the necessities — a few sheets of paper and a pencil each.

I asked Mrs. Melton for the list from all four grades and told her I would take care of it the next day. She smiled and gave me the lists.

The next day, we brought the supplies in and gave them to the office with instructions to give them to the boys.

As Christmas neared, the thought of John, his brothers and family weighed heavily on my mind. What would they do? Surely they would not have money for gifts.

I asked Mrs. Melton if she could get me their address.

At first she refused, reminding me that there was a policy that protected the privacy of the students, but because she knew me from my work at the school and involvement on the PTA board, she slipped a piece of paper into my hand and whispered, "Don't tell anyone I gave it to you."

When my family began to set the stage for our traditional Christmas Eve, which was usually held at my house, I simply told them all that my husband, the kids and I did not want gifts, but instead we would prefer to have groceries and gifts for our "family."

As the girls and I shopped throughout the holiday season, they delighted in picking things out for the four boys. Gina was especially interested in things for John.

Christmas Eve came and my family began to arrive. Each of them had bags of food and gifts wrapped for the children. My living room was full and the excitement was contagious.

Finally, at 9:00, we decided it was time to take our treasures to them. My brothers, dad, uncles and nephews loaded up their trucks and set out for the apartment complex address that Mrs. Melton gave us.

They knocked on the door and a little boy appeared. They asked for his mother or dad and he ran away. The guys waited until a young man, hardly more than a child himself, came to the door. He looked at the men standing there, with arms full of gifts and bags full of groceries, and couldn't say a word. The men pushed past him and went straight to the kitchen counter to set the bags down.

There was no furniture. It was an empty one-bedroom apartment with a few blankets on the floor and a small TV where they obviously spent their time. A Christmas tree was the result of the kids bringing in a bush they had found in the field behind the complex. A few paper decorations made in their classrooms made it look like a real Christmas tree. Nothing was underneath.

The boys and their parents stood without speaking as the men sat down bag after bag. They finally asked who had sent them, how did they know them and so on. But the men just left them with shouts of "Merry Christmas!"

When the guys got back to my house they didn't say a word. They couldn't.

To break the silence, my aunt stood up and began to sing "Silent Night," and we all joined in.

When school resumed, Gina came home daily telling of John's new clothes and how the other children now played with him and treated him like the rest of the children.

She never told a soul at school about what we did, but every Christmas since that one she will say to me, "Mom, I wonder what happened to John and his family? While I'm not quite sure of the answer, I'd like to think that John and his family were somehow helped by my daughter's gift.

~Linda Snelson
Chicken Soup for the Soul Christmas Treasury

An Angel Among Us

The manner of giving is worth more than the gift.
~Pierre Corneille, Le Menteur

I come from a large family of nine brothers and sisters, and all of us have kids of our own. On each Christmas night, our entire family gathers at my oldest sister's home, exchanging gifts, watching the nativity skit put on by the smaller children, eating, singing and enjoying a visit from Santa himself.

The Christmas of 1988, my husband Bob and I had four children. Peter was eleven, Leigh-Ann was nine, Laura was six and Matthew was two. When Santa arrived, Matthew parked himself on Santa's lap and pretty much remained dazzled by him for the rest of the evening. Anyone who had their picture taken with Santa that Christmas also had their picture taken with little Matthew.

Little did any of us know how precious those photos with Santa and Matthew would become. Five days after Christmas, our sweet little Matthew died in an accident at home. We were devastated. We were lucky to have strong support from our families and friends to help us through. I learned that the first year after a death is the hardest, as there are so many firsts to get through without your loved one. Birthdays and special occasions become sad, instead of joyous.

When our first Christmas without Matthew approached, it was hard for me to get into the holiday spirit. Bob and I could hardly face putting up the decorations or shopping for special gifts for everyone.

But we went through the motions for Peter, Leigh-Ann and Laura. Then, on December 13th, something extraordinary happened to raise our spirits when we didn't think it was possible.

We were just finishing dinner when we heard a knock on the front door. When we went to answer it, no one was there. However, on the front porch was a card and gift. We opened the card and read that the gift-giver wanted to remain anonymous; he or she just wanted to help us get through a rough time by cheering us up.

In the gift bag was a cassette of favorite Christmas music, which was in a little cardboard Christmas tree. The card described it as being "a cartridge in a pine tree," a twist on the "partridge in a pear tree" verse in the song "The Twelve Days of Christmas." We thought that it was a very clever gift, and the thoughtfulness of our "elf" touched our hearts. We put the cassette in our player and, song by song, the spirit of Christmas began to warm our hearts.

That was the beginning of a series of gifts from the clever giver, one for each day until Christmas. Each gift followed the theme of "The Twelve Days of Christmas" in a creative way. The kids especially liked "seven swans a-swimming," which was a basket of swan-shaped soaps plus passes to the local swimming pool, giving the kids something to look forward to when the warm days of spring arrived. "Eight maids a-milking" included eight bottles of chocolate milk, eggnog and regular milk in glass bottles with paper faces, handmade aprons and caps. Every day was something very special. The "five golden rings" came one morning just in time for breakfast—five glazed doughnuts just waiting to be eaten.

We would get calls from our family, neighbors and friends who would want to know what we had received that day. Together, we would chuckle at the ingenuity and marvel at the thoughtfulness as we enjoyed each surprise. We were so caught up in the excitement and curiosity of what would possibly come next, that our grief didn't have much of a chance to rob us of the spirit of Christmas. What our elf did was absolutely miraculous.

Each year since then, as we decorate our Christmas tree, we place on it the decorations we received that Christmas while we play the song "The Twelve Days of Christmas." We give thanks for our elf who was, we finally realized, our very own Christmas angel. We never did find out who it was, although we have our suspicions. We actually prefer to keep it that way. It remains a wondrous and magical experience—as mysterious and blessed as the very first Christmas.

~Rita Hampton
Chicken Soup for the Soul Christmas Treasury for Kids

A Christmas Dinner

My work calls for me to venture to the farthest reaches of the world, but one of my most memorable encounters occurred while traveling close to home.

A few years ago, a group of my far-flung friends decided to gather in Connecticut to celebrate Christmas.

I was to buy all the soft drinks, champagne and wine, and a doctor friend would get the turkey and trimmings.

On our way from New York City to Connecticut, my friend and I stopped in for a Christmas Eve party in upstate New York. As we left, I ran into the doctor and casually asked him what size bird he had bought. His eyes widened with surprise—he had bought all the drinks.

So here we were on a snowy Christmas Eve, with sufficient drinks to serve a cruise ship but not one piece of food for twelve hungry people! We searched around, but every supermarket was closed. Finally, just before midnight, we found ourselves at a gas station quick-food shop.

The manager was willing to sell us cold sandwiches. Other than potato chips, cheese and crackers, he didn't have much else. I was very agitated and disappointed. It was going to be a rather miserable Christmas dinner. The only bright spot was that he did have two cans of cranberry jelly!

In the midst of my panic, an elderly lady stepped from behind one of the aisles.

"I couldn't help overhearing your dilemma," she said, "If you follow me home, I would happily give you our dinner. We have plenty of turkey, potatoes, yams, pumpkins and vegetables."

"Oh no, we couldn't do that!" I replied.

"But you see, we no longer need it," she explained, "Earlier today we managed to get a flight to Jamaica — to see our family down there, for the holidays."

We couldn't say no to such kindness. We thanked her and followed her car. The journey seemed endless as we meandered through back roads and dimly lit streets. Eventually, we reached this kind woman's house.

We followed her in and, sure enough, she removed a turkey and all the trimmings from the fridge. Despite our attempt to reimburse her for her generosity, she refused our money.

"This is just meant to be," she said. "I don't need it anymore — and you do."

So we accepted her gift, asked her for her name and address, and went on our way.

The next day we impressed and surprised our friends by presenting them with a complete feast and telling them our amazing story about the old lady's help. Despite the last-minute scramble, Christmas dinner turned out to be a great success.

Before we left Connecticut, we went to a department store, picked out a gift and drove to the lady's home to leave our small token of appreciation.

We searched and searched but we couldn't find her place. We couldn't find the street address on any maps. The name she had given us wasn't listed anywhere. Baffled, we questioned several local store owners, yet no one knew of the elderly lady. Even the gas station manager told us that he had never seen her before. Every effort we made to locate our Christmas angel failed.

As I returned home, I pondered our bizarre encounter with this beneficent woman. Who was this lady who had appeared just in time to help out two desperate strangers, only to disappear with the night?

Years later, when I look back upon that particular holiday season, I recall the joy of gathering with friends from across the world and an amazing little old lady whose generosity embodied the very meaning of the Christmas spirit.

~Robin Leach
Chicken Soup for the Traveler's Soul

Rosemary's Remarkable Gift

I didn't see any way to escape the deep bitterness. Even with Christmas approaching, it followed me like a shadow. Sitting by my nine-month-old son's hospital bed on the pediatric floor of our local hospital, I wondered how I could possibly get my joy back. My husband Jerry wasn't bitter—he hardly stopped smiling. His time was divided between our three other children at home, being cared for by grandparents, work and the hospital. Lately, it seemed he was spending enormous time and energy trying to talk me out of being bitter. My answer remained, "It should have never happened."

I'd made two trips to the pediatrician's office with Jeremy during the week. His fever was 105 degrees. The doctor was convinced from the onset that he had the flu since there was an epidemic. From the very beginning, I couldn't shake this gut-level feeling that my son had a far more serious illness. I made a third trip with Jeremy to the emergency room at two in the morning when his fever shot up again. The doctor didn't come, but instructed a nurse over the phone that Jeremy only had the flu and gave orders for a fever shot. I phoned his office several times the next day suggesting an antibiotic—praying for penicillin.

On the fourth night of Jeremy's sickness, he cried literally all night. I cried with him, rocking him, praying out loud and forever looking out our den window for a hint of dawn. When it finally arrived, Jeremy stopped crying. He hardly moved and was quiet and limp, running the high fever again. Now he struggled noisily for breath and his entire head was swollen grotesquely. A large, bluish/purple hard circle had appeared on his right cheek.

Jerry and I rushed him to the pediatrician's office without conversation. Words were too scary. We happened to see a physician friend as we hurried down the hall to our doctor's office. He warned us not to even consider changing doctors with a child as sick as Jeremy. Time was too critical. When our pediatrician finally saw Jeremy, he sent us with STAT orders for him to be admitted to the hospital. It was December 18th. We left the car parked in a no parking zone and I ran, carrying Jeremy bundled in a blanket as Jerry hurried ahead, opening doors for us. We ran right past admitting in the lobby, and rather than waiting for the elevator, we sprinted up three flights of stairs. On the pediatric floor, someone directed us to a tiny examining room where they took Jeremy from my arms and placed him on a small stainless steel table in the center of the room covered with a sheet. He didn't move at all and his breathing was very shallow. His brown eyes seemed fixed on the ceiling light directly over his head. His red hair was wet with perspiration.

"I'm not getting a pulse," a nurse called out. Someone in white took his temperature as a lab technician reported that his veins had collapsed. The walls were light green—sickening green—and the huge black and white squares on the floor made me feel dizzy. The shelves were neatly stocked with all kinds of medical supplies. But was it too late? Where did they keep the penicillin? If I could have stolen some and given it to him, I would have.

"Temp's 106.3," someone announced. Why was everything moving in slow motion? My prayer remained simple, uncomplicated, Please, God! Our minister had arrived and prayed quietly but fervently behind us. When it appeared that Jeremy was... gone, this blessed nurse gave him an injection that I'll always believe was unauthorized. She had also phoned our pediatrician, but he never arrived. Jeremy didn't cry or move when he got the shot in his chubby leg.

She picked him up, and he flopped around like a rag doll. She ran with him down the hall to an oversized sink. Everyone in the room followed her. No one spoke. I heard my heart pounding like a giant drum and my mouth was so dry I couldn't swallow. The nurse placed Jeremy in the sink and began packing him in crushed ice. Others helped get the ice from a brown and beige ice machine nearby. "Get it on his head," she barked at me. At last I could do something, if it wasn't too late, and I piled ice on his little, hot head until she said sternly, "That's enough." Dear God, how she tried. I'll never forget you, I thought.

His scream was sudden, strong and the most beautiful sound I'd ever heard. Jeremy stabilized rather quickly after our pediatrician ordered massive injections of penicillin. He still hadn't come to the hospital. In less than an hour, Jeremy stood in his bed, holding onto a bottle and laughing. Even so, the nurses kept a very close eye on him. After dark that evening, our pediatrician strolled into the room and, standing near the door with his arms folded, chatted briefly, as though nothing traumatic had happened. I knew if I opened my mouth or even looked at him, I might never stop screaming. I fixed my eyes on the chrome bars of Jeremy's baby bed and didn't look up.

Jerry said and did all the proper parental things, smiling from ear to ear and nodding. The doctor explained that when the test results were in, we'd know what the problem was. I clenched my teeth to keep from bellowing, "You are the problem." Even after the doctor left, Jerry kept smiling and beaming. How I envied him. I couldn't even fake one smile. Down deep inside me I felt the huge chunk of frozen bitterness. It had no intention of breaking up and leaving. "It shouldn't have ever happened," I said sternly to my husband over and over.

Jerry went home at night to be with our children and I slept near Jeremy. Or I tried to. When I'd lie down on the makeshift bed and get nearly to sleep, bitterness intruded and I'd wake up and relive that horrible experience in the tiny examining room at the end of the hall.

As Christmas closed in, the children were dismissed until only Jeremy and one other patient remained. On our fifth night in the hospital, a nurse suggested that I might like to pull Jeremy in a little red wagon with wooden sides. Almost mechanically, I pulled him for hours up and down the halls of the pediatric floor. Each time I approached that small examining room with the door open, I'd get this sick, angry feeling and couldn't bring myself to look inside it. I even began turning my face the other way. After a while, I made an attempt to just glance at it, but it represented too much needless pain and horror. So I pulled Jeremy and my bitterness through the halls, avoiding that room as one would a plague.

As I lifted Jeremy from the wagon later that afternoon, I noticed that the door to the room next to us was ajar. I looked inside. A small girl in bed peered out at us. When our eyes met, she looked away. "Hi," I really tried to give her a smile. She wouldn't look at me. Her name was on the door. "Rosemary?" She looked hesitantly. "If you'd ever want to come out and stroll with Jeremy and me, we'd love to have you." There was a tiny wheelchair parked outside her room.

The next morning when I came out into the hall with Jeremy on my hip, Rosemary sat in the wheelchair by our door, staring straight ahead. "Hey, Rosemary," I said. She didn't answer or even glance at me, but instead began to roll her chair alongside Jeremy in the wagon. I didn't attempt to talk to her. She seemed content just to roll along with us down the mostly empty halls. Jeremy reached out to her, and she held his hand. A nurse came and put her back in bed before lunch. When she came out of Rosemary's room, I asked, "Is she going to be okay?"

"She's in and out of here all the time. It's her second home. She's mildly retarded and has a crippling disease, plus other major health problems. She usually doesn't take to strangers."

"What are her chances?" The nurse went back to her station. I followed, "Do her parents come often?"

"They both work two jobs and have a house full of children."

"But tomorrow's Christmas." The nurse answered the phone and I pulled Jeremy in the wagon back to his room. Throughout the day I'd go outside his room to find Rosemary waiting, sort of like a miniature soldier on duty. I learned to listen for the squeak of her chair. Christmas Eve I went out in the hall, totally empty except for Rosemary and an artificial tree with colored lights. Reindeer were taped to the pale green walls, but Christmas was nowhere around. "Do you want to come and watch me bathe Jeremy?"

She nodded and rolled alongside us. I helped her wedge her small chair into the bathroom. As I sat on the edge of the tub, running the water and holding Jeremy, he began to squirm and reach for Rosemary. Looking back now, I suppose he was getting tired of me. I'd held onto him for a week.

"Let me hold Jeremy for you," Rosemary offered matter-of-factly. Startled, I looked up at her. Her soft brown eyes locked onto mine. I knew I had to trust her without a moment's hesitation. If I didn't trust her right then, I might never trust anyone again.

I tried to sound casual as I handed Jeremy to Rosemary. "Hold him tight, okay?"

"I got him," she beamed as she encircled him firmly with her small arms, holding him secure. Jeremy snuggled up against her, grabbing onto one of her huge pigtails. They smiled at each other as though they were old friends. She sort of rocked him back and forth, humming all the while.

"I can take him now, Rosemary. The water's ready. You were right here when I needed you the most. Thanks."

"You're welcome. He's a good boy."

After Jeremy and Rosemary were both sleeping, I asked the nurse if I could have Jerry bring Rosemary some gifts the next day—Christmas. The nurse was quite obviously pleased. Jerry seemed very willing to go out late on Christmas Eve to look for gifts, but I realized that everything would be picked over. "Jerry, ask Julie if she'll let Rosemary have the Chatty Cathy doll we have for her. Tell her I'll make it up to her." Chatty Cathy dolls were a big item that year. I'd gotten Julie's in October. Our oldest child, at eight, was sort of a number-two mother to Jeremy. After we hung up, I stared out Jeremy's window at the lights below. I even saw a few Christmas trees.

Even so, it was the strangest Christmas Eve I'd ever experienced as I continued my tug-of-war with bitterness. It should have never happened, the agonizing thought bombarded me like well-aimed stones, hitting their mark. As I crawled on the cot by Jeremy's bed for the seventh night, I finally asked God to somehow allow me to let go of the bitterness so I could celebrate Christmas. I didn't really see how he could manage it.

Jerry arrived bright and early with the Chatty Cathy doll and other wrapped gifts. Behind him was Jeremy's pediatrician, who announced that Jeremy was doing so well, he could go home. His mysterious illness turned out to be a rare form of Ludwig's angina. The doctors hadn't seen a case like his in over fifteen years. Jerry went to the business office, and Jeremy and I headed for Rosemary's room.

She couldn't believe the doll was for her. I demonstrated how to pull the string in the doll's back, and Rosemary looked stunned, then delighted as the doll asked, "What is the color of my dress? Can you tie your shoes?"

Rosemary laughed out loud and said, "Your dress is red like Jeremy boy's hair, and I can tie my shoes real good." I didn't know what to do next, so I just stood there holding Jeremy and smiling with this huge knot in my throat. "You gon' be just fine, Jeremy boy, and you going home. You be good for your Mama—you hear?" I sat down on the edge of her bed and retied the ribbon on one of her pigtails and then hugged her to me. Jeremy grabbed onto one of her fat pigtails as well as the doll. As I carefully pried his hands away, I handed the doll back to Rosemary.

"Let him have it," she insisted.

"No, Rosemary, she belongs to you."

"But I want to give him something for Christmas—something to remember me by."

"Oh, Rosemary, you've given us both so much. I couldn't have made it without you." I brushed away tears. Something deep inside of me suddenly felt soft and gentle, and Christmas seemed close by. "We could never forget you. When Jeremy gets bigger, I'm going to tell him about a very beautiful little girl named Rosemary and the Christmas we shared. Why, I may even write a story about you."

"Me! A story about me!" She thumped her small frame over and over. I nodded, unable to speak.

"And you gon' tell Jeremy boy about me—you won't forget?"

I shook my head and managed, "I promise." I handed the doll back to her, pretending humor, "Boys don't play with dolls much."

"Okay. I'll keep her, then. I sure do like her."

I stood up, turned and hurried from the room, carrying Jeremy down the long green hall for the last time. We headed for the elevator, but stopped abruptly outside that tiny examining room. Shifting him to my other hip, I stood still and stared long and hard. Then I entered the room, my eyes fastened onto the pint-sized examining table. I looked down at the black and white squares on the floor—the medical equipment neatly stacked on green shelves. But everything in the room, even that terrifying memory seemed drenched with one churning emotion.

Gratitude.

I breathed it in deeply, almost greedily. "Thank you, God, for letting us keep Jeremy. Thank you for sending your son. Thank you for Rosemary... and her remarkable gift this Christmas."

~Marion Bond West
Chicken Soup for the Soul Christmas Treasury

Author's note: Jeremy recovered fully from Ludwig's angina (not heart-related). We found another pediatrician shortly after he was dismissed from the hospital.

A Christmas Gift

We can do no great things—
only small things with great love.
~Mother Teresa

It was a half-hour before midnight on December 24th. I was a ticket-counter supervisor for a major airline and was looking forward to the end of my shift at Stapleton International Airport in Denver, Colorado. My wife was waiting up for me so we could exchange gifts, as was our tradition on Christmas Eve.

A very frantic and worried gentleman approached me. He asked how he could get home to Cheyenne, Wyoming. He had just arrived from Philadelphia and missed his connecting flight. I pointed him to the ground transportation area. There he could either hire a limousine or rent a car from the various agencies.

He told me that it was extremely important for him to be in Cheyenne for Christmas. I wished him well, and he went on his way. I called my wife to let her know I would be home shortly.

About fifteen minutes later, the same gentleman returned and informed me that all the buses were full and there were no cars or limousines available. Again he asked if I had any suggestions. The most logical option was to offer him a room in a hotel for the night and get him on the first flight to Cheyenne in the morning. When I suggested this, tears starting running down his cheeks.

He explained that his son was seventeen years old and weighed forty pounds. He had spina bifida and was not expected to live another year. He expected that this would likely be the last Christmas with his son and the thought that he would not be there to greet him on Christmas morning was unbearable.

"What's your name, Sir?" I asked.

"Harris, Tom Harris," he replied, his face filled with desperation.

I contacted all of the ground transportation providers and the car rental agencies. Nothing. What was I to do? There was no other choice.

I told Tom to go to the claim area, collect his luggage and wait for me. I called my wife Kathy and told her not to wait up for me. I was driving to Cheyenne, and I would explain everything in the morning. Something had come up that was more important than our exchanging gifts on Christmas Eve.

The drive to Cheyenne was quiet, thoughtful. Tom offered to compensate me for my time and the fuel. I appreciated his gesture, but it wasn't necessary.

We arrived at the airport in Cheyenne around 2:30 A.M. I helped Tom unload his luggage and wished him a Merry Christmas. His wife was meeting him and had not yet arrived.

We shook hands. As I got into my car, I looked back at him. He was the only customer in the airport. I noticed how peaceful and quiet this was compared to the hectic, crowded airport in Denver. Pulling away, I waved goodbye and he waved back. He looked tired and relieved. I wondered how long he would have to wait for his wife to pick him up. She was driving quite a distance.

Kathy was waiting up for me. Before we went to bed, we traded gifts and then our conversation concerned Tom. We imagined his family on Christmas morning as Tom and his wife watched their son open his last Christmas presents. For Kathy and me, there was no question that driving Tom to Cheyenne was the only option. She would have done the same thing.

A couple of days later, I received a Christmas card with a picture of Tom and his family. In it, Tom thanked me for the special gift he had received that holiday season, but I knew the best gift was mine.

~Bob White
Chicken Soup for the Traveler's Soul

25

The Unexpected Gift

It is Christmas in the heart that
puts Christmas in the air.
~W.T. Ellis

First the snow came lightly. I watched it out the window, the flakes flying in the wind the bus made as it sped from Cincinnati, where we lived, to Canton, Ohio, where we were going to spend Christmas with my uncle and cousins. My brother and I were traveling alone because our parents were on the way from Pittsburgh, where they had gone to take care of things after my grandmother died. It was a family emergency, and though my mother did not like the idea of leaving us with her best friend, or having us travel alone, she did not have much choice.

Soon we would all be together in my uncle's house playing the rowdy games and eating too many sugar cookies, which my Aunt Alice made in the shape of snowmen. They always had little stubby hands and feet too. For some reason I liked to eat the feet first. My brother always ate the cherry nose.

I had the window seat for this leg of the trip. My mother always made us trade off to avoid fighting about it and we did that even when we were by ourselves. There was a very big woman sitting across from us who talked to us at the last stop. She thought we were young to be traveling alone and she bought us each a doughnut even though she seemed poor. Her name, she said, was Mrs. Margaret Mills and her husband was dead. I don't know why she told us that.

Before long, the snow got heavier and heavier and the bus began to slow down. It slowed and slowed and before long it was just kind of crawling along and the world outside had turned completely white. I heard the driver talking on his radio about what we should do. So I woke up my brother in case we were about to hit a snowdrift and be boarded by bandits. He always hoped for some big adventure that just never seemed to come our way. Now might be his chance, I thought.

The other passengers began to stir about and go stand in line for the bathroom and make each other nervous. I gave my brother my seat and he kept his face plastered to the glass.

"Look, look," he would say every once in awhile. "More snow. More snow."

It was about an hour later that we eased into a gas station that had a little restaurant shaped like a railroad car attached to it. We all bundled up as best we could, pulled our hats down over our ears and ran for shelter. The wind was making a very weird sound... like a bird screeching. Finally we were all inside and the bus driver told us we were likely to have to spend the night here and might make it out in the morning if the storm stopped and the plows came through.

Now I was frightened and my brother was crying. I told him we would be all right and the weird woman took us to the counter and ordered hot chocolate. My mother had pinned a card inside my coat pocket — she pinned it there because I was always losing things I needed, like mittens — with my uncle's name, address and phone number.

While we were having hot chocolate, the bus driver asked us if we had a phone number for whoever was going to meet us and I gave him the card.

People were very upset. After all, we were about to spend Christmas with a handful of strangers and no one wanted to do that. All the joy and anticipation of being with family and friends was replaced by disappointment and sadness. We were a sorry lot. Some people drank coffee and some ate chicken salad sandwiches and some just sat staring at their folded hands.

I wanted to talk to my parents, and just as I had that thought, the bus driver called me and I went to the phone. He had my aunt on the line. My parents were out at church with my cousins and Aunt Alice was very calm about our situation. She said we would be all right and that we should do what the bus driver said. And that we should not leave the place where we were because my family would come get us in the morning when the roads were plowed.

That made me feel a lot better. But my brother was hard to console. He wanted to be home, to be singing carols while Aunt Alice played the piano, to be having the kind of Christmas Eve we loved. I didn't know what to do to help him and it was beginning to make me mad that he was crying all the time.

Then a strange thing happened. People began to talk to each other and to us. And then they began to laugh and tell stories about their families and where they'd been and where they were going. The man who owned the restaurant turned on the lights of the Christmas tree he had in the corner of the room. They were shaped like candles. And together with the colored lights that bordered the big front window, the room began to seem a little festive. I hoped it all would cheer my brother up, but it did not.

"What are we going to do? I want to see Mama, I want to have cookies, I want to sing the manger song with Aunt Alice, I... I... " and then he would lean against me and cry some more.

The weird woman watched us from time to time. I thought she disliked his sniveling as much as I did, but finally she came to the booth were we were sitting by ourselves and said, "I believe I'll just join you, if you don't mind."

She sat down before I could say anything and she took up quite a lot of space doing it, too.

Then one of the strangest things I have ever seen happened. Her face, which I thought was a little scary—she had a very big nose and this huge neck—softened and gentled as she looked at my brother. And then she began to sing. Out of her strange body came one of the loveliest sounds I've ever heard. She put her arm around my brother and pulled him close to her. And softly, very softly, she sang as though singing just for us, "Away in a manger, no crib for a bed, the little Lord Jesus laid down his sweet head."

He looked up at her. I think he was startled at first to hear his favorite carol sung to him by a strange woman in a snowbound bus stop. But soon the sadness left his face. Soon he put his hand in hers. And then they sang together, louder now, "The stars in the bright sky looked down where he lay, the little Lord Jesus asleep on the hay."

After that a young man unpacked his guitar and the bus driver pulled out a harmonica, and before long, everyone was singing just about every Christmas carol you ever heard in your life. We sang and drank hot cocoa with marshmallows and ate cupcakes until people finally settled down for the evening, huddled in the booths, sitting on the floor, leaning against each other for comfort and support. And so we spent Christmas Eve.

The roads were cleared by eleven the next morning and we said goodbye to everyone on the bus. Our parents had called the restaurant and were on their way to pick us up. The last person we saw was Mrs. Mills. She hugged us and I thanked her. Then she bent over and kissed us both on the forehead. "I'll never forget you two boys. You were my Christmas present. That's the way I'll always think of you." Then she got on the bus and I never saw her again.

Later that night, when we were all comfortable and warm before the fire at Aunt Alice's, I asked my dad what the strange woman could have meant. I'd told him the whole story, of course, except for the part about getting mad at my brother for crying so much.

He said, "That's the thing about a true gift. You can only give it. You never know how much it means to another person."

"But what was our gift, dad? We didn't give her a present or anything."

"I don't have any way of knowing that. It might have been your cute faces. It might have been that you liked her, or weren't afraid of her because of the way she looked. Or it might have been that you sang along with her in a strange place she never planned to be in. Just be grateful that you had something to give that woman, something she treasured and would remember. Make that a part of who you are and that will be your gift to me."

And then Aunt Alice went to the piano and we, all of us, began our annual caroling, the singing of songs together that I liked better than almost anything in the world. But what I was thinking about most that evening was Mrs. Margaret Mills and what a wonderful voice she had. And as I thought about her, I missed her. Truly missed her. And I hoped that wherever she was, she was singing for someone who liked her as much as I did.

~W. W. Meade
Chicken Soup for the Soul Christmas Treasury

26

I'm Not Scrooge...
I'm Just Broke!

There are people who have money
and then there are people who are rich in friends.
~Coco Chanel

It's said that you can never have too many friends, but Christmas was just a week away and I had five people left to shop for on my Christmas list and only three dollars to my name. How do you tell your mother, brother and three friends that you can only spend sixty cents on each of them?

"Let's set a price limit on our gifts this year," I suggested to my best friend, Joanie.

"That's a good idea," Joanie agreed. "How about nothing over five dollars?"

"How about nothing over sixty cents?" I felt like the biggest cheapskate in the world.

"I guess this is where I'm supposed to say it's not the gift, it's the thought that counts," Joanie smiled. "But don't blame me if all you get is a stick of gum!"

It is almost impossible to buy anything for under sixty cents, so it was really going to have to be very small gifts with very big thoughts. I'd never spent so much time or effort trying to come up with the right gift for the right person.

Finally, Christmas Day arrived, and I was worried how people would feel about my "cheap" gifts.

I gave my mother a scented candle with a note that said, "You are the brightest light in my life." She almost cried when she read the note.

I gave my brother a wooden ruler. On the back of it I'd painted, "No brother in the world could measure up to you." He gave me a bag of sugar and had written on it, "You're sweet." He'd never said anything like that to me before.

For Joanie, I painted an old pair of shoes gold and stuck dried flowers in them with a note that said, "No one could ever fill your shoes." She gave me a feather and a Band-Aid. She said I always tickled her funny bone and made her laugh until her sides ached.

To my other two friends, I gave one a paper fan and wrote on it, "I'm your biggest fan." To the other, I gave a calculator that cost one dollar and I painted a message on the back, "You can always count on me." They gave me a rusty horseshoe for luck and a bundle of sticks tied with a red ribbon because "friends stick together."

I don't remember all the other gifts that I got from people last Christmas, but I remember every one of the "cheap" gifts.

My brother thinks I'm sweet. My mother knows she is the most important person in my life. Joanie thinks I'm funny and I make her laugh, which is important because her dad moved away last year and she misses him and is sad sometimes.

I was worried I wouldn't have enough money for Christmas gifts, but I gave gifts to five people and still had twenty cents left over. We all still talk about our "cheap" gifts and how much fun it was to come up with a gift that cost pennies but told someone how we really felt about them. On my bookshelf, I still have a bag of sugar, a feather, a horseshoe and a bundle of sticks... and they are priceless.

~Storm Stafford
Chicken Soup for the Soul Christmas Treasury for Kids

With Gladness
and Glue

While Christmas shopping in a jewelry store, I discovered a clearance table of gilded ornaments. Detailed and delicate in design, each had a personality all its own. I sorted among the hundreds of filigreed masterpieces, picked out a few and took them home.

Deciding they were much too pretty to disappear among the clutter of a Christmas tree, I used them instead to decorate small eight-inch wreaths. When I stood back to admire my handiwork, a thought crossed my mind: Wouldn't some of our family and friends like these, too?

I raced back to the jewelry store to discover that the stack of ornaments had been reduced even further. This time I bought dozens as I thought of the many people who might enjoy one for the holidays.

Armed with a glue gun and bright ribbons of every color, I eagerly began my creative project. The wreaths multiplied like measles and dotted every flat surface in our house. For days, my family tiptoed around, elbowed their way through and slept among the miniature masterpieces.

While I tied dainty bows and glued golden ornaments, my mind wandered to Christmases past, and I pondered how special each had been. I thought about others perhaps not so fortunate. Some people in our community didn't have a family to share the joy of Christmas. Some didn't bother with holiday decorations. Some never left their homes to celebrate the season.

I nodded my head in determined satisfaction. They would be at the top of my list to receive a little wreath. My husband joined me in the plan, and we set out together to put it into action.

We visited the aged. We visited the widowed. We visited the lonely. Each one was thrilled with our cheery stops and immediately hung our small gifts—often the only signs of celebration in their homes.

After several days, I realized we had made and given almost two hundred wreaths. Decorated with love and delivered with delight, they filled many homes and hearts with the joy of Christmas.

And I came to the simple realization that we were actually the ones who received the greatest blessing that year. We had found our Christmas spirit in the doing.

~Nancy B. Gibbs
Chicken Soup for the Soul Christmas Treasury

28

A Special Breakfast

For it is in giving that we receive.
~Saint Francis of Assisi

Until last year, the greatest sorrow of my life was that my wife Alice and I couldn't have any children. To make up for this in a small way, we always invited all the children on our street to our house each Christmas morning for breakfast.

We would decorate the house with snowflakes and angels in the windows, a nativity scene and a Christmas tree in the living room, and other ornaments that we hoped would appeal to the children. When our young guests arrived—there were usually ten or fifteen of them—we said grace and served them such delicacies as orange juice garnished with a candy cane. And after the meal we gave each of the youngsters a wrapped toy or game. We used to look forward to these breakfasts with the joyful impatience of children.

But last year, about six weeks before Christmas, Alice died. I could not concentrate at work. I could not force myself to cook anything but the simplest dishes. Sometimes I would sit for hours without moving, and then suddenly find myself crying for no apparent reason.

I decided not to invite the children over for the traditional Christmas breakfast. But Kathy and Peter, my next door neighbors, asked me to join them and their three children for dinner on

Christmas Eve. As soon as I arrived and had my coat off, Kathy asked me, "Do you have any milk at your house?"

"Yes," I replied. "If you need some, I'll go right away."

"Oh, that's all right. Come and sit down. The kids have been waiting for you. Just give Peter your keys."

So I sat down, prepared for a nice chat with eight-year-old Beth and six-year-old Jimmy. (Their little sister was upstairs sleeping.) But my words wouldn't come. What if Beth and Jimmy should ask me about my Christmas breakfast? How could I explain to them? Would they think I was just selfish or self-pitying? I began to think they would. Worse, I began to think they would be right.

But neither of them mentioned the breakfast. At first I felt relieved, but then I started to wonder if they remembered it or cared about it. As they prattled on about their toys, their friends and Christmas, I thought they would be reminded of our breakfast tradition, and yet they said nothing. This was strange, I thought, but the more we talked, the more I became convinced that they remembered the breakfast but didn't want to embarrass Grandpa Melowski (as they called me) by bringing it up.

Dinner was soon ready and afterward we all went to late Mass. After Mass, the Zacks let me out of their car in front of my house. I thanked them and wished them all merry Christmas as I walked toward my front door. Only then did I notice that Peter had left a light on when he borrowed the milk — and that someone had decorated my windows with snowflakes and angels!

When I opened the door, I saw that the whole house had been transformed with a Christmas tree, a nativity scene, candles and all the other decorations of the season. On the dining room table was Alice's green Christmas tablecloth and her pinecone centerpiece. What a kind gesture! At that moment, I wished that I could still put on the breakfast, but I had made no preparations.

Early the next morning, a five-year-old with a package of sweet rolls rang my bell. Before I could ask him what was going on, he was joined by two of his friends, one with a pound of bacon, the other with a pitcher of orange juice. Within fifteen minutes, my house was alive with all the children on my street, and I had all the food I needed for the usual festive breakfast. I was tremendously pleased, although in the back of my mind I still feared that I would disappoint my guests. I knew my spur-of-the-moment party was missing one important ingredient.

At about nine-thirty, though, I had another surprise. Kathy Zack came to my back door.

"How's the breakfast?" she asked.

"I'm having the time of my life," I answered.

"I brought something for you," she said, setting a shopping bag on the counter.

"More food?"

"No," she said. "Take a look."

Inside the bag were individually wrapped packages, each bearing the name of one of the children and signed, "Merry Christmas from Grandpa Melowski."

My happiness was complete. It was more than just knowing that the children would receive their customary gifts and wouldn't be disappointed; it was the feeling that everyone cared.

I like to think it's significant that I received a gift of love on the same day that the world received a sign of God's love two thousand years ago in Bethlehem. I never found out who to thank for my Christmas present. I said my "Thank you" in my prayers that night—and that spoke of my gratitude more than anything I could ever say to my neighbors.

~Harold Melowski as told to Alan Struthers Jr.
Chicken Soup for the Christian Family Soul

$\mathcal{A}$ Secret for Mom

As I contemplate the arrival of the holidays, I think about all the warm and wonderful Christmases as a child, and I feel a smile cross my face. They were truly a time to remember. As I grew older, the Christmas memories become less vivid and more of a sad and depressing time for me... until last year. It was then that I believe I learned how to recapture that childhood wonder and joy I felt as a child.

Every year I flounder, never knowing what to buy my mother for Christmas. Another robe and slippers, perfume, sweaters? All nice gifts, but they just don't say I love you like they should. I wanted something different, something she would love for the rest of her life. Something that would put that beautiful smile back on her face and the quickness in her step. She lives alone, and much as I may want to spend time with her, I can only manage an occasional visit with the schedule I keep. So I made the decision to become her Secret Santa. Little did I know that this would be just what the doctor ordered.

I went out and bought all sorts of small gifts and then headed to the more expensive areas of the mall. I picked up little nothings, things that I knew only my mother would love. I took them home and wrapped each one differently. Then I went to my computer and made a card for each one. It went according to the song "The Twelve Days of Christmas." Then I began my adventure. The first day was so exciting, I dropped it off and put it in the screen door. Then I hurried home and called her, pretending to inquire about her health. She was bubbling over. Someone had left a gift for her and signed it "Secret Santa."

The next day, the same scenario played out. After four or five days, I went to her house, and my heart just broke. She had laid out all the gifts on her kitchen table and was showing them to everyone at the apartment complex. Wrappings and all were spread out and each one had the note attached. She never stopped talking about this secret admirer the entire duration of my visit. Her eyes sparkled, and her voice was lilting. She was in seventh heaven. Every day, she would call me with news of the new gift she found when she woke up. Then she decided to try to catch the person responsible and slept on the couch with the door cracked open. So I left it later that day, and she worried that the gifts weren't coming anymore. She had me just as excited as she was. On the last day, the note told her to be dressed on that Saturday, and she was to go to Applebee's for dinner. There she would meet her Secret Santa. She went wild. The note also told her to ask her daughter Susan to bring her (that's me). It said she would know her Secret Santa by the red ribbon she would be wearing. So I picked her up and off we went.

When we arrived, the hostess seated us at a table, and my mom looked around. She lost the smile and asked when she was going to meet her Secret Santa. I slowly took off my coat, and there was the red ribbon. She began to cry and fuss over how much I spent and how I did this. She was happier than I have ever seen her.

When it was all said and done, I thought about how good I felt, and just as quickly, I remembered something very important. When I was a child, it was my mother who taught me that it is better to give than to receive. Reality slapped me hard. All these years when I had been sad during the holidays was most likely because I was looking at the "getting" instead of the "giving." I was humbled by this realization, and now I am certain, Mom does know best....

~Susan Spence
Chicken Soup for the Mother & Daughter Soul

30

The Wreath

Perhaps the best Yuletide decoration
is being wreathed in smiles.
~Author Unknown

For their Christmas holiday project, Cassie's Blue Bird troop planned to visit a nursing home.

"Folks in nursing homes are often too old or too sick to be home alone," Mrs. Peters, the group leader, told the little girls. "Maybe they have no relatives; maybe families are far away or unable to help. We're going to cheer them with carols and bring them gifts we've made."

Placing the last flower on her wreath, Cassie wondered about the person whose name she drew—Mabel—somewhere between sixty and eighty. Not yet ten, Cassie had difficulty identifying with "old." Her grandparents played golf, traveled a lot and had plenty of loving relatives.

Outside, a car horn blared. Cassie scooped up her wreath and rushed to join her friends. The Blue Birds, a junior version of Camp Fire Girls, soon arrived at a modest cottage. A matron greeted them enthusiastically.

"The folks are just so looking forward to your visit," she said with a smile.

Stepping onto the cottage's smooth linoleum floor, Cassie

sniffed a strong disinfectant odor. Mrs. Peters sounded a pitch on her harmonica and led the troop in "We Wish You a Merry Christmas."

Singing along, Cassie gazed at one wrinkled face after another: some smiling, some sad, some apathetic. One elderly woman turned her face to the wall. As the matron announced the little girls would be circulating among the residents with gifts, a man in a wheelchair spun forward. He wagged his finger fiercely at the visitors.

"What right do you have coming here, reminding us of families we don't have?" he shouted. "Once a year somebody comes here. Take your do-gooding pity and get out!"

Wide-eyed, some of the girls backed away, but Mrs. Peters coaxed them forward again as the matron calmed the grumbling man.

Shaken but determined, Cassie asked a group of card players, "Please, where can I find Mabel?"

A lady with bright orange hair gestured toward the window.

"Over there," she said cheerfully. "And don't pay these grouches any mind. You kids are okay."

Timidly clutching her wreath, Cassie approached the straight-backed figure surrounded by soft winter light.

"Mabel?"

The gray head with a proud French roll at its crown didn't move. Mabel — if this was Mabel — continued gazing out the window at the darkening California desert. Cassie set her wreath on the worn, polished surface of a table by her side. Taking a deep breath, she stared at it, as if memorizing every leaf.

"I made this wreath for you," she said. "I know it's just homemade, but there is a story for every twig and flower. I came to tell you about them.

"The base is made from pine branches — some were easy to bend, and some I had to soak in water to shape the frame. It's all natural and gathering the flowers was fun, because I remember where each one grew."

Her courage up now, Cassie talked faster, touching the wreath as she spoke.

"The wild sunflowers are from a vacant lot by my house. Someone is going to build new homes there, so by spring the sunflowers will be all gone. These dried desert flowers—the mustard, sage and lavender—smell so good, and they'll last a long time. Rabbit foot fern is from my patio garden, and so is the baby's breath. I caught the gold and red maple leaves when they blew across our lawn. I found a few little pinecones, too. And in the center is a star white cactus flower. Mom says it's kind of unusual for this time of year."

Slowly, Mabel turned around. Eyes undimmed by age searched Cassie's.

"I sit by this window," she said quietly, "because I miss the outdoors so. Thank you for bringing it inside."

A trembling hand, clustered with brown spots, reached over and grasped Cassie's. "I, too, remember where the flowers grew. Merry Christmas, child."

~Sherri Andervich
Chicken Soup for the Gardener's Soul

31

The Not-So-White Christmas Gift

Do all the good you can,
by all the means you can,
in all the ways you can...
as long as ever you can.
~John W. Desley

Through the front window of the drugstore where we both worked as assistant managers, I could see Lamar eagerly awaiting my arrival, his breath condensing on the glass as he peered out at me. A deal we had struck back in November had him working Christmas Day and me New Year's.

The weather outside was typical of Memphis at this time of the year. Lamar and I always hoped for a white Christmas, but this one had rolled by just like the previous twenty—cold and foggy, with nary a snowflake in sight.

As I pushed into the warmth of the store, Lamar looked relieved.

"Rough day?" I inquired.

Gesturing to the front cash register, Lamar moaned, "We had lines fifteen-deep yesterday. I've never seen so many people trying to buy batteries and film. Oh well, I guess that's one of the joys of working Christmas day."

"What do you want me to do today?" I asked.

"It will probably slow down around six tonight. The night after Christmas is usually dead. Then you can straighten this disaster of a toy aisle." He stooped to pick up a stray stuffed animal, which he shoved into my belly. "And do something with this animal."

That little plush dog had become our Christmas mascot. We seemed to be forever picking it up off the floor. Five, maybe ten, times a day. It hadn't been a pretty toy to begin with. Now its long shaggy fur had become matted and soiled, as gray as the day outside, grimed with dust from the floor and dirt from the hands of children who had held it while their mothers waited for prescriptions to be filled. The toy had been marked down many times, without any takers. In that bright shiny world of Smurfs and Barbie dolls and G.I. Joes, I guess a little dog with dirty white fur just wasn't the plaything of choice. Still, every kid in Memphis must have squeezed that puppy at least once that Christmas season.

The afternoon bustled by with refunds, exchanges and the sale of half-price Christmas decorations, but at six o'clock, just as Lamar had predicted, business came to a halt. Out of sheer boredom, I went to work on the toy aisle. The first toy I encountered, of course, was that fluffy dog with the droopy ears, staring up at me from the floor one more time. I started to throw it away and write it off the inventory, but, I changed my mind and stuck it back on the shelf. Sentimental, I guess.

"Excuse me." A voice interrupted my deliberations. "Are you the manager?" I turned and saw a slender young woman with a little boy of five standing quietly beside her.

"I'm the assistant manager," I said. "How may I help you?"

The lady looked down for a moment, then put her chin up and said with something like a rasp in her voice, "My son hasn't had any Christmas. I was hoping you might have something marked down now. Something I could afford?"

I had grown cynical at the occasional homeless person's plea for quarters, but in her voice, I heard a note of sincerity and a pride that made her ache at having to ask such a question.

I looked down at the little boy, standing there so self-controlled in the midst of all those toys.

"I'm just marking the toys down now. What is it you're looking for?"

The young woman brightened, as though she had finally encountered someone who would listen. "I don't have much money, but I'd like to buy my son something special."

The boy's face lit up at his mother's words. Speaking directly to him, I said, "You pick out the best toy you could want for Christmas, okay?"

He glanced at his mother, and when she nodded her assent, he grinned ear to ear. I waited, curious to see which of the season's most popular toys he would choose. Maybe a race car set, or a basketball.

Instead, he walked right to that gruff old dog and hugged it as tightly as ever I had seen a kid clutch a toy. I acted as if I were brushing the hair out of my eyes, while I surreptitiously wiped away a tear.

"How much is that dog?" his mother asked, unfastening the clasp on a small, black coin purse.

"It's no charge," I said. "You'd be doing me a favor by taking it away."

"No, I can't do that," she insisted. "I want to pay for my son's Christmas present."

From the intense look in her eyes, I knew that she wanted to give her child a gift as much as he wanted to receive one.

"It's a dollar," I said.

She pulled a crumpled bill from her purse and handed it to me. Then she turned to her son and said, "You can take the dog home with you now. It's yours."

Once again I fumbled with the hair around my eyes, as the little boy beamed ecstatically. His mother smiled, too, and silently mouthed "Thank you" as they left the store.

Through the window, I watched them make their way into the Memphis evening. There still wasn't a snowflake in sight, but as I turned back to the toy aisle, I found, smiling, that I had gotten that old white-Christmas feeling after all.

—Harrison Kelly
A Second Chicken Soup for the Woman's Soul

Chapter
4

Christmas Cheer

Holiday Humor

Humor has a way of bringing people together.
It unites people. In fact, I'm rather serious when I suggest that
someone should plant a few whoopee cushions in the United Nations.

~Ron Dentinger

32

Christmas Love

There has been only one Christmas—
the rest are anniversaries.
~W.J. Cameron

Every year, I promised it would be different. Each December, I vowed to make Christmas a calm and peaceful experience. But, once again, in spite of my plans, chaos prevailed. I had cut back on what I deemed nonessential obligations: extensive card writing, endless baking, Martha Stewart decorating, and, yes, even the all-American pastime, overspending. Yet still I found myself exhausted, unable to appreciate the precious family moments, and, of course, the true meaning of Christmas.

My son, Nicholas, was in kindergarten that year. It was an exciting season for a six-year-old, filled with hopes, dreams and laughter. For weeks, he'd been memorizing songs for his school's upcoming Winter Pageant.

I didn't have the heart to tell him I'd be working the night of the production. Not willing to miss his shining moment, I spoke with his teacher. She assured me there'd be a dress rehearsal in the morning, and that all parents unable to attend the evening presentation were welcome to enjoy it then. Fortunately, Nicholas seemed happy with the compromise.

So, just as I promised, I filed in ten minutes early, found a spot on the cafeteria floor and sat down. When I looked around the room,

I saw a handful of parents quietly scampering to their seats. I began to wonder why they, too, were attending a dress rehearsal, but chalked it up to the chaotic schedules of modern family life.

As I waited, the students were led into the building. Each class, accompanied by their teacher, sat crossed-legged on the floor. The children would become members of the audience as each group, one by one, rose to perform their song. Because the public school system had long stopped referring to the holiday as "Christmas," I didn't expect anything other than fun, commercial entertainment. The Winter Pageant was filled with songs of reindeer, Santa Claus, snow-flakes and good cheer. The melodies were fun, cute and lighthearted. But nowhere to be found was even the hint of an innocent babe, a manger, or Christ's precious, sacred gifts of life, hope and joy.

When my son's class rose to sing "Christmas Love," I was slightly taken aback by its bold title. However, within moments, I settled in to watch them proudly begin their number. Nicholas was aglow, as were all of his classmates, adorned in fuzzy mittens, red sweaters and bright snowcaps upon their heads. Those in the front row, center stage, held up large letters, one by one, to spell out the title of the song. As the class would sing "C is for Christmas," a child would hold up the letter C. Then, "H is for Happy," and on and on, until each child holding up his or her portion had presented the complete message, "Christmas Love."

The performance was going smoothly, until suddenly, we noticed her, a small, quiet girl in the front row holding the letter M, upside-down! She was entirely unaware that reversed, her letter M appeared as a W. She fidgeted from side to side, until she had moved away from her mark entirely. The audience of children snickered at this little one's mistakes. In her innocence, she had no idea they were laughing at her and stood tall, proudly holding her W.

You can only imagine the difficulty in calming an audience of young, giggling children. Although many teachers tried to shush them, the laughter continued. It continued, that is, until the moment the last letter was raised, and we all saw it together. A hush came over the audience and eyes began to widen. In that instant, we finally understood the reason we were there, why we celebrated in the first place, why even in the chaos, there was a purpose for our festivities. For, when the last letter was held high, the message read loud and clear, "CHRIST WAS LOVE." And, I believe, He still is.

~Candy Chand
Chicken Soup for the Christian Family Soul

Taffy Twist

"How's it look?" my mother asked me. I stared into the boiling pink goo bubbling up in the pan. My mom had decided that we should have an "old-fashioned" Christmas this year, and we were experimenting with making taffy for the first time in our lives.

"I think it's ready," I said. The candy thermometer read 265 degrees. My mother checked it.

"It's definitely ready," she said. "Let's pour it out."

My little sister, Janet, had a large cookie sheet buttered and ready to go. My brother Mike and his best friend, Jimmy, looked on as my mother took the hot pan off the stove and poured the pink taffy slowly onto the cookie sheet. It looked shiny and delicious.

"While we wait for that to cool, let's pull this one," my mom said, pointing to the white taffy we'd made earlier.

"Yeah!" we shouted. It was the moment we'd been waiting for. My mom cut the white taffy into two halves and gave one hunk to Mike and Jimmy, and the other hunk to Janet and me. As teams, we began pulling on opposite sides of our taffy, making long stringy lengths, folding it in half and pulling it out again. We did this over and over until our sticky taffy turned smooth and satiny. It was hot work, but no one minded on such a cold December night in Alaska. It made us feel cozy even though huge snowflakes spun past the streetlights outside.

Now that the taffy was pulled, we rolled it into one big ball. From there, we took small pieces and formed them into little taffy "snakes." When the pink taffy was cool enough, we repeated the process.

"Now," my mother said, "watch this." She picked up a length of white taffy and a length of pink taffy and twisted them together. She pinched the ends and formed a crook at the top. "It's a candy cane!" she said.

"How cool!" we said, excited to be making our own candy canes from scratch. We got busy twisting the taffy and soon had a large batch of candy canes ready. We took them out to the living room and hung them one by one on our Christmas tree. Our tree was decorated with homemade ornaments in the spirit of an old-fashioned Christmas and the freshly made candy canes added just the right touch. We took a moment to admire our handiwork and then headed back into the kitchen to clean up our mess.

After the last pan had been washed and dried and the kitchen was tidied up, we returned to the living room to enjoy our creations and relax in front of the fire. But when we entered the living room, the sight of our tree made us stop and stare in amazement.

The homemade taffy candy canes were now two and three feet long! They oozed from branch to branch like thick pink and white spider webs.

"Oh no!" my mother shrieked. "The heat from the fireplace is melting the taffy!"

Mike stifled a laugh. That did it. In an instant, we were all hysterical with laughter as we watched the blobs of taffy slowly plop onto the carpet.

The next year at Christmas, we bought candy canes from the store.

~Sandra J. Payne
Chicken Soup for the Soul Christmas Treasury for Kids

Martha's Christmas Wonderland

Humor is, in fact, a prelude to faith, and laughter is the beginning of prayer.
~Reinhold Niebuhr

The Christmas season is one of my favorite times of year. I always thought I did a pretty good job of celebrating it by putting up lots of holiday decorations throughout the house—but that was before I met my friend Martha. I was amazed at how she magically transformed their entire home into a Christmas extravaganza. I had no idea you could put so many garlands and ornaments and lights on a tree and still have it look good, let alone stand up. Everyone marveled at the wonderland she created.

One day Martha told our friend Maureen the reason she went to such lengths to celebrate Christmas. She said it was because she had never really had much of one when she was growing up. In fact, she said her family had never even had a Christmas tree.

Maureen was deeply moved by Martha's missing out on this childhood experience. She reached over, touched her lightly on the arm and said, "Oh, Martha, were you poor?"

Martha looked at her in a puzzled sort of way, then said, "No! We were Jewish!"

~Nancy Mueller
Chicken Soup for the Soul The Book of Christmas Virtues

Not Alone

"What do you think of God," the teacher asked.
After a pause, the young pupil replied,
"He's not a think, he's a feel."
~Paul Frost

hristmas was only two weeks away. I usually loved the Christmas season and all the joy it brings, but this year any joy I exhibited would be forced. It was the first Christmas for my small daughters and me since my husband had announced he was not happy and had moved away. It was our first Christmas without him.

"Since the divorce..." everything seemed to be referenced by this event. I never wanted to be a single parent, but that is what I had recently become. The responsibility of caring for my two little girls was sobering. As their only safety net, I felt vulnerable. Rampaging through my mind were questions such as: What if I get sick? What if I cannot find a teaching job? Who will take care of the girls if they become ill, and I am at work? What if I make the wrong financial decisions? I was fearful of how I would possibly handle all these challenges alone. And somehow, this first Christmas without my husband made my aloneness even more pronounced.

The girls' father left us for what he called "a better life." It was not better for us. I was frantically taking twenty-one hours of college courses, including student teaching, in an attempt to finish my

degree in one semester. I had put off obtaining this teaching certifica-
tion to have the girls, but now I desperately needed it before I could
even seek employment in my field. And until I finished, I was forced
to live in a city far away from family and friends. I could not afford
to spread it out over another semester; so despite the heavy load, I
pushed forward.

The fall semester had been exhausting. I tried not to leave my
young daughters with the sitter more than was absolutely necessary,
and I felt it my duty to be cheerful and ready for interaction when I
picked them up. That meant I did no studying or assignments until
after they were in bed for the night. I lost considerable weight and
was truly just running on fumes during that last week of the semester.
There was little time to eat or sleep. The stress and sadness I felt were
almost unbearable, and with all my family in another state, I felt I
was facing it all alone.

The few hours of sleep I had each night were so welcome that
it was difficult to even stir when my alarm blasted me awake each
morning. Yet this night, a strange sound startled me out of my deep
sleep. I had heard a loud thump. As I tried to shake off the effects
of sleep, I heard the familiar sound of the heater coming on, but
now something else penetrated my groggy state. A muffled voice was
speaking, and it was coming from the direction of my bedroom closet.
The closet door was closed, but I could still hear someone talking,
asking a question that I couldn't quite make out. All my senses came
alive, heightened by fear. My eyes widened, trying unsuccessfully to
pierce the darkness and make sense of the situation. I strained to
hear. It clearly was not the voice of either of my little daughters. As
the grogginess left, I realized with increasing alarm that there was a
stranger's voice in my walk-in closet!

I lay very still, too terrified to move. I was like a rabbit that
freezes, almost without breathing, in the hope he is camouflaged
and the hunter cannot see him. I did not want to move, but then I
remembered that I was no camouflaged rabbit. I was a mother—a
mother with two little girls to protect. There was no one else in the
house to help. Those sweet babies were my sole responsibility, and I

was not going to let some intruder get to them. I had to think clearly and act quickly. I renewed my efforts to analyze the muffled voice. My heart was still pounding, but I decided the voice did not seem to be coming any closer to the bed, nor did it seem quite so ominous. However, it did have an eerie singsong cadence.

Since the divorce, I was down to one phone, which was in the kitchen on the other side of the house. A run there would leave my sleeping babies in the adjacent bedroom unprotected. I ruled out a plan to make a run for the phone, but something had to be done, and it was up to me to do it. I decided to confront this intruder myself. That decision caused a trusted old habit to kick in. I sent an arrow prayer to God: "God, I'm in trouble. Please help me."

With my heart pounding, I inched my way across my bed, dropped to the floor, pulled out the gun I had purchased for protection from the bedside table and crept toward the closet door. It was time to find out who was having this conversation in my closet. Fortunately, the closet light switch was outside the door. I flipped on the light. With lightning speed and far too much force, I flung the door open. Still wearing my short nightgown, I spread my legs and took a bold "gun stance," much like you might see on a Charlie's Angels movie poster, and pointed my gun in the direction of the voice.

That's when I saw it.

Lying on the carpeted floor was an overturned, brightly wrapped Christmas present. Now I could clearly hear the repetitive message it was emitting: "Hello. I'm Mickey Mouse. Do you want to play?"

Again. "Hello. I'm Mickey Mouse. Do you want to play?"

Reality hit that I was pointing a gun at my daughter's wrapped Christmas gift, a prerecorded Disney talking telephone. A week before, I had installed the battery, wrapped the phone and hidden it on the highest closet shelf until it was time to put it under the tree. Somehow it had slipped off the shelf, flipped over and activated a button that produced this one-sided conversation from Mickey.

Mickey's muffled voice droned on.

"Hello. I'm Mickey Mouse. Do you want to play?"

Stepping into the closet, I lowered the gun and slid my back down the wall until I was sitting on the floor. The overturned talking package was directly in front of me. The crisis was over, and as relief flooded over me, I found myself crying and laughing at the same time. Crying in relief that the exaggerated fear I had conjured in my mind was unfounded, and laughing at the ridiculousness of the situation. I had terrified myself over a toy!

Sitting on that closet floor, God reminded me in a most humorous way that I was not alone — never had been and never would be. Through this noisy toy still talking away, he let me know that with him by my side, I had the courage to face the thumps in the night and any other challenge life would bring my daughters' or my way. I had feared being alone, but this night's experience taught me a precious truth about that fear: God is my refuge and he would never leave me. No matter my situation in life, I was not alone, and the spirit of Christmas could fill my home.

I reached over and righted my daughter's toppled Christmas gift. This released the depressed button and finally Mickey was silenced. And so were my fears.

~Jennifer Clark Vihel
Chicken Soup for the Single Parent's Soul

The Lost Ball

The other sports are just sports.
Baseball is a love.
~Bryant Gumbel, 1981

This story is about a little kid and an autographed baseball. It's a story about that awful feeling in your stomach when you lose your prized possession.

This story is also about rediscovering the joy of childhood, no matter how old you are, and this story is about brotherhood.

The story starts around Christmastime 1954.

My oldest brother, Jerry, was less than a month old. My parents wanted to buy him something special, and they learned about a promotion at a local department store. Bob Turley, a pitcher with the first-year Baltimore Orioles of the American League, was signing baseballs one afternoon. An autographed baseball seemed like a perfect, inexpensive keepsake so my parents waited in line for Turley's autograph.

When it was time for Turley to sign my parents' ball, my mother mentioned that it was for her newborn. Turley responded that he, too, had a new baby.

That was enough for my mother, who could make small talk with a brick wall. For the next few minutes, Turley and my mother talked about newborns while my father rolled his eyes and the rest of the line waited.

My mother will never forget that encounter, always remembering what a nice man Turley was, but that's only part of this story.

Now it's 1965.

Jerry is ten and his younger brother, Chuck, is about eight. They want to play catch in the back alley, but they can't find an old ball to use. So they make a mistake that thousands of little boys and girls have made over the years.

"Let's use the autographed ball."

They promise not to drop it. But, eventually, the inevitable happens. One overthrows the other, and the baseball skips down the steep alley. The two boys run after it as fast as they can. When they reach the end of the alley, though, the ball has disappeared. Two older boys say they saw the ball hit the sewer grate and fall down into the sewer.

Jerry and Chuck check out the scene. They find nothing except that sick feeling in their stomachs.

Flash forward to Thanksgiving 1991. My family has eaten turkey and stuffing and watched football.

Now it's time to sit in the living room and talk—our favorite pastime. As it always does, the conversation eventually turns to baseball. And to the Baltimore Orioles.

Six weeks before, the team had hosted its last game in venerable Memorial Stadium, which was being replaced by Oriole Park at Camden Yards. Many former Orioles had been invited back to say goodbye to the old ballpark, including Turley, the man who threw the first pitch for the Orioles in their first game in Memorial.

The mention of Turley's name brings the old stories rushing back. First, my mother and the tale of the department store line. And then the sigh from Jerry Jr.

"Are you going to cry again about how you lost that ball?" I chide my brother.

"I didn't lose it," he responds with the high-pitched voice of a ten-year-old. "Those older kids—they stole it. I know it didn't go down the sewer."

My family burst into laughter.

Twenty-eight years had passed, but the memory still pains my brother. He's a successful businessman with a wonderful wife and two beautiful daughters. He can buy as many autographed baseballs as he wants.

But that's not the point. He'll never forget the ball that got away.

"Do you know how silly you sound?" I ask him.

A slight smile crosses his lips.

"You don't understand," he says in an anguished voice. "Those older kids stole my ball."

We laugh for a few more minutes at Jerry's expense before the subject changes to something else, but his anguish stays with me. He is my big brother, after all.

Two weeks later, I devise a plan. It seems like a long shot, but it is worth a try. I make some phone calls. And some more phone calls.

Finally, I find the man I am looking for. He laughs when I tell him the story of the old ball. He graciously agrees to help me out.

On December 24th, the package arrives. And, on Christmas Day, we all meet at my brother's house.

After opening all of the other presents, I hand Jerry a small box. Our mother readies her camera. His wife giggles.

"What is this?" he asks as he lifts a baseball out of the box. "Is this for real?"

I nod.

"This is unbelievable," Jerry says, laughing as his face turns red.

"Well," our mother says, "read it aloud."

My brother clears his throat.

"To Jerry. Don't lose this one. Your friend, Bob Turley."

~Dan Connolly
Chicken Soup for the Baseball Lover's Soul

An Untraditional Holiday Tale

As kids, my sister and I were enemies. Three years my junior, Wendy would borrow my clothes and leave them scattered on the floor. We'd fight about who got to use the bathroom first and how much hot water was left. At times, we'd be locked in hair-pulling brawls.

As we grew up, dislike turned into tolerance, acceptance and then friendship. Today, she's not only my best friend but also my partner in crime as we try to undo the nutty traditions my parents won't give up. There's one in particular we've tried to buck; each year we're unsuccessful.

For more years than I can remember, Wendy and I have read *The Night Before Christmas* aloud to our family on Christmas Eve. The routine repeats itself each year.

After midnight church service on Christmas Eve, Wendy and I are instructed to go upstairs, where we find new pajamas. Then, clad in our new duds, we scamper downstairs for a late-night snack of homemade cookies and wine, sit on the fireplace, and read from the book that belonged to my grandmother.

Wendy's twenty-seven; I'm three years older. We're still reading the story. In fact, we're still receiving new pajamas, although Victoria's Secret has replaced the OshKosh.

Every year, we vow to quit reading. When we tell my parents

we're too old for this, they laugh. "Santa Claus won't come tonight if there's no reading," my mom says. She's not kidding.

Santa still leaves us presents in exchange for milk and cookies, although the milk's long since been replaced by beer. In fact, the Easter Bunny still hides our baskets, but that's another story.

Admittedly, Wendy and I have sunk so low as to make our reading obnoxious, hoping this would force us out of this yearly duty. One year, we read in country twang. The next year, we read one word at a time, slowly. Another year, we read as fast as we could. Our family calls the variety cute and won't consider ending the tradition.

So Wendy and I decided to get even. Seven years ago, we planned our first revenge.

We were giving my parents a grill, and rather than just give it to them, we wanted them to work for it, punishment for those years of reading.

When my parents opened their present that year, they found a riddle. Solve the riddle and they'd find another clue leading them closer to their present. Thirty minutes later, after running around the house, they located the grill on the porch.

We still had to read the next year. So we got meaner.

We filled a box the size of a mattress with Styrofoam peanuts. Inside three peanuts, we stuck a rolled-up message that directed my parents to their present. Luck struck, unfortunately, for after fifteen minutes of searching, my dad located a coded peanut.

A year later, we employed intellect for our payback scheme.

The box my parents opened contained a booby-trapped Twister board. To find their present, my parents had to make it to one corner of the board. Getting there required successfully passing through a maze of challenges. After completing each challenge, my parents could move to the next spot.

Wendy and I spent a day putting the maze together, but it was worth it. On Christmas morning, my parents sang "Jingle Bells" with their noses plugged, kissed our two cats (which you couldn't have paid them enough to do ordinarily), stood on their heads, and yes, read *The Night Before Christmas*.

We weren't excused from our duty.

Wendy and I have since made my parents play our version of *Let's Make a Deal*. They traded away everything except a bag of kitty litter. Two hours later, when Santa called to say there'd been a technical error, my parents found a new television.

The next Christmas, we put together a huge jigsaw puzzle, scribbled their present on the back (a trip to San Francisco), disassembled the puzzle, and then watched them spend the next several hours putting it together. The following year, they had to complete a list of crazy activities before they received a map, which directed them to their presents. In our pajamas, we piled into the car and drove to a friend's house where we'd stashed their gifts.

Last year, they played our version of Who Wants to Win Their Christmas Present, modeled after *Who Wants to Be a Millionaire*. Our rules were different, though: Goof up and they had to perform certain activities before they could play again. So they ran around the outside of the house in their bathrobes, clenched my dog's pig-ear treat between their teeth, and did twenty push-ups on the floor.

Our plan for revenge has obviously backfired. My parents enjoy their payback so much—they even look forward to it—that our goofy way of giving gifts has now become a tradition of its own.

That means Wendy and I will be stuck reading *The Night Before Christmas* forever. If only the story would change. But it doesn't, and maybe that's the point. As much as I hate to admit it, I would never trade the reading for the hours I spend with my sister planning new, zany ways to give my parents their Christmas present.

At least Wendy and I will never have to shop for PJs again.

~Karen Asp
Chicken Soup for the Sister's Soul

38

Deck the Halls... and Save Some Tinsel for the Goat!

Our perfect companions never have fewer than four feet.
~Colette

"It followed me home, Mom, can I keep it?"

If you live in the city, this usually means your child has brought home a stray kitten or a puppy. If you live in the country, it could mean your child has brought home anything from a chicken to a pig. Today it was a goat.

"Isn't she beautiful, Mom?" Peter hugged the smelly, black nanny goat who looked at me with blank eyes that showed no sign of intelligence.

"She looks very valuable, I'm sure some farmer has lost her and wants her back." I hoped that was true.

"I'll put an ad in the lost and found, and if nobody claims her in a week, can I keep her?" he begged.

"Okay," I agreed, not realizing I had just destroyed my entire life.

No one claimed the goat even though I ran the ad an extra week. Some very smart farmer had dumped her on our doorstep and wasn't about to admit it and get stuck with the goat again.

Nanny goat ate every living thing in the yard except the cat. She mowed the flowers to the ground, ate the weeping willow tree my husband had given me on our anniversary and she tap-danced on the hood of my car. No fence was high enough or tight enough to keep her in the pasture.

Nanny grew and grew and it became obvious she was pregnant. On Thanksgiving Day, she produced triplets. That night, an ice storm came sweeping through the Ozarks and the goats had to be moved into the house to keep them from freezing to death.

That was also the night our new minister came to visit. He said he'd never known anyone who kept goats in their living room before. He only stayed a few minutes. He said he wanted to get home before the roads got too slick. Nanny chewing on his shoelaces probably didn't help.

We discovered a goat only four hours old can jump on a chair, bounce on a sofa and slide across the coffee table forty-two times an hour. Triplets can do 126 jumps, bounces and slides per hour. Nanny sat in the recliner, chewed her cud and showed no signs of intelligence.

The Christmas parade was just around the corner and what animal reminds us all of Christmas more than a goat and three baby goats? My husband promised to take the goats to the parade in his truck, but he was working at the auction and running late. I had to get four children and four goats to town or they would miss the parade.

I'd have to be crazy to load my children and the goats into my station wagon and drive six miles to town just so they could be in a Christmas parade.

Nanny loved riding in the car, but she insisted on a window seat. She sat upright with a seat belt holding her securely in place. Three of the children each held a baby goat in their lap. As other cars passed us, people stared and pointed and I hoped they knew I had four goats in my car and not four very ugly children.

When we arrived in town, Peter dressed the four goats in tinsel, bobbles and bells, and walked down the street behind the band and the float with Santa Claus riding on it.

The band struck up "Hark! the Herald Angels Sing" and the goats bolted through the middle of the trumpet players and made short work of the elves. Santa jumped off the float and helped us corner the goats in the doorway of the donut shop.

The goats were dragged back to the street and placed at the front of the parade to keep them as far away from the band as possible.

Peter and his goats won the first place trophy for the most unusual entry. Nanny's picture was in the newspaper, and she looked brilliant.

If you look closely at the newspaper picture, you can see me in the background, showing no sign of intelligence.

Time has passed, and Peter's goat herd has grown to over thirty. These smelly, wonderful animals have changed our lives and Christmas just doesn't seem like Christmas until someone asks, "Who's going to hang up the stockings on the mantle, and who's going to decorate the goats?"

~April Knight
Chicken Soup for the Soul Christmas Treasury

39

Surprise Santa

Never miss an opportunity to make others happy.
~Author Unknown

few days before Christmas, a devout Christian couple held the hands of their young son and walked briskly to their nearby church. But the boy pulled back a bit, slowed and came to an abrupt halt.

"Santa," he whispered. "Santa!"

The four-year-old broke free of his parents' grasp and ran toward an elderly gentleman with a long, flowing white beard.

Tugging on the stranger's coattail, the youngster begged, "Santa, will you bring me a teddy bear for Christmas?"

Embarrassed, the couple started to apologize, but the man merely waved them aside. Instead, he patted their son on the head, nodded once, winked wryly at the youngster and—without a word—went on his way.

On Christmas morning, a knock interrupted the family's festivities. In the doorway stood the old man holding out a large bear with a plaid bow around its neck.

"I didn't want the little fellow to be disappointed on his holiday," he explained with an awkward grimace and turned to leave.

Uncomfortable and stunned, the parents could only stutter a weak, "Uh, th-thanks. And M-merry Christmas to you... Rabbi."

~Henry Boye
Chicken Soup for the Soul The Book of Christmas Virtues

Chapter 5

Christmas Cheer

Special Holiday Memories

There is no ideal Christmas;
only the Christmas you decide to make
as a reflection of your values, desires, affections, traditions.

~Bill McKibben

Away in a Manger

The emotion which has no vent in tears may make other organs weep.
~Henry Maudsley

One afternoon about a week before Christmas, my family of four piled into our minivan to run an errand, and this question came from a small voice in the back seat: "Dad," began my five-year-old son, Patrick, "how come I've never seen you cry?"

Just like that. No preamble. No warning. Surprised, I mumbled something about crying when he wasn't around, but I knew that Patrick had put his young finger on the largest obstacle to my own peace and contentment—the dragon-filled moat separating me from the fullest human expression of joy, sadness and anger. Simply put, I could not cry.

I am scarcely the only man for whom this is true. We men have been conditioned to believe that stoicism is the embodiment of strength. We have traveled through life with stiff upper lips, secretly dying within.

For most of my adult life, I have battled depression. Doctors have said much of my problem is physiological, and they have treated it with medication. But I know that my illness is also attributable to years of swallowing rage, sadness and even joy.

Strange as it seems, in this world where macho is everything, drunkenness and depression are safer ways than tears for many men to deal with feelings. I could only hope the same debilitating handicap would not be passed to the next generation.

So the following day, when Patrick and I were in the van after playing at a park, I thanked him for his curiosity. Tears are a good thing, I told him, for boys and girls alike. Crying is God's way of healing people when they're sad. "I'm glad you can cry whenever you're sad," I said. "Sometimes daddies have a harder time showing how they feel. Someday I hope I do better."

Patrick nodded. In truth, I held out little hope. But in the days before Christmas, I prayed that somehow I could connect with the dusty core of my own emotions.

"I was wondering if Patrick would sing a verse of 'Away in a Manger' during the service on Christmas Eve," the church youth director asked in a message left on our answering machine.

My wife Catherine and I struggled to contain our excitement. Our son's first solo.

Catherine delicately broached the possibility, reminding Patrick how beautifully he sang, telling him how much fun it would be. Patrick himself seemed less convinced and frowned. "You know, Mom," he said, "sometimes when I have to do something important, I get kind of scared."

Grown-ups feel that way, too, he was assured, but the decision was left to him. His deliberations took only a few minutes.

"Okay," Patrick said. "I'll do it." From the time he was an infant, Patrick has enjoyed an unusual passion for music. By age four he could pound out several bars of Wagner's "Ride of the Valkyries" on the piano.

For the next week, Patrick practiced his stanza several times with his mother. A rehearsal at the church went well. Still, I could only envision myself at age five, singing into a microphone before hundreds of people. When Christmas Eve arrived, my expectations were limited.

Catherine, our daughter Melanie and I sat with the congregation in darkness as a spotlight found my son, standing alone at the microphone. He was dressed in white, with a pair of angel wings.

Slowly, confidently, Patrick hit every note. As his voice washed over the people, he seemed a true angel, a true bestower of Christmas miracles.

There was eternity in Patrick's voice that night, a beauty rich enough to penetrate any reserve. At the sound of my son, heavy tears welled at the corners of my eyes.

His song was soon over, and the congregation applauded. Catherine brushed away tears. Melanie sobbed next to me.

After the service I moved to congratulate Patrick, but he had more urgent priorities. "Mom," he said as his costume was stripped away, "I have to go to the bathroom."

As Patrick disappeared, the pastor wished me a merry Christmas, but emotion choked off my reply. Outside the sanctuary I received congratulations from fellow church members.

I found my son as he emerged from the bathroom. "Patrick, I need to talk to you about something," I said, smiling. I took him by the hand and led him into a room where we could be alone. I knelt to his height and admired his young face, the large blue eyes, the dusting of freckles on his nose and cheeks, the dimple on one side.

He looked at my moist eyes quizzically.

"Patrick, do you remember when you asked me why you had never seen me cry?"

He nodded.

"Well, I'm crying now."

"Why, Dad?"

"Your singing was so wonderful it made me cry."

Patrick smiled proudly and flew into my arms.

"Sometimes," my son said into my shoulder, "life is so beautiful you have to cry."

Our moment together was over too soon. Untold treasures awaited our five-year-old beneath the tree at home but I wasn't ready for the traditional plunge into Christmas greed yet. I handed Catherine the keys and set off for the mile-long hike home.

The night was cold and crisp. I crossed a park and admired the full moon hanging low over a neighborhood brightly lit in the colors of the season. As I turned toward home, I met a car moving slowly down the street, a family taking in the area's Christmas lights. Someone inside rolled down a window.

"Merry Christmas," a child's voice yelled out to me.

"Merry Christmas," I yelled back. And the tears began to flow all over again.

~Tim Madigan
Chicken Soup for the Soul Christmas Treasury

Don't You Just Feel Like Singing?

According to Westlake Lutheran Church's tradition, our small but spirited band of off-tune singers left the church for a night of singing and good cheer for the sick members of our church. But it was quickly apparent that, because few were sick this year, we'd be back to the cider and cookies all too soon. It was time for some merry magic to weave an insightful strategy.

After finishing our repertoire of songs at the last home, our group of teens and good-natured sponsors huddled together at my request. "I've a got a crazy idea," I said. "Let's go caroling at the supermarket."

The blank stares of the teens were matched only by the alarmed and skeptical look of my wife. Not one for making a scene in public, particularly in her market, she was ready with a quick veto. But before she could speak, I shared the rest of my plan.

"No," I said, "it won't be our usual caroling experience." My voice turned almost secretive as if plotting a fiendish act. "Each of us goes into the market alone. We each take a cart and march through the store. Then we meet in the fruits-and-nuts section." The kids were excited, but my wife's expression said otherwise.

My voice picking up speed as the plan emerged, I continued, "We meet in the produce section. Then I'll turn to you and shout, 'Don't you just feel like singing?' Then so as not to leave me alone and looking like a fool, you say, 'Yes!' At that precise moment, we break into song with 'We Wish You a Merry Christmas'!" That seemed to be the only song we were able to hit on key with any regularity.

Before my wife could turn the tide, we were off to Von's market with a renewed sense of mission. We wandered the aisles with our empty carts, trying to look normal. My wife, on the other hand, chose to wander a bit further away, hoping not to be identified with this band of crazy Lutherans.

Although my plan was well thought-out, I was not prepared for the multitude of shoppers already in the fruits-and-nuts section.

There is no way this is going to be a clean performance, I thought. There are too many unsuspecting shoppers in the way to gather our throng of singers. I looked across the aisle at my wife, whose look reflected more horror than support. The teens were confused and unsure of what to do. Wearing my "Just Do It!" sneakers, I knew there was only one alternative — stick to the plan.

My enthusiastic question reached the ears of a woman in front of me, right about the time her hand reached a ripe tomato. With as much sincerity and Christmas cheer as I could muster, I looked her in the eye and asked, "Don't you just feel like singing?" The woman recoiled as if attacked, and the unsuspecting tomato fell victim to her death grip.

She looked confused, as if trying to figure out whether I was a mad-hatter or serial killer. As a somewhat shocked and strained smile appeared on her lips, she uttered cautiously, "Well... yes!"

With her guarded approval, I turned to the throng in the produce section. With arms open wide, I asked, "Don't the rest of you just feel like singing?"

As the voices of our small but spirited band of off-tune singers blended with the glassy-eyed crowd, they shouted, "Yes!" in unison.

At my direction, we all turned and faced the checkout lines, singing, "We wish you a Merry Christmas, We wish you a Merry Christmas, We wish you a Merry Christmas, and a Happy New Year!"

In a flash, like elves scurrying for cover, our merry band left our carts and immediately ran for the doors, leaving the explanations to the puzzled participants.

Today, many of those young people now work in church groups across the country. We still get an occasional call from a "teen" — now in an older person's body — who will leave a message on our answering machine: "We did a Von's!"

These are the best memories of all.

~Terry Paulson, Ph.D.
Chicken Soup for the Volunteer's Soul

Listen To What I Hear

May Peace be your gift at Christmas
and your blessing all year through!
~Author Unknown

The phone call always came last minute.

"So when are we taking the boys Christmas caroling?" asked my neighbor Mary, cheerful beyond measure with only five days left before Christmas.

Christmas caroling? Was she crazy? The December 25th deadline for shopping, wrapping, baking, and cleaning loomed with Scrooge-like orneriness.

Who had time to sing?

Yet passing up the opportunity to take my three young sons and her little guy out into the crisp night air to belt out Christmas carols for our neighbors would haunt me like the ghost of Christmas past.

"How does the 23rd look?" I asked, mustering as much enthusiasm as I could.

"Perfect!" said Mary, who doubles as a highly organized art teacher. "I'll send out flyers for our neighbors to leave their porch lights on if they'd like us to stop. You bring the hot chocolate."

With that she hung up. There was no backing out now. The event was rolling along like the final verses of the "Hallelujah Chorus."

"When are we going Christmas caroling?" asked an eager son hovering nearby.

"The day after tomorrow," I answered.

"I get the sleigh bells this year!" all three yelled together.

Two days later, the mystery of a winter night bloomed dark, frosty, and beckoning. The three boys and I stuffed ourselves in as much warm clothing as allowed us to move, filled the thermos with hot chocolate, grabbed a bag of cups and marshmallows, and snatched the sleigh bells from the mantle.

Just about the time we started to sweat, Mary called to say they were on their way.

"Meet you at the end of the driveway," she said.

"Let's go!" the boys yelled, dashing out the door into the welcome blast of cold night air.

Across the street and down the hill came Mary and Brad.

As we gathered in the road, the boys let out whoops of joy at the sight that greeted us.

"Wow! Look at that!" Brad said.

Mary's flyer had done the trick. Beacons of porch lights, like a string of constellations, twinkled around our horseshoe-shaped lane directing us to a waiting audience.

"We better do a warm-up before we go," Mary suggested.

Like a rowdy Midwestern version of an English boys' choir, our four guys launched into a rousing rendition of "Jingle Bells," our caroling opener, ringing their bells with enough gusto to spook even Marley's ghost.

As they hit the last note, they were off and running to the nearest house to see who could push the doorbell first. Mary and I lagged behind struggling to keep up with their energy.

As soon as a neighbor swung open the storm door, the boys broke into song. One by one, more friendly faces began to pop up behind the first one until we had a small ensemble bobbing with our beat. Ending our short medley with "We Wish You a Merry Christmas," the boys were rewarded with candy canes and Christmas cookies.

Of course, Mary and I had to have some too.

Then it was onto the next welcoming porch light as more

shivering neighbors shouted to family members, "Come quickly, come quickly, it's the Christmas carolers!"

After five or six houses, our throats were ready for a short intermission. Sipping the soothing hot cocoa, we looked skyward through the sculptured arms of a huge old oak tree, studied the stars, and embraced the sudden stillness of the night.

In that simple moment, I found the peace of Christmas.

Soon the rustle of jingling bells indicated it was time to move on. One of our favorite stops was at Bill and Paula's. Although Bill's speech was impaired from a stroke, he opened the door like a king welcoming his favorite minstrels to his court. Paula appeared right behind him with an array of cookies made just for us.

The boys' repertoire for Bill differed slightly from the rest. They knew his favorite song was "Silent Night," and they sang it with all the sweet, awkward tenderness that their innocent young voices could muster.

Like the crystalline beauty of a snowflake drifting through a moonlit night, a moment of magic hung in the air as the boys ended their song. With misted eyes, Bill broke into enthusiastic applause and with great effort called each boy by name.

"J-John, B-Bob, T-Tom and B-Brad, that was wonderful!" he joyfully proclaimed.

The boys beamed with the happy awareness that somehow they had given a gift.

As our guys grew older, musical instruments began to replace the bells. Two trombones, a trumpet, and a drummer made up a caroling band, with Mary and me as back-up singers.

Some years we sang in soft snowfall and some years the nights were so cold the boys' instruments stuck to their lips. Sometimes visiting grandmothers trudged along beside us, and occasionally the new voices of other children who had moved into neighborhood joined the swell. Once we even sang "Away in a Manager" to a neighbor's stabled horse.

Always there were porch lights beckoning and sweet songs answering

Sometime during the teenage years, the caroling phone call stopped coming. Band concerts, dates, and sports took over the boys' busy schedules, and we all moved on to other Christmas activities.

Like the imperceptible beat of angel wings, time flew by. Our boys became young men, Bill passed on, and after twenty-six years as my neighbor, Mary moved away.

Yet even now, when the hectic holidays threaten to turn me into a Humbug, I'll step out into the night and look up through the gnarled arms of an old oak to the sparkling stars. The cold quiet warms my soul. And if I listen closely, I can hear the peace of Christmas in the whisper of young boys' voices serenading back to me, "All is calm, all is bright."

The echo, forever, will be a hymn in my heart.

~Marnie O. Mamminga
Chicken Soup for the Mother and Son Soul

Working Christmas Day

The best of all gifts around any Christmas tree:
the presence of a happy family all wrapped up in each other.
~Burton Hillis

*I*t was an unusually quiet day in the emergency room on December 25th. Quiet, that is, except for the nurses who were standing around the nurses' station grumbling about having to work Christmas Day.

I was triage nurse that day and had just been out to the waiting room to clean up. Since there were no patients waiting to be seen at the time, I came back to the nurses' station for a cup of hot cider from the crockpot someone had brought in for Christmas. Just then an admitting clerk came back and told me I had five patients waiting to be evaluated.

I whined, "Five? How did I get five? I was just out there and no one was in the waiting room."

"Well, there are five signed in." So I went straight out and called the first name. Five bodies showed up at my triage desk, a pale petite woman and four small children in somewhat rumpled clothing.

"Are you all sick?" I asked suspiciously.

"Yes," she said weakly and lowered her head.

"Okay," I replied, unconvinced, "who's first?" One by one they sat down, and I asked the usual preliminary questions. When it came to descriptions of their presenting problems, things got a little vague. Two of the children had headaches, but the headaches weren't accompanied by the normal body language of holding the head or trying to keep it still or squinting or grimacing. Two children had earaches, but only one could tell me which ear was affected. The mother complained of a cough but seemed to work to produce it.

Something was wrong with the picture. Our hospital policy, however, was not to turn away any patient, so we would see them. When I explained to the mother that it might be a little while before a doctor saw her because, even though the waiting room was empty, ambulances had brought in several, more critical patients, in the back, she responded, "Take your time; it's warm in here." She turned and, with a smile, guided her brood into the waiting room.

On a hunch (call it nursing judgment), I checked the chart after the admitting clerk had finished registering the family. No address—they were homeless. The waiting room was warm.

I looked out at the family huddled by the Christmas tree. The littlest one was pointing at the television and exclaiming something to her mother. The oldest one was looking at her reflection in an ornament on the Christmas tree.

I went back to the nurses' station and mentioned we had a homeless family in the waiting room—a mother and four children between four and ten years of age. The nurses, grumbling about working Christmas, turned to compassion for a family just trying to get warm on Christmas. The team went into action, much as we do when there's a medical emergency. But this one was a Christmas emergency.

We were all offered a free meal in the hospital cafeteria on Christmas Day, so we claimed that meal and prepared a banquet for our Christmas guests.

We needed presents. We put together oranges and apples in a basket one of our vendors had brought the department for

Christmas. We made little goodie bags of stickers we borrowed from the X-ray department, candy that one of the doctors had brought the nurses, crayons the hospital had from a recent coloring contest, nurse bear buttons the hospital had given the nurses at annual training day and little fuzzy bears that nurses clipped onto their stethoscopes. We also found a mug, a package of powdered cocoa and a few other odds and ends. We pulled ribbon and wrapping paper and bells off the department's decorations that we had all contributed to. As seriously as we met the physical needs of the patients that came to us that day, our team worked to meet the needs, and exceed the expectations, of a family who just wanted to be warm on Christmas Day.

We took turns joining the Christmas party in the waiting room. Each nurse took his or her lunch break with the family, choosing to spend his or her "off-duty" time with these people whose laughter and delightful chatter became quite contagious.

When it was my turn, I sat with them at the little banquet table we had created in the waiting room. We talked for a while about dreams. The four children were telling me about what they wanted to be when they grow up. The six-year-old started the conversation. "I want to be a nurse and help people," she declared.

After the four children had shared their dreams, I looked at the mom. She smiled and said, "I just want my family to be safe, warm and content—just like they are right now."

The "party" lasted most of the shift, before we were able to locate a shelter that would take the family in on Christmas Day. The mother had asked that their charts be pulled, so these patients were not seen that day in the emergency department. But they were treated.

As they walked to the door to leave, the four-year-old came running back, gave me a hug and whispered, "Thanks for being our angels today." As she ran back to join her family, they all waved one more time before the door closed. I turned around slowly to get back to work, a little embarrassed for the tears in my eyes. There stood a group of my coworkers, one with a box of tissues, which she passed around to each nurse who worked a Christmas Day she will never forget.

~Victoria Schlintz
Chicken Soup for the Nurse's Soul

The Christmas Mouse

Animals are such agreeable friends —
they ask no questions, they pass no criticisms.
~George Eliot

Once upon a time, we lived in part of a massive, hundred-plus-year-old stone building with an interesting past. Located at a fork in the road at the top of a ridge in rural Lockport, New York, it had once been a blacksmith shop; before that, we heard, it had served as a stagecoach stop. Though it resembled a fortress, it was a grand old place and we loved it. It had character and charm — and leaks, drafts and holes. Pipes froze. So did we. Our cats regularly left us tiny, gory gifts, remnants of the house mice that entered as they pleased after we were asleep.

One special Christmas, we had emerged from some difficult times, and I, after the summer's cancer surgery, had a new awareness of the worth of each day, as well as a deeper appreciation of love and family. It was an especially excellent Christmas because all six of our children were with us. Although we didn't know it then, my husband, David, and I would move to Florida the following summer, and never once since that Christmas have we all managed to be gathered in the same place at the same time.

At one end of the big area that served as living room, dining room and kitchen, I was putting dinner together. Things were noisy, what with the Christmas music on the stereo, the clatter in the kitchen corner, and nine young adults horsing around (a few had brought friends). The cats, in typical cat fashion, had absented themselves upstairs, away from the hullabaloo.

Just then, out of the corner of my eye, I caught a small, unexpected movement and turned to focus on an astonishing sight. There in the midst of all this uproar, smack in the middle of a kitty bowl on the floor, sat a tiny, exquisite deer mouse eating dry cat food. Incredulous, I stared, but didn't say a word. For one thing, I wanted to make sure he wasn't a figment of my imagination; for another, I'll admit, I wanted to keep him to myself for a few minutes. He was very charming.

Up on his haunches he sat, chubby rear firmly planted, little front paws holding a piece of cat food. The pieces were round, with holes in the middle; our mouse firmly clutched his morsel with a hand on each side, looking for all the world like a little fat guy munching a doughnut. When he finished one, he'd help himself to another, turning it about and adjusting it in his small fingers till it was perfectly situated, then he'd start nibbling again.

I squatted down and looked at him, catching his shiny dark eye. We gazed at each other, then he looked away and nonchalantly went on eating. It was time to call in the witnesses.

"Hey!" I softly called to the assembled multitude. "Come and look at this." When eventually I got their attention, I thought it would be all over—he'd run and hide from the mob advancing on him. Not so! He sat right there while eleven bent-over people stood in a circle, gawking (not silently, either) at him. He glanced confidently at the crowd, gave his doughnut a quarter-turn, and kept munching.

We were amazed. He wasn't in the least afraid of us. What made the little guy so brave? Some of us brought cameras into the circle, and while the flashes popped, the mouse proceeded serenely onward with his Christmas feast. From time to time, he paused to regard us with that sparkly, confiding glance, as the pile of food in the bowl grew smaller.

For some time we watched in delight while he, apparently bottomless, stuffed himself with goodies. However, enchanted as I was to entertain him, I was uneasily aware that it was also dinnertime for the resident Predators Two. When the cats appeared on the scene, as they were bound to any minute, our Christmas mouse could be seriously hurt or killed in the ensuing pandemonium, even if we were able to prevent the cats from transforming the diner into dinner (a perfectly appropriate denouement from their point of view).

I leaned closer. "Listen," I murmured, "we have been honored. But now you have to go back outside with the other mice. Good company though you are, your life is in jeopardy here. If you will permit, I will escort you."

With that, I reached into the dish and picked him up. He neither attempted to bite nor gave way to panic, but sat in my hand, calm and comfortable, awaiting developments, front paws resting on my thumb. I had not expected this; I thought there would be fear, protest, a struggle. Instead, he looked at me, a veritable paradigm of the intelligent, friendly fairy-tale mouse, exactly like something out of a Disney movie.

"What are you, really?" I silently inquired. "Are you really a mouse?" The cool, rational part of me jeered at the question, yet there was something undeniably uncanny about this Christmas visitor.

I carried him outdoors, followed by the family. It had grown dark—one of those blue-and-white Northern winter nights with snow on the ground, the air crisp and sharp.

Squatting down near the cover of bushes in back of the house, I released him. He sat on my palm and looked about, taking his time. Then he jumped to my shoulder and for a long moment we sat there, I in the snow and he on my shoulder, woman and mouse together looking out into the night. Finally, with a mighty leap for one so small, he flew through the air, landed in the shadow of the bushes out of sight and was gone. We humans stayed outside for a while, wishing him well and feeling a little lonely.

His visit left us with astonishment that has never diminished, the more so because, as country people, we knew perfectly well that wild mice are terrified of humans. Furthermore, deer mice are particularly timid; unlike common house mice, they avoid inhabited homes. Engaging and winsome they may be (in the wild, they are known to sing), but not with our kind.

These rare, luminous occasions when wild things in their right minds cross the line that separates us leave us full of wonder. We resonate with remembrance of something ancient and beautiful. As all together we surrounded him, his little wild presence silently conveyed joy, peace, trust and wonder. He was a delightful mystery and a tiny miracle.

~Diane M. Smith
Chicken Soup for the Pet Lover's Soul

The Christmas Cookie Can

You give but little when you give of your possessions.
It is when you give of yourself that you truly give.
~Kahlil Gibran, The Prophet

*I*t was almost Christmas again, and I was in my father's home... one last time. My dad had died a few months before, and the home that we had grown up in had been sold. My sister and I were cleaning out the attic.

I picked up an old Christmas cookie can that my dad had used to store extra Christmas light bulbs. As I stood there, holding the can, the memory of a past Christmas swirled through my mind like the snowflakes outside the attic window swirling towards the ground.

I was eleven years old, and with Christmas only a week away, I woke up one morning to a perfect day for sledding.

It had snowed all night, and my friends would be hurtling down the sledding hill at the end of our street. It wasn't what you would call a great challenge, but we all had fun, and I couldn't wait to try out the fresh layer of snow on the runs.

Before I could go anywhere, my mom reminded me that I had to shovel the walkways around the house. It seemed like forever, but after about an hour and a half I was finally finished. I went into the house to get a glass of water and my sled. Just as I got to the front door to leave, the phone rang.

"Joey will be right over," my mom said in reply to someone.

Geez, not now, I thought. The guys are waiting for me. I opened the front door, but there just wasn't enough time to get away.

"Joey, Mrs. Bergensen wants you to shovel her sidewalk," my mother stated.

"Mom," I groaned, "tell her I'll do it this afternoon." I started to walk out the door.

"No, you'll do it now. This afternoon you'll be too tired or too cold. I told her you would be right over, so get going."

My mother sure is free with my time, I thought to myself, as I walked around the corner to the old lady's house. I knocked on her door.

The door opened, and there was Mrs. Bergensen with this bright smile on her old face.

"Joey, thanks for coming over. I was hoping someone would come by, but no one did."

I didn't reply, just shook my head and started shoveling. I was pretty mad and wanted to take it out on Mrs. Bergensen. Sure, you were hoping someone would come by. Why would they? You're just an old lady, I fumed in my mind. At first, my anger helped me work pretty fast, but the snow was heavy.

Then I started thinking about Mrs. Bergensen and how her husband had died years ago. I figured she must feel lonely living all by herself. I wondered how long it had taken her to get that old. Then I started wondering if she was going to pay me anything for my work, and if she did, how much she was going to give me. Let's see, maybe $2.50, with a fifty-cent tip thrown in. She likes me. She could have called Jerry, the kid across the street, but she called me. Yep, I'll be getting some bucks! I started to work hard again.

It took me about another hour to finish. Finally, it was done. Okay, time for some money! I knocked on her door.

"Well, Joey, you did an outstanding job and so fast!" I started to grin. "Could you just shovel a path to my garbage cans?"

"Oh... sure," I said. My grin faded. "I'll have it done in a few minutes." Those few minutes lasted another half-hour. This has to be worth another buck at least, I thought. Maybe more. Maybe I'll get five bucks altogether. I knocked on her door again.

"I guess you want to get paid?"

"Yes, ma'am," I replied.

"Well, how much do I owe you?" she asked. Suddenly, I was tongue-tied.

"Well, here. Here's a dollar and a fifty-cent tip. How's that?"

"Oh, that's fine," I replied. I left, dragging my shovel behind me. Yeah, right, that's fine. All that work for a buck fifty. What a lousy cheapskate. My feet were freezing, and my cheeks and ears were stinging from the icy weather.

I went home. The thought of being out in the cold no longer appealed to me.

"Aren't you going sledding?" my mom asked as I dragged in the front door.

"No, I'm too tired." I sat down in front of the TV and spent the rest of the day watching some dumb movie.

Later in the week, Mrs. Bergensen came over and told my mom what a good job I had done for her. She asked if I would come over to shovel her sidewalks every time it snowed. She brought with her a can loaded with homemade Christmas cookies. They were all for me.

As I sat holding that can in my lap and munching the cookies, I figured that shoveling her sidewalk had been a way for me to give her a Christmas gift, one that she could really use. It couldn't be easy for her being all alone with no one to help her. It was what Christmas was really all about... giving what you could. Mrs. Bergensen gave me the cookies she made, and I gave her my time. And hard work! I started to feel better about the whole thing, including Mrs. Bergensen.

That summer, Mrs. Bergensen died, and it ended up that I never had to shovel her sidewalk again.

Now, years later, standing in my family's attic and holding that Christmas can, I could almost see Mrs. Bergensen's face and how she had been so glad to see me. I decided to keep the can to remind myself of what I had figured out so many years ago, about the true meaning of Christmas. I dumped the old light bulbs that were in it into the trash. As I did so, the piece of paper that had been used as the layer between the cookies and the bottom of the can floated into the trash as well. It was then that I saw something taped to the inside of the can.

It was an envelope that said, "Dear Joe, thank you and have a Merry Christmas!" I opened the yellowed envelope to find a twenty-dollar bill... a gift to me, with love, from Mrs. Bergensen... the cheapskate.

~Joseph J. Gurneak
Chicken Soup for the Soul Christmas Treasury for Kids

Chicken Soup for the Soul

Homestead Holiday

I had so wanted to celebrate Christmas at the two-hundred-year-old farmhouse, surrounded by the love of the dear relatives who had labored to preserve it. A delightful throwback to an era of simplicity—no phones to jangle nerves, no electric lights to glare in eyes—the place veritably shouted, "Christmas!" But first things first; we had to settle in.

"Let's make it easier for our folks to get up," I said to my cousins on our first morning at the old homestead.

We drew well water in tall buckets and carried split logs chin high. Soon a kettle whistled on the cast-iron stove. In each bedroom, we poured warm water into the pitchers of porcelain wash sets.

Our efforts paid off. Our sleepy-eyed parents climbed out of Victorian beds to chat over cinnamon rolls and coffee.

We girls cranked the Victrola in the parlor and pedaled the empty spinning wheel in the hall. Everything about this place was a novelty. We read century-old magazines in the barn and memorized epitaphs in the family cemetery.

We bathed in the fresh waters of Connor Pond and shared teen secrets on the two-holers at "the end of the line." We purchased a block of ice for the antique box in the shed and even scrubbed down the "Grouch House" for would-be guests.

But we wanted so much more.

We wanted Christmas!

"It might be a little odd," one cousin said.

"Sure would," echoed the other.

"Let's ignore that," I said.

Cross-legged on the antique bed in our upstairs hideaway, we plotted how we could pull it off.

"We'll handcraft decorations for the tree," said one cousin.

"We'll pick up gifts in the village... even a holiday meal," chimed the other.

"And we'll send out invitations," I said.

The wide plank flooring quivered under our combined energy.

On stationery found in the parlor desk, we composed rhymed couplets penned in our best script. Convinced Keats would be proud, we lost no time in posting them.

We begged our moms to pick up a few items at the grocery store — okay, maybe not a turkey, but how about a holiday brunch with eggs Benedict and a fresh fruit cup? "And don't forget maple syrup for waffles!"

We popped corn in a pan and strung garlands, yet so much was missing. There were no ornaments to be found anywhere. We poked through brush along a New England stone wall and fell upon a treasure trove of cones, seedpods and nuts. We tied loops around red-berry sprigs and green crabapple stems. Scissors soon fashioned white paper into snowflakes and tinfoil into a star.

Thoughts of the tree encouraged us — but the mailbox didn't. Every afternoon, we rode down the mountain to check it. Still no reply to our invitations — even though the event was upon us.

On the morning of the anticipated day, our folks distracted us with an excursion to the mountains. We arrived home late and tired.

Dad went in first to light the kerosene lamps. When the windows were aglow, we girls ambled upstairs. We stopped at the sound of bells.

"What is it?" I craned over the stairwell.

"Ho, ho, ho," resounded in the distance.

"It's got to be Chesley!" Dad said, lamp in hand, as he peered out the front door into the darkness.

Chesley and Barbara, I thought. The guests are arriving!

I jumped down the stairs in time to see a fully regaled Santa leap into the lamplight. A prim Mrs. Claus joined him by the house.

"You didn't think it was a dumb idea, after all!" we girls shouted.

"Oh, we thought it was wonderful," they said.

Such gameness of spirit spurred us cousins to action. We chopped down a forest fir, placed it in the sitting room and smothered it with our handmade treasures.

Before the crackling fire in the hearth, Mrs. Claus rocked while Santa distributed our carefully selected gifts.

Chocolate mints, knickknacks and a dainty handkerchief... even Roy Tan cigars for Dad.

The impossible had actually happened: a farmhouse Christmas... in August!

True, this was a most uncommon New Hampshire Christmas. Instead of frost nipping at our toes, perspiration beaded our foreheads. Rather than windows iced shut, fragrant breezes blew past. In place of quietly falling snow, a chorus of crickets performed. Where snowsuits would have hung, swimsuits dried on pegs.

Yet the love of celebrating, which knew no season, abounded. And therein lay the joy.

~Margaret Lang
Chicken Soup for the Soul The Book of Christmas Virtues

Chocolate-Covered Cherries

Editors' Note: This Christmas letter was sent to friends and family along with a box of chocolate-covered cherries.

What a terrible way to spend Christmas! My oldest son, Cameron, had been diagnosed with acute myeloblastic leukemia the previous June. After a harrowing ride in a military helicopter to Walter Reed Hospital, three rounds of horrendous chemotherapy, an excruciating lung resection, and a disappointing bone marrow search, we were at Duke University Hospital. Cameron had undergone a cord blood transplant, a last-ditch effort to save his life, in early December. Now, here it was Christmas Eve.

Spending Christmas in the small room on Ward 9200 seemed strange — so different from our usual holiday setting at home. We had always spent weeks on our favorite holiday project: baking cookies. Now the cookies were sent from family and friends, since I tried to spend all my time with Cameron, helping to ease the long, tedious hours. He had been in isolation for weeks, because the chemotherapy and drugs they used to make his new bone marrow engraft left him with no immune system. When presents had arrived in the mail, we hadn't waited for Christmas, but had opened them immediately—anything to create a bright moment in that dull and painful time.

Always in the past, 6:00 P.M. on Christmas Eve was the "Magic Hour." This was the time when everyone in my family, in Iowa, Wisconsin, California and Washington, D.C., opened our presents. We all did this at exactly the same time, somehow bringing the family together, even though we lived so far apart. Cameron's father, stepmother, sister and brother also opened presents at their house at that time.

This year, the Magic Hour would find just Cameron and me in a small, almost-bare hospital room, since most decorations weren't allowed in the sterile environment.

We sat together, listening to the drone of the HEPA filter and the beeping of the six infusion pumps hooked to a catheter in his heart, as Cameron waited until 6:00 P.M. exactly, to open the few presents I had saved for him. He insisted we follow this small tradition, to create some semblance of normalcy—all of which had been abruptly abandoned six months earlier. I watched him open the presents. His favorite was a Hug Me Elmo toy that said, "I love you," when squeezed.

All too quickly, Christmas was over. Or so I thought.

Cameron carefully reached over the side of his hospital bed and handed me a small green box. It was wrapped beautifully, obviously by a gift store, with perfect edges and a folded piece of ribbon held down with a gold embossed sticker.

Surprised, I said, "For me?"

"Mom, it wouldn't be Christmas unless you have something to unwrap, too," he replied.

For a moment, I was speechless. Finally I asked, "But, how did you get this? Did you ask a nurse to run down to the gift store?"

Cameron leaned back in his bed, and gave me his most devilish smile. "Nope. Yesterday, when you went home for a few hours to take a shower, I sneaked downstairs."

"CAMERON! You aren't supposed to leave the floor! You know you're susceptible to almost any germ. They let you leave the ward?"

"Nope!" His smile was even bigger now. "They weren't looking. I just walked out."

This was no small feat, because since the cord blood transplant, Cameron had grown weaker. He could barely walk, and certainly not unassisted. It took every ounce of strength just to cruise the small ward halls, pushing the heavy IV pole hung with medication and a pain pump. How could he possibly have made it nine floors to the gift store?

"Don't worry, Mom. I wore my mask, and I used the cane. Man, they really chewed me out when I got back. I couldn't sneak back in, since they'd been looking for me."

I couldn't look up. I held the box even tighter now and had already started to cry.

"Open it! It's not much, but it wouldn't be Christmas if you didn't have something from me to unwrap."

I opened the box of gift-store-wrapped chocolate-covered cherries. "They are your favorite, right?" he asked hopefully.

I finally looked at my poor eighteen-year-old baby. Cameron had begun all this suffering almost immediately after his high school graduation. Did he know how much he was teaching me about what being a family really meant? "Oh, absolutely my favorite!"

Cameron chuckled a little bit, "See, we still have our traditions—even in here."

"Cameron, this is the best present I've ever received... ever," I told him, and I meant every word. "Let's start a new tradition. Every Christmas, let's only give each other a box of chocolate-covered cherries, and we'll reminisce about the year we spent Christmas at Duke University Hospital battling leukemia. We'll remember how horrible it all was and how glad we are that it is finally over."

We made that pact right then and there, as we shared the box of chocolate-covered cherries. What a wonderful way to spend Christmas!

Cameron died two months later, after two unsuccessful cord blood transplants. He was so brave—never giving in, never giving up.

This will be my first Christmas without him and the first Christmas without something from him to unwrap.

This is my gift to you. A box of chocolate-covered cherries. And when you open it, I hope it will remind you what the holidays are really about... being with your friends and family... recreating traditions, maybe starting some new ones... but most of all—love.

What a beautiful way to spend Christmas.

~Dawn Holt
Chicken Soup for the Mother's Soul 2

48

A Gift-Wrapped Memory

Creativity is inventing, experimenting, growing, taking risks,
breaking rules, making mistakes and having fun.
~Mary Lou Cook

very holiday season since I was a teenager, Dad asked, "Do you remember that Christmas Eve? Remember those two little children who asked us for carfare?"

Yes, I remembered. Even if my father had not reminded me of that strange event every season for more than thirty-five years, I would have remembered.

It was 1935, a typical Christmas Eve in St. Louis, Missouri. Streetcars clang-clanged their warnings. Shoppers rushed in and out of stores for last-minute gifts. Even then, mothers forgot a few ingredients absolutely necessary to complete the family Christmas dinner. Mother had sent Dad and me on such a mission.

Our frosty breaths made a parallel trail behind us as we hurried from the car to her favorite grocery store on Delmar Avenue. Mother liked Moll's because its shelves were stocked with exotic condiments and fancy foods.

Up and down the aisles we hurried, selecting anise and cardamom for Christmas breakfast bread, double whipping cream and jumbo pecans for pumpkin pies, and day-old bread for a fat gobbler's stuffing. We checked the last item off Mother's list and paid the cashier.

Once again we braced our backs for the frigid cold. As we stepped out of the store, a small voice asked, "Please, would you give us a dime for carfare so we can go home?"

Taken aback, Dad stopped. Our eyes met those of a little girl around nine years old. She was holding the gloveless hand of her six-year-old brother.

"Where do you live?" Dad asked.

"On Easton Avenue" was the reply.

We were amazed. Here it was night — Christmas Eve night — and these two children were more than three miles from home.

"What are you doing so far from home?" Dad asked her.

"We had only enough money to ride the streetcar here," she said. "We came to ask for money to buy food for Christmas. But no one gave us any and we are afraid to walk home." Then she told us that their father was blind, their mother was sick, and there were five other children at home.

My dad was a strong-willed urban businessman. But his heart was soft and warm, just like the little girl's brown eyes. "Well, the first thing I think we should do is shop for groceries," he announced, taking her hand. Her brother promptly reached for mine.

Once again we hurried up and down Moll's aisles. This time Dad selected two plump chickens, potatoes, carrots, milk, bread, oranges, apples, bananas, candy and nuts. When we left the store, we had two huge sacks of groceries to carry to the car and two small trusting children in tow.

They gave us directions to Easton Avenue. "Home" was upstairs in a large, old brick building. The first floor housed commercial establishments, while rental units were on the second. A bare light bulb on a long cord hung from the ceiling at the landing, swaying slightly as we climbed the long flight of worn wooden steps to their apartment.

The little girl and her brother burst through the door announcing the arrival of two sacks of groceries. The family was just as she had described: The father was blind and the mother was ill in bed. Five other children, most of them with colds, were on the floor.

Dad introduced himself. First on one foot and then the other, concerned that he would embarrass the father, he continued, "Uh... er... Merry Christmas." He set the groceries on a table.

The father said, "Thank you. My name is Earl Withers."

"Withers?" Dad turned sharply. "You wouldn't know Hal Withers, would you?"

"Sure do. He's my uncle."

Both Dad and I were stunned. My aunt was married to Hal Withers. Although we were not blood relatives, we felt related to Uncle Hal. How could the sad plight of this family be? Why were they in such need when they had so many relatives living in the same city? A strange coincidence, indeed.

Or was it?

Through the years the incident haunted us. Each succeeding year seemed to reveal a different answer to the question, "What was the meaning of that Christmas Eve?"

At first, the phrase repeatedly quoted by elderly aunts, "God works in strange and mysterious ways," surfaced. Perhaps Dad acted out the Good Samaritan role. That was it! God had a job for us to do and fortunately we did it.

Another year passed. It was not a satisfactory answer. What was? If I am my brother's keeper, am I also my wife's sister's husband's brother's blind son's keeper? That was it! This tied the incident into a neat package.

Yet it didn't. The years rolled by, and each year Dad and I would again toss the question around. Then Dad, who was born in the Christmas season of 1881, died in the Christmas season of 1972. Every December since, though, I still hear him ask me, "Do you remember that Christmas Eve?"

Yes, Dad. I remember. And I believe I finally have the answer. We were the ones blessed when two children innocently gave a middle-aged father and his teenaged daughter the true meaning of Christmas: It is more blessed to give than to receive.

This gift-wrapped memory became the most beautiful Christmas I ever celebrated. I think it was your best one, too, Dad.

~Dorothy DuNard
A 5th Portion of Chicken Soup for the Soul

49

The Best Christmas
I Never Had

The best way to cheer yourself up is to
try to cheer somebody else up.
~Mark Twain

My sister, Yvonne, was fourteen the year our home and everything in it was destroyed. I was seventeen. Our home was heated by a wood-burning stove, and every fall, my family and I would mark dead trees, cut them down, haul the wood and stack it in the basement. The week before Christmas, the basement was half full of dry wood.

Yvonne and I were home from school, and she did as either of us had done a thousand times before: checked the furnace, tossed a few more logs on the fire and slammed the door shut.

At the time, I was upstairs sulking. I had a sink full of dishes to wash, homework to tackle and my grandfather, after a lonely day at home, wouldn't leave me alone. Stomping around the kitchen, listening to him chatter, I thought about how I couldn't wait to get out of this house, this town. Lightning could strike this very spot and I wouldn't care. Or so I thought.

The house seemed a little smoky, but that wasn't unusual. It often became that way after the furnace had a few new logs to chew up. I simply waved the smoke away and kept doing dishes and daydreaming of getting away from my family. My sister's cats were no help; they were as starved for affection as Grandpa, and kept twining around my ankles.

My sister wandered in and said, "Don't you think it's a little too smoky in here?"

I shrugged sullenly and kept washing dishes. But after another minute, we knew something was wrong. The smoke was much too thick. My sister and I looked at each other, then at our grandfather. He was the adult, but he lived with us because he couldn't take care of himself. If there were decisions to be made, my sister and I—high school students—would make them. The thought was daunting, to say the least.

Without a word to each other, we went outside and opened the garage door (foolish in retrospect) and stared in disbelief as smoke and flames boiled out.

We had no time for tears or hysterics. That would come later. Instead, we both turned and ran up the hill. My sister shot through the kitchen door and raced for Grandpa's coat while I searched frantically for my keys. "There's a fire, Grandpa," I said abruptly. Where in the world had I put my purse? "We have to get out."

"Oh. Okay," he agreed. Amiable as a child, Grandpa stood still while my sister jerked him into his coat. She made sure he was warm and tightly bundled, forced warm slippers on his feet and hustled him out the door. I was so busy wondering where my keys were and trying the phone, which was dead, I never noticed that in her great care to make sure our grandfather was protected from the elements, she had neglected her own coat and boots.

I glanced out the window, blinking from the smoke. December in Minnesota was no joke... and no place for two teenagers and an old man to await help. If I could find my keys, I could get back down to the garage and probably, if the flames hadn't spread that far, back the van out of the garage. We could wait for help in relative comfort, and at least my mom's van could be saved.

Memory flashed; I had tossed my purse in my room when I'd come home. My room was at the end of a long hallway, far from the kitchen. Daughter and granddaughter of professional firefighters, I should have known better. But things were happening so quickly—my little sister and my grandfather were standing in the snow, shivering—I had to get the van. So I started for my room, the worst decision I've ever made.

The smoke was gag-inducing, a thick gray-black. It smelled like a thousand campfires and I tried not to think about what was being destroyed: my family's pictures, their clothes, furniture. I'd gone three steps and couldn't see, couldn't hear, couldn't breathe. How was I going to make it all the way to my room?

I wasn't, of course. I instantly knew two things: if I went down that hallway, I would die. Number two, what was I still doing in this inferno? Ten-year-olds were taught better. My sister was probably terrified, and in another moment, she'd come after me. How stupid could I be?

I stumbled back to the kitchen, took one last glance around my home, then went out into the snow.

Yvonne was sobbing, watching our house burn to the foundation. Grandpa was patting her absently. "That's what insurance is for," he said. A veteran of the New York City Fire Department, I couldn't imagine how many house fires he had fought. For the first time, I could see him as a real person and not my aged, feeble grandfather who took up entirely too much of my time with his endless pleas for me to sit down and talk to him.

"I'm going to the neighbors' to call for help," Yvonne said abruptly. She was wearing a sweater, jeans and slippers. I was in sweatpants, a T-shirt and socks. The closest neighbor was down the length of our driveway and across the highway, about a mile.

"Okay," I said. "Be careful crossing the...." But she was gone, already running through the snow and down the driveway.

Then I remembered Yvonne's three cats, which were, I guessed, trapped in the house. When she remembered them, I thought, she would go right out of her mind.

It seemed she was only gone for a moment before I saw her puffing up the driveway. "I called," she gasped, "they're on their way."

"You should have stayed with the neighbors and gotten warm," I said, mad at myself because I hadn't told her to stay put.

She gave me a look. "I couldn't leave you out here in the cold."

"Actually, I'm not that..." I began, when suddenly Yvonne clapped her hands to her face and screamed.

"Oh my God, the cats!" she shrieked, then burst into hoarse sobs.

"It's okay, Yvonne, it's okay, I saw them get out," I said frantically, reaching for her. I could tell she didn't believe me, but she didn't say anything more, just wept steadily and ignored my fervent assurances — my lies.

As it swiftly grew dark, our burning house lit up the sky. It was as beautiful as it was awful. And the smell... to this day, whenever someone lights a fire in a fireplace, I have to leave the room briefly. A lot of people find fireplaces soothing, but to me the smell of burning wood brings back the sense of desolation and the sound of my sister's sobs.

We could hear sirens in the distance and moved out of the way as two fire trucks and the sheriff pulled in. The sheriff screeched to a halt and beckoned to us. In another minute he was talking to my grandfather while Yvonne and I sat in the back of the police car, getting warm.

After a long moment, Yvonne sighed. "I just finished my Christmas shopping yesterday."

I snorted... and the snort became a giggle, and the giggle bloomed into a laugh. That got my sister going, and we laughed until we cried and then laughed some more.

"I got you the CD you wanted," I told her.

"Really?" she said. "I bought you a new Walkman."

We listed all the things we had bought for friends and family that were now burning to cinders. Instead of being depressing, it was probably the highlight of the evening. The sheriff interrupted our spiritual gift-giving to open the door and say, "Your parents are here."

We scrambled out and raced down the driveway. If I live to be one thousand, I'll never forget my mother's face at that moment: bloodless and terrified. She saw us and opened her arms. We hurled ourselves at her, though we were both considerably taller than she was and nearly toppled her back into the snow. Dad looked us over, satisfied too that we weren't hurt, and some of the tension went out of his shoulders. "What are you crying about?" he asked, pretending annoyance. "We've got insurance. And now we'll get a new house for Christmas."

"Dad... for Christmas... I got you those fishing lures you wanted but..."

He grinned. "That reminds me. I picked up your presents on the way home." He stepped to the truck and pulled out two garment bags. Inside were the gorgeous jackets Yvonne and I had been longing for since we'd fallen in love with them at the mall.

We shrugged into them, ankle-deep in snow, while the house crackled and burned in front of us. It was a strange way to receive a Christmas present, but neither of us was complaining.

"We'll have to come back here tomorrow," Dad said. "It's going to be depressing and stinky and muddy and frozen and disgusting and sad. Most of our stuff will be destroyed. But they're only things. They can't love you back. The important thing is that we're all okay. The house could burn down a thousand times and I wouldn't care, as long as you guys were all right."

He looked at us again and walked away, head down, hands in his pockets. Mom told us later he had driven ninety miles an hour once he'd seen the smoke, that they both gripped the other's hand while he raced to the house. Not knowing if we were out safe was the worst moment of her life.

Later we found out the pipe leading from the furnace to the wall had collapsed, spilling flaming coals all over our basement. If it had happened at 2:00 A.M., we all would have died of smoke inhalation. In less than half an hour, our house transformed from a safe haven to a death trap. Asleep, we would have had no chance.

We lived in a motel for more than a month, and we spent Christmas Day in my grandmother's crowded apartment eating take-out because she was too tired to cook. For Christmas, Yvonne and I got our jackets and nothing else. My parents got nothing except the headache of dealing with insurance companies. All the wonderful things my family had bought for me had been destroyed in less time than it takes to do a sink full of dishes. But through it all I had gained long-overdue appreciation for my family. We were together. That was really all that mattered.

I'll always remember it as the best Christmas I never had.

~MaryJanice Davidson
Chicken Soup for the Preteen Soul

Sing We Noel

*T*he year of my tenth birthday marked the first time that our entire family had jobs. Dad had been laid off from his regular employment, but found painting and carpentry work all around town. Mom sewed fancy dresses and baked pies for folks of means, and I worked after school and weekends for Mrs. Brenner, a neighbor who raised cocker spaniels. I loved my job, especially the care and feeding of her frisky litters of puppies. Proudly, I gave my earnings to Mom to help out, but the job was such fun, I would have worked for no pay at all.

I was content during these "hard times" to wear thrift-shop dresses and faded jeans. I waved goodbye to puppies going to fancy homes with no remorse. But all that changed when the Christmas litter arrived in the puppy house. These six would be the last available pups until after Christmas.

As I stepped into the house for their first feeding, my heart flip-flopped. One shiny red puppy with sad brown eyes wagged her tail and bounced forward to greet me.

"Looks as if you have a friend already," Mrs. Brenner chuckled. "You'll be in charge of her feedings."

"Noel," I whispered, holding the pup close to my heart, sensing instantly that she was special. Each day that followed forged an inexplicable bond between us.

Christmas was approaching, and one night at dinner, I was bubbling over about all of Noel's special qualities for about the hundredth time.

"Listen, Kiddo." Dad put down his fork. "Perhaps someday you can have a puppy of your own, but now times are very hard. You know I've been laid off at the plant. If it wasn't for the job I've had this month remodeling Mrs. Brenner's kitchen, I don't know what we'd do."

"I know, Dad, I know," I whispered. I couldn't bear the pained expression on his face.

"We'll have to brave it out this year," he sighed.

By Christmas Eve, only Noel and a large male remained. "They're being picked up later," Mrs. Brenner explained. "I know the family taking Noel," she continued. "She'll be raised with tons of love."

No one could love her as much as I do, I thought. No one.

"Can you come tomorrow morning? I'll be weaning new pups the day after Christmas. Mop the floor with pine, and spread fresh bedding for the new litter. Would you be a dear and feed the kennel dogs, too? I'll have a house full of guests. Oh, and ask your dad to stop over with you. One of the kitchen cabinet doors needs a little adjustment. He did such a beautiful job that I'll enjoy showing it off!"

I nodded my head, barely focusing on her words. The new puppies would be cute, but there'd never be another Noel. Never. The thought of someone else raising my puppy was almost too much to bear.

Christmas morning, after church, we opened our meager gifts. Mom modeled the apron I made her in home economics with a flair befitting a Paris gown. Dad raved about the watchband I gave him. It wasn't even real leather, but he replaced his frayed band and admired it as if it were golden. He handed me the book *Beautiful Joe*, and I hugged them both. They had no gifts for each other. What a sad Christmas, with all of us pretending that it wasn't.

After breakfast, Dad and I changed clothes to go to Mrs. Brenner's. On our short walk, we chatted and waved to passing neighbors, each of us deliberately avoiding the subjects of Christmas and puppies.

Dad waved goodbye as he headed toward the Brenners' kitchen

door. I walked directly to the puppy house in the backyard. It was strangely silent, no puppy growls, tiny barks or rustling paper. It felt as sad and dreary as I did. My head gave the order to begin cleaning, but in my heart I wanted to sit down on the lonely floor and bawl.

It's funny looking back at childhood days. Some events are fuzzy, the details sketchy and faces indistinct. But I remember returning home that Christmas afternoon so clearly; entering the kitchen with the aroma of pot roast simmering on the stove, Mom clearing her throat and calling to Dad, who suddenly appeared in the dining room doorway.

With an odd huskiness in his voice, he whispered, "Merry Christmas, Kiddo," and smiling, he gently placed Noel, clad in a red bow, into my arms. My parents' love for me merged with my overwhelming love for Noel and sprang from my heart, like a sparkling fountain of joy. At that moment it became, without a doubt, absolutely the most wonderful Christmas I have ever had.

~Toni Fulco
Chicken Soup for the Pet Lover's Soul

My Most
Memorable Christmas

"**R**aus mit du, Schwine Hund!" ("Out with you, you pig of a dog!") These were the words I remember hearing every morning of the eight months I spent in Stalag 7-A, the German prisoner-of-war camp located in Moosburgh, Germany, fifteen kilometers from Munich.

To discourage escape attempts, we were not allowed shoelaces, socks or belts. Very few of us had underwear. Of my own GI clothing, all that remained were the wool pants and shoes I hit Omaha Beach with on D-Day.

Most of the thousands of POWs in our camp were issued old French flannel Army shirts, woolen trench coats and a woolen blanket with more holes in it than material. The trench coat they gave me must have been made for a seven-foot-tall French soldier. It dragged on the ground, and I could hardly walk in it.

Using a piece of sharp tin from a can received in an American Red Cross food parcel, I cut the coat off between my ankles and knees, and used a piece to make a ski mask, with holes for eyes, nose and mouth. With the material left over, I sewed a pouch into my coat to sneak loot from work details into the prison camp.

The blanket was more like a horse blanket, and the odor seemed to confirm it. Some of the POWs were lucky enough to find or steal burlap and other materials to make extra blankets and clothing.

Thanks to the ingenuity of a British POW, each man made his own miniature cookstove out of tin cans from the Red Cross food parcels.

Our barracks were thin-walled, unheated buildings without water or electricity. We slept in bunks stacked three high, made of salvaged wood, with bug-infested straw mattresses. To take the chill out of the air, we lit candles found or stolen on work details in Munich.

Although the winter of 1944 in Europe was the coldest in quite some time, we were still looking forward to Christmas Day. The word was that we would be allowed to lie around and take it easy with no work details.

On the days we didn't work, the guys mostly played cards, read or talked about going home. During one of those days when we were killing time, I suggested putting on a Christmas play to boost morale. Everyone thought it a good idea, except for one man, whom I'll call Joe.

Joe was more depressed than any man in the barracks. Most of us felt he was suicidal. Maybe the play would give him something to think about, we thought, instead of focusing on the loneliness and despair that was eating at him.

The word spread, and the idea caught on like wildfire. Committees were formed, and our barracks leader — a natural-born catalyst — was chosen as director. We never did find out how he managed to get the lumber to build the stage and benches for the audience.

Everyone continued to scrounge things suitable for making music, decorations or something to eat and drink. When things were brought in, they'd be hidden under mattresses or floorboards, or buried.

As Christmas drew near, the anticipation and enthusiasm grew more contagious and magical. An ex-stage director was found among the POWs. Choirs were formed, and a magician, impersonators, comedians, actors, writers, ushers and stagehands stepped forward. So many people volunteered, they couldn't all be put to work.

The GIs who smoked, chipped in one cigarette each to bribe the guard for a Christmas tree. Ornaments were made of tin, paper, wood and cloth, and someone scrounged several cans of paint to color them.

Raisins, prunes, sugar, chocolate and powdered milk from Red Cross food parcels were hoarded for six weeks. They would be added to several loaves of black bread to make a pudding that would be given to each man as he came to watch the show. The rest of the raisins, prunes and sugar would be brewed into a strong alcoholic drink that would be cut with water and portioned out to each man. By Christmas Eve, all was ready.

The building we used to present the show held one hundred men at a time. We scheduled the show hourly, so all the men in our section of the camp could see it. Where the energy in our weakened bodies came from, I'll never know. I suppose our determination to generate some happiness for our fellow GIs spurred us on. It wasn't only Joe who needed it. We all needed it.

The first show was at 8 A.M. Christmas Day. The opening hymn, "O Come All Ye Faithful," brought so many tears, we thought we'd have to stop the show. And there in the very first row of the choir was Joe, singing his head off.

The music and laughter could be heard throughout the camp. After the audience filed out of our third show, we heard the distinctive thump of German boots coming through the door. In came a German colonel, two majors, three captains, numerous lieutenants and about sixty enlisted men.

We feared they had come to put an end to our Christmas celebration. Instead, they trooped to the front benches and sat down. The colonel then motioned us to proceed with the show.

The head usher, who spoke fluent German, climbed on the stage and dedicated the opening hymn to the German officers and enlisted men. Then the ushers passed out a slice of pudding and a drink to each German soldier.

The Germans were overwhelmed to see that people in our situation could treat their enemy with such kindness. Some on both sides cried, including me.

After the performance, the German guards shook our hands and thanked us, saying "Sehr gut" and "Danke shöne." There were tears and happy smiles on their faces, as well as our own. All animosities were put aside that Christmas morning.

The next day, however, things went back to normal. Except with Joe. From that day forward, Joe was a new man. I noticed he smiled more, took part in our conversations and card games and even went out of his way to help other prisoners who were feeling hopeless and depressed.

The show had worked. The spirit of Christmas had entered Joe's lonely heart, as well as ours, and never left.

~Gene DuVall
Chicken Soup for the Veteran's Soul

A Surprise Wedding

Over the years, my wife, Sue, expressed interest in renewing our wedding vows. It was not something she talked about frequently, but she brought it up on such special occasions as weddings or anniversaries.

Like most macho men, I believed that once was enough. But as time passed, since it still seemed important to her, I began to relent: "Honey, I might consider it someday, but only if it's just you and me—maybe on vacation somewhere." (I really didn't need an audience for something like this.)

Then, four years ago, Sue had a cancerous mole removed from her leg. The diagnosis: malignant melanoma.

My attitude at that time was that the mole wasn't so bad. After all, it was removed and the cancer was gone. I knew little, however, about this cancer's ability to resurface.

In November, Sue found a new lump on the same leg as before—it turned out to be a swollen lymph gland—and the biopsy again revealed malignant melanoma. Sue went in for surgery and had numerous lymph glands removed from her leg and abdomen. The doctors had good news: The cancer had not spread beyond the two lymph glands—the one that was swollen and one next to it.

One week after Sue's diagnosis, however, her father was diagnosed with cancer—not the best week my wife has ever had.

In December of that year, like every year, I struggled with what to get my wife for Christmas, but even more than usual. Sue always said that she wanted "something personal." When the cancer returned, it made me think long and hard about what our future might be like. I wondered about what I might get her for Christmas that would be personal, show her how much I loved her and express what she means to me and to our family.

I'm the kind of guy that thinks of grand things I would like to do for my wife but rarely gets around to doing them. That year I really searched my soul—and the thought of renewing our wedding vows suddenly took on more meaning. This was a way to show her I truly wanted to do it all over again.

Then I thought of the verse "In sickness and in health" and began to cry. I'm glad I was alone.

Even with all Sue had been through—and maybe because of it—she wanted to host Christmas Eve at our house this year. It was only going to be a small group of relatives. It seemed to me that this would be the perfect time to renew our vows, so I recruited Karen, my sister-in-law, to help me. I called everyone and told them to come two hours early. I said I had a surprise for Sue but didn't tell anyone what it was. I didn't want this gift to be spoiled.

I called on our neighbor, Jean Partridge, a justice of the peace. We had never really stopped and talked or gotten to know one another, and I hoped she would be willing to come over on Christmas Eve. She said she was busy that night and had to arrive at her daughter's house by six o'clock. My heart sank. As I turned to walk away, Jean asked, "Why do you need a justice of the peace on Christmas Eve, Don?"

"I want to get married to my wife again," I answered. "It's a surprise wedding." I hesitated, then asked, "Do you think you could marry us at four o'clock and still be on time for your daughter's Christmas Eve celebration?" I told Jean what the ceremony meant to me and would mean to my wife at this particular time. I told her about Sue's health problem. I explained all this so in case I started to cry, she'd understand why. After that, she said that she might have to toss down a shot to calm her nerves before the wedding, too.

"I'll be there at four," she smiled.

A great wave of joy swept over me. I had found a way to show how much I loved Sue—and this time, instead of just thinking about it, I was going to make it happen.

I finally found something unique and meaningful to give my wife on Christmas. The only other people I told were Sue's parents, since I really wanted them to be there. When they heard the plan, there was only silence on the phone for a few long moments. Then Sue's dad, who had his good and bad days due to his own illness, declared in an emotional voice that he would be there no matter how he was feeling.

I realized that I also needed fluff—or should I say, some schmaltz—all the details that women think of and men usually don't consider. I had my youngest son, Shaun, get a song off the Internet—the same song that was played in church when we were married twenty-three years earlier. Sean made a CD for me so I could play it when she walked in the door. Oh, and flowers—I got a wristlet for Sue, a flower for my lapel and two poinsettias for the mantel. And I got a cake, champagne, glasses, boxes and boxes of Kleenex, and disposable cameras. I even bought some special rings.

In the flower shop, a small snowman statue caught my eye. I picked it up and saw that it was some sort of jewelry holder. This snowman had a small sign he was holding and on that sign was the word "hope." I thought how perfect it was, and my eyes welled up with tears again. I've been crying a lot, lately, for a macho man.

That afternoon, everything was in place. Karen, my sister-in-law, took Sue out to visit a sick relative. When she returned, she looked puzzled to see everyone at our home two hours early. After all, she had to get the food ready for our guests.

"What's going on?" she asked, a little upset.

The rest I'm going to leave to your imagination.

Just picture this: Our wedding song begins to play, people are taking pictures of Sue and me, and the tears and champagne are beginning to flow.

And I said, "Honey, Merry Christmas. I love you. Will you marry me again tonight?"

~Don Flynn
Chicken Soup to Inspire the Body & Soul

Christmas
with TwylaRose

When I adopted TwylaRose, a retired racing greyhound, I promised myself I would treat her like a dog and not like a four-legged imitation human. She was my first dog and I had my standards. There'd be no dressing up in human clothes, no Christmas photographs with Santa, no joint shopping trips, no jewelry and no baby talk. I resolved to preserve her dog-ness and my dignity.

Those high sentiments crashed, one by one, beginning with the restrictions against baby talk. Though I didn't actually make goo-goo sounds on the way home from the kennel, I brimmed over with pet names: Pumpkin, Sweetie, Girlfriend, Honeybunch, Boo... I hadn't expected to feel so much or to feel it so quickly. The skinny anxious creature in the backseat spoke directly to my heart. Our first hour together transformed me into her friend and protector, parent and pal, teacher and student, sister and most dedicated fan.

As our first Halloween approached, a friend bought a top hat and tails costume for her own dog. Theoretically, I couldn't have been more opposed to the idea but it got me thinking. I enjoy Halloween and it didn't seem right to leave TwylaRose out of the festivities.

Since she came from the long line of hounds that lived as royalty with the pharaohs, I dressed her as Anubis, the deity in Egyptian mythology whose task it was to lead the deceased into the other world. Anubis appears in tomb paintings as a half-human, half-greyhound figure that weighs the human heart against its own truth in the form of a feather.

Being helped through that final passage by a god with the canine qualities of faithfulness and surefooted instinct appealed to me. I assured myself that TwylaRose as Anubis was not only a species-appropriate character, but one that was inspirational and educational as well.

I sewed a golden-brown sequined body suit and a small matching bag to hold the feather. Of course no one had a clue about who she was supposed to be. Even when I explained, no one much cared and TwylaRose seemed indifferent, but I enjoyed recounting the mythology and I loved the flash of sunlight off those sequins.

During that first year, I had become friends with three women who also had adopted retired racers. Our four greys became The Pack: TwylaRose, Ike, Pepper and Christa. With humans in tow, they met several times a week.

Nothing pleased the greyhounds so much as being together. They sniffed butts, stood flank to flank in greeting and draped their long necks over each other. When it was too hot or too cold to walk, we met at someone's home where the greys vied for squeaky toys or came to us for stroking, then settled into naps. Doggy play dates became part of my reality and an extended human/canine family formed.

When Christmas approached, somebody suggested we have The Pack's picture taken with Santa Claus. My early resolutions echoed against the idea but I felt the tug: Wouldn't it be sweet? Wouldn't it be fun? Wouldn't it be nice to have a picture of The Pack?

I cast around for an excuse to break my own rule. Since I am no fan of Christmas excesses, I reasoned, the photo could be my Wegman-like comment on the season. Everyone else wants to go and it would be rude of me to resist. I said I'd do it for the good of the group. Of course, I lied. Deep down, I wanted to immortalize our Pack. I wanted to include them in our celebration of winter, like the family members they were. So I went along. I even tied a wide red ribbon around TwylaRose's neck and stiffened it with a shot of spray starch.

And so we found ourselves at PetSmart one Saturday morning just before Christmas. A large pet supply chain store, PetSmart welcomes dogs to shop along with their humans. It hosts events like meet-and-greets during which various rescue groups show their dogs and take applications for adoption. In December, they host Santa.

The store was rich with the scents of dogs as well as the subtle perfume of live snakes, kittens, iguana, parakeets and parrots. It was a huge cavernous place with fluorescent light pouring down on a crowd of shoppers and their sniffing animal companions, frantic from overstimulation. Exotic birds, parrots and canaries layered the air with their cries and Burl Ives tied it all up in a fat red ribbon with his hearty and optimistic rendition of "Jingle Bell Rock."

Just inside the door, Ike began trembling so hard his tags rattled. Pepper and TwylaRose lunged in opposite directions, and Christa hid her tail and froze. We had arrived early to avoid the crowd. Santa's white plastic bench waited at the center of the store. We stood second in line. Christa eyed the Chihuahua ahead of us, her predator instinct stirring. Pepper's anxiety turned to gas, heralding intestinal distress. By now, Ike was vibrating and TwylaRose had lowered her head and was pulling toward the door.

A man dressed as Santa slunk in from a back room. He was human, small and shapeless. He didn't look like the Santa in the Macy's Thanksgiving Day Parade. His shoulders rounded and his face hung expressionless until it disappeared into a tired, synthetic beard.

I felt empathy for Santa. I wouldn't want to spend my Saturday posing with overwrought dogs and trying to please their doting owners. Our Santa coped by exhibiting an indifference of mythic proportions. He sat down. The feisty Chihuahua sprinted toward him and spun at his feet. Santa stared straight ahead. The human scooped up her darling and plopped him onto Santa's lap. She crouched just outside of camera range and cheered her pup on. The Polaroid flashed and it was our turn.

Trembling, farting, panting, scanning the environment for danger, tongues hanging out, ears up to monitor sounds, the greys approached for the group picture.

Santa sat there limp while we arranged the greyhounds around him, TwylaRose beside him on the bench and Christa up on the other side. TwylaRose jumped down and I lifted her up again. We draped Santa's arms over each of the girls and wrapped the fingers of his gloved hands around their collars. We arranged Ike to the right of his knees and Pepper to the left. We backed out of camera sight, holding our collective breath. Pepper broke for the door. We set him back into place.

One camera flash and it was done. We each have a copy. There is Pepper looking for the exit, Ike with his long, long tongue panting into the camera, TwylaRose whose red bow had slipped down her neck and Christa smiling at the lens.

I still believe TwylaRose deserves respect for who she is. There are still no dog pajamas in the house, though on cold nights I do throw a light blanket over her. I shop alone at the pet store. The baby talk comes and goes and mixes with adult conversations. Every Christmas, I bring out the picture of The Pack with Santa. I'm learning about what it is to be a greyhound, racing and retired. And she participates when I involve us in human adventures. I may have trashed my standards but I've come to understand that tasting each other's lives is the point, and love, not foolishness, enables that to happen.

~Emma Mellon
Chicken Soup for the Soul Celebrates Dogs

Student Teacher

How beautiful a day can be
When kindness touches it!
~George Elliston

I was a little nervous about my students remembering the more difficult songs. I thought that we didn't rehearse enough to do the songs justice. However, I was sadly mistaken. My students performed brilliantly. Even Bing Crosby himself couldn't have done a better job on that warm Arizona winter day. My students sang with an honest heart and with simple intentions. I believe that this is what made them shine through as beautifully as they did.

My class and I were on a field trip to Chris Ridge Retirement Home and Care Center in Phoenix, Arizona. We were there to sing holiday songs to those who might need a little cheering up during this holiday season. There were three floors in this care center. The first two floors were for residents who needed a little extra help in taking care of themselves. The third floor was an Alzheimer's unit. This is was a lock-down floor, where the patients have completely lost all recollection of their previous lives and loved ones. Most on this floor seemed to wander around in a dazed and confused state. The lock-down was to prevent any of the residents from wandering off and getting lost in the busy city. This floor made my students the most nervous.

We sang beautifully on the first two floors. The residents loved our songs and our cards that we left with them. My students were truly feeling the holiday spirit as we entered the elevator to take us to the third floor. Their apprehensions quickly set in as we stepped off the elevator and onto the lobby of the third floor unit. As the residents were put into their chairs for our performance, my selfish mind asked itself, What good will we do here? These people don't even recognize that we are even here. How are they going to appreciate our singing?

As we began singing, most of the residents stared off at the walls or floor. It seemed as though my premonition was going to be right. However, one lady in a wheelchair caught my eye. She was sitting by the door. She was in her wheelchair and singing songs to herself. They weren't the songs that we were singing, at least they didn't sound like it. And as we got louder with each festive song, she did likewise. The louder we got, the louder she got. As she was singing, she was also reaching out to us with her hands and body. I knew that I should have gone over to her, but I thought that my responsibilities were to my students. There were people who worked at the care center that could attend to her, I thought. As our songs continued, I eventually stopped feeling guilty about not giving her the attention she needed. It took one of my students to demonstrate to me what the holiday season is really all about.

Justin Proctor is a good kid. In his heart, he shines forth with his genuine personality. Justin noticed the same lady by the door. The difference between us is that he acted on her needs, and I didn't. During the last song, "Silent Night," the lady was singing the loudest that her lungs could let her. She was reaching out as far as she could, almost to the point of falling out of her wheelchair. Justin stopped singing. He walked over to her and grabbed her hand and held it during the rest of the song. He looked this aged lady in her eyes and with his actions said, "You are important and I will take my time to let you know that."

This tired elderly lady seemed to regain, if only for a moment, what she had lost—her memory. She stopped singing and held his hand. She then took her other hand and put it up to his face. She touched his cheek. Tears began to fall down her wrinkled face, as the memories—for that brief moment—began to rush back into her mind. No words can completely portray that poignant moment. It took a boy to teach me, a man, about kindness and love. Justin's example of complete, selfless compassion towards another was a lesson that I will never forget. He was the teacher that day and I consider myself lucky to have witnessed his lesson.

~Mike Ashton
Chicken Soup for the Soul Celebrates Teachers

The Cowboy Suit

If evolution really works, how come mothers only have two hands?
~Milton Berle

Christmas was a wonderful time for me in 1962 when we had just moved from Alabama to Texas. The tree didn't have a lot of gifts under it, but there was one big one with my name on it.

Finally, Christmas morning rolled around, and we gathered around the little tree to open gifts. I grabbed mine with eager hands and ripped it open to find a genuine cowboy suit, just like they wore in Texas. It had a big, ten-gallon hat, chaps, a leather vest, a badge, a pair of cowboy boots and a two-pistol holster. I was blessed. All my sisters got were silly old dolls. I could think of nothing better for Christmas, except maybe a Superman suit with cape and all. The thoughts of a super hero leaping tall buildings would have to wait another year, but in the meantime, I was going to be a cowboy sheriff. I pinned on the silver badge with pride.

Dad seemed to enjoy my gift more than his new shirts and blue jeans. Being an adult was tough, and all he could do now is play with the toys his son got for Christmas. My dad was a big western fan, and we watched those cowboy movies together. I loved the Lone Ranger and Will Rogers. I shot up a whole roll of caps in no time working on my quick draw, with Dad's coaching, of course.

I went to bed that night thinking of slinging those two six-shooters and twirling those pistols in grand fashion, just like Roy Rogers. I could smell the gunpowder.

The next morning arrived bright and early. I was out of bed, loading my two six-shooters and donning the whole cowboy suit to include the boots. You know the kind—no matter which way you put them on, they always look like they are on the wrong feet. I was ready for a shootout, and I knew right where it was going to happen. I got my imaginary friend, Will Rogers, and we started for the old barn. I knew Mom was there milking the cow. She'd be surprised when I stepped into the barn and started my shootout. I just knew Mom would beam with pride.

Stepping in, I noticed the cow busy eating hay and Mom sitting on a stool squeezing squirts of milk into a bucket on the dirt floor. She was so busy with her chore, she didn't notice my arrival.

I stood there, fully dressed, cowboy hat and all. The only thing missing was a good set of spurs on my boots, but not to worry. I stood bowlegged as if I had been riding a horse for about a week anyway. I looked into the barn, imagining that at the other end stood five mean, old cowboys with black hats and dirty-looking, as though they needed a shave and a good scrubbing with Mom's scrub brush.

I raised my hands ready above each pistol to await their move. I said, "Mean Joe Whiskey, I'm here to run you out of town. Either get on your horses right now or make your move." I waited about a minute, and then I caught a movement that told me the bad guys were going for their guns.

It happened so quickly. I whipped my two six-shooters out and started shooting. Bam! Bam! Bam! Maybe the cow didn't like cowboys. Maybe it didn't like cap pistols either. Anyway, it spun around, knocking my mother to the floor. The mad cow tossed the stool and milk bucket against the wall, then turned on me and my shiny six-shooters. It lowered its head, and for the first time I saw those sharp, dangerous horns. The cow plowed toward me in a rage of steam and snorts. I stood there, frozen, helpless, watching death charge right at me.

Maybe I closed my eyes or perhaps I just blinked, but how my mother passed that cow still amazes me. Was she really that fast, or could she fly? All I knew was I was looking at a set of mean-looking horns on an even meaner-looking cow, and out of nowhere came those hands that lifted me into the air—not only into the air, but rising up to clear the gate to the field and land on the other side. Immediately, I heard the raging cow collide with the gate.

It left a dent that would remain there as a reminder that a super hero was leaping that Christmas after all.

~G. E. Dabbs
Chicken Soup for the Mother and Son Soul

Holiday Traditions

For centuries men have kept an appointment with Christmas.
Christmas means fellowship, traditions, feasting,
giving and receiving and a time of good cheer.

~W.J. Ronald Tucker

56

Tending the Home Fires

May the spirit of Christmas bring you peace,
The gladness of Christmas give you hope,
The warmth of Christmas grant you love.
~Author Unknown

Our hardworking parents always did their best to provide memorable holidays for their family of seven.

Weeks before Christmas, my father pulled double and even triple shifts at the cement mill to make sure there would be presents under the tree. Coated in ashes and soot, he'd drag into the house each night, bone-weary from cleaning out smokestacks. Besides one full-time job as city clerk and another one mothering us, Mom did all the things necessary back in the 1960s to make our budget stretch: sewing clothing into the wee hours of the morning, mending hand-me-downs, packing school lunches and laundering cloth diapers.

Even so, my parents emphasized the memory-making moments: designing elaborate macaroni ornaments to decorate the tree, hanging dozens of cheery greeting cards from loved ones around our bedroom doorframes, and singing carols as we hauled aging boxes of decorations from the basement to the living room. In mid-December, Mom gathered her baking sheets, her huge wooden rolling pin and her kids to spend an entire day in the cramped kitchen baking and decorating sugar cookies.

And she always delegated one duty to me.

Because our scant living room had no fireplace to hang stockings, we used a cardboard-kit substitute. It was my job to assemble it each year, that special place where Santa would soon leave his few presents for us.

Against one wall, I unfolded the fireplace front. Then I placed and balanced the black cardboard mantle that bore wounds from dozens of punctures where we'd thumbtacked our stockings during holidays past. After I inserted a red light bulb into the hole near the metal spinner, I plugged in the cord so the logs would "burn."

Satisfied at last, I settled to the floor in my favorite nook across from the fireplace—directly in front of a furnace vent. I knew the warm air blew from the basement, but in my mind, the heat spread from the cardboard logs to ignite my imagination. It was there that I spun my boyish dreams and lived my foolish fantasies.

The years drifted on, and so did I.

When all of us kids were grown and on our own, our parents hit the jackpot. I mean, really hit the jackpot. In a big way. They won over two million dollars in the Illinois State Lottery!

As instant millionaires, the first thing they did was look for a new place to live. My father insisted on only two musts: an attached garage and... a working fireplace. My mom wanted more space. And they found it: a beautiful two-story house with four bedrooms, a spacious kitchen, a dining area, a two-car garage, a roomy basement—and a living room with a working fireplace.

In December after their move, we all came home for our first holiday together in years. While everyone lazed and chatted by the fireside on Christmas Eve, I rose to my feet to stroll through the house on a private tour.

Mom had decorated with recently purchased crystal ornaments and a hand-carved Santa from Germany. Embroidered holiday doilies graced new end tables, and expensive wrapping paper enveloped dozens of presents under the beautifully lit tree. From top to bottom, the place murmured, "New. Gorgeous. Tasteful." It certainly wasn't home as I remembered it.

Near the stairwell, I glanced up... and did a double take. Perched at the top, like a forgotten old friend I might bump into on the corner, stood the raggedy cardboard fireplace. With a smile as wide as Mom's rolling pin, I climbed the stairs and sank to the top step as a wave of boyhood memories washed over me.

Before long, Mom found me upstairs and stood silently at my side. I looked up, waiting for her eyes to meet mine.

"You kept it, this old fireplace in your new home. Why?"

After a long moment, she placed her hand on my shoulder and bent toward me. "Because I don't ever want any of us to forget the simple joys of Christmas," she whispered.

And I nodded in understanding, pleased that I could still feel the warmth radiating from the old, cardboard fireplace.

~Jim West
Chicken Soup for the Soul The Book of Christmas Virtues

57

The Melding

God made so many different kinds of people.
Why would he allow only one way to serve him?
~Martin Buber

My husband and I came from different religious backgrounds—mine Christian, his Jewish—and moreover, we were both fiery and determined individuals. Consequently, our first few years together tested our ability to respect and combine our two religious traditions with love and understanding. I remember raising the subject of a Christmas tree the first December after our marriage.

"Christmas tree?" LeRoy exclaimed incredulously. "Listen, there are two things I won't do. Buying a ham is one of them. Buying a Christmas tree is the other."

"If I can grate my knuckles while making potato latkes and clean up drippy candles at Chanukah, you can suffer through a Christmas tree!" I snapped back.

"No way," he retorted. "Remember last month? Whom do I meet at the grocery store when I have nothing but a ham in my cart? The rabbi. If we went shopping for a Christmas tree together, the whole synagogue would probably pass by on a bus while I was loading it into the trunk! Forget it!"

Naturally, we got a tree. A big, beautiful, feathery spruce that claimed half the living room in our tiny apartment. Or, as LeRoy scornfully referred to it in front of our Jewish friends, a "moldy-green matzo ball with colored lights." However, despite LeRoy's professed antagonism, when Christmas morning arrived, I noticed that the number of gifts beneath the tree had doubled and the tags they bore were written in LeRoy's hand.

By the time our daughter Erica was born, we had faced and solved many of the problems of an interfaith marriage and agreed to combine our heritages in an effort to provide the best for our children. By the time Shauna arrived three years later, we had settled into a way of life that was comfortable for both of us, although a bit unusual. Holly around the menorah. chicken soup, matzo balls with oregano, and potato latkes for Christmas dinner. Merry Chanukah. Fa-la-la-la. Happy Christmas. Shalom. We were discovering that peace means the same in any language.

At holiday time, our home was decorated with a potpourri of blue-and-white streamers, menorah lights, Advent calendars and a crèche. Our friends from both traditions joined in the spirit. A Christian neighbor brought us a glass mobile made of multiple Stars of David from the Holy Land. Our Jewish friends made and gave us many ornaments for the tree.

I became adept at reciting Hebrew prayers and explained Chanukah to both girls' classes every year. When LeRoy bought me a beautiful homemade guitar one Christmas, the first thing I taught myself to play and sing was a Jewish folk song. Dressed in a blue velvet shirt with buttons from Israel and a matching yarmulke (the skullcap worn by Jewish men at religious functions) that I had made him, LeRoy learned to warble off-key versions of the better-known carols.

One year, my husband brought home a little blue wooden Star of David. "This is for your tree," he stated crisply. "I want it to be the first ornament hung every year."

"I'll see to it personally, General," I quickly assured him, and from then on, it adorned the top of our tree.

One disconcerted Christian friend asked me, "Don't you feel hypocritical placing a Star of David on the top of your Christmas tree?"

"No," I replied and meant it. "Jesus was Jewish. And there was a star shining high over a stable. Remember?"

By this time, Chanukah had become almost as much a symbol of freedom and light to me as Christmas. And Christmas had become increasingly meaningful as the birthday of one so special that he gave light and freedom to everyone. As people of all races and religions gathered in our home, we found that their differences enriched our lives. The holidays seemed to become even more joyous.

Then, not long after we had celebrated our eleventh wedding anniversary, my forty-two-year-old husband suffered three heart attacks within two months. On December 17th, our daughters and I crowded onto his narrow hospital bed in the intensive care unit to sing Chanukah and Christmas songs. The next night, the first night of Chanukah, I was driving to a friend's house where Erica and Shauna would kindle the first Chanukah lights. Suddenly, in my mind, I saw a dazzling burst of light, and then the image of a smiling, healthy LeRoy. When we reached our friend's house, I learned that at sundown, LeRoy had leaned over and whispered, "Shalom, shalom" to his rabbi, who was seated by his hospital bed. Then LeRoy's soul had departed this earth.

The following evening, friends and relatives arrived at our home to sit shivah, the Jewish period of mourning.

In the lights provided by the silver menorah's candles and the twinkling Christmas tree, Jewish men in yarmulkes and prayer shawls bowed their heads and opened worn copies of the Old Testament. The doorbell rang. I opened the door and found members of Erica's fourth-grade class assembled there. As they began to sing "Silent Night," my daughters rushed to stand beside me in the doorway. I gathered Shauna and Erica into my arms. Behind us, we could hear the comforting Hebrew words chanted by men LeRoy had loved. In front of us, Erica's schoolmates sang the ancient carol in their clear, childish voices. The love radiating from these two traditions gave sudden, special meaning to LeRoy's and my marriage. In that one moment, my grief fell away, and I felt LeRoy's presence.

"Shalom, my love," I whispered.

"Sleep in heavenly peace," the children sang sweetly and triumphantly.

"Daddy's with God now, isn't he?" Shauna asked.

"Yes," I told her firmly. "Whatever road he took to get there, he's certainly with God."

Twenty Chanukahs and twenty Christmases have come and gone since that night, but the love that fused our hearts and lives remains vibrant in our home. Every December, the prayers of Chanukah as well as of Christmas still echo through the house, and the green holly encircles the silver menorah on the windowsill. The little blue Star of David still takes its lofty place as the first ornament placed on the Christmas tree, shining from on high—as did the star above that stable in Bethlehem so long ago—to proclaim peace on earth, good-will to men.

~Isabel Bearman Bucher
A Second Chicken Soup for the Woman's Soul

Away from
the Manger

O Christmas Sun! What holy task is thine!
To fold a world in the embrace of God!
~Guy Wetmore Carryl

"Okay, that's the last of it." Michael stacked the final box in my entry hall.

I surveyed the tattered, dusty containers with anticipation. To me, these Christmas decorations from Michael's childhood, in storage since his mother's death, signified our future together as a couple. We were sharing all sorts of holiday activities—parties, shopping and, now, decorating. In a few months we'd be married, and I was eager to create some traditions of our own. I yearned for meaningful practices, significant and unique to the two of us.

Opening the crates was a start.

"Hey, here's our old nativity set." Michael pulled out a well-packed box. "Mom always put it under the Christmas tree."

I carefully unwrapped Mary and Joseph and the manger. Stuffed deep in the newspapers was a stable. I placed it on the floor beneath the tree and arranged three wise men, a shepherd boy, a lamb and a cow. All accounted for, except...

I double-checked the loose packing and looked under the wadded newspapers, hoping to find the missing figure. Nothing.

"Honey," I called to Michael, who was busily arranging Santa's toyshop in the dining room. "I can't find Jesus."

Walking to my side, he playfully squeezed my shoulder. "Excuse me?"

"The baby Jesus for the nativity. He's not here!" I rummaged through more wrappings.

Michael's expression tensed. "He's here. He has to be. He was here the last Christmas Mom was alive."

Hours later, all the boxes were unpacked, but Jesus never appeared. Michael regretfully suggested we pack the nativity scene back in the crate.

"No," I said. "I'll find a baby that matches the set tomorrow."

We kissed good night, and Michael went home.

The next day, I stuffed the manger into my purse and headed to the hobby store during my lunch hour. No Jesus there. After work, I searched for him at several other stores only to discover that baby Jesus wasn't sold separately. I considered buying another nativity just to replace the Jesus in Michael's, but none of the infants fit the manger.

Michael arrived for dinner a few days later, and I broke the news to him. After we ate, I began to repack the figurines in their box. Michael stilled my hands with his.

"I think we should leave it up."

"Honey, we can't. There's no baby," I replied. "We can't have a nativity without Jesus."

"Wait a minute." Michael pulled me away from the tree. "Now look from back here."

He pointed. "At first glance, you don't notice anything missing. It's not until you look closely that you see the Christ Child is gone."

I cocked my head and looked at the scene. He was right. "But I don't get your point."

"Amid the decorations, shopping lists and parties, sometimes we lose sight of Jesus," he explained. "Somehow, he gets lost in the midst of Christmas."

And then I understood.

So began our first Christmas tradition—significant and unique to our family. Each year, we position the treasured figures in their customary places. The manger remains empty. It's our gentle reminder to look for Christ at Christmas.

~Stephanie Welcher Thompson
Chicken Soup for the Soul The Book of Christmas Virtues

Traditions

I think I've discovered the secret of life—
you just hang around until you get used to it.
~Charles Schulz

Holiday traditions have always had great importance in my home. My children love Christmas and all the rituals associated with this special time of year.

My husband died suddenly, and at the age of thirty-eight, I was a widow. One week later, I gave birth to our third child and only son, whom I named after his father.

When the first holiday season without David rolled around, I was determined, for the children, to keep all the Christmas traditions that my late husband and I had established. Every year on Thanksgiving morning, our home was transformed into Christmas City, with beautiful ceramic churches, rinks with free-moving skaters and musical houses we collected at the annual holiday craft fair. Beautiful lights wound together with greenery adorned the staircase and fireplace of our home. My husband would set up the tree with lights and the angel on the top, and the children and I would place the ornaments and tinsel on it. When it was completely decorated, our daughters, Nicole and Amanda, would turn on the angel light. It was magical for them, and we always looked forward to the coming of Christmas.

That first Christmas season somehow came and went effortlessly.

With the help of friends, we managed to get the tree in just the right spot and decorate it. Everything went off without a hitch.

By the second year, I was feeling confident that I could do all the Christmas preparations by myself. Through the year, I had asked for help from many friends who graciously lent a hand with whatever I needed, and I was incredibly grateful. However, it was painfully apparent that all my friends had plenty to do at their own homes, so I worked on being more independent. Raising a seven-year-old, a five-year-old and a one-year-old is challenging in and of itself, but adding a traditional holiday season with everyday activities? Brutal! Despite my good intentions, Thanksgiving Day came and went without the traditional decoration ceremony. Time flew by, and before I knew it, I realized it was only a few days before Christmas! There were no presents and no decorations whatsoever.

I was discouraged and overwhelmed. The only present I wanted was the look of joy on my children's faces as they opened their presents on Christmas morning. I had to pull it together for them. That night, once the children were in bed, I ran up and down the attic stairs carrying boxes, ceramic decorations and the tree, which was so heavy that I could only carry it down one flight of stairs. So I set it up in the family room on that level. I worked until two in the morning decorating the house. The children were delighted with the result when they awakened, but I was spent.

The night before Christmas Eve, I managed to get a sitter so I could go Christmas shopping. I went from one store to another canvassing the mall for presents for my children, friends and family. I call it "power-shopping," and luckily, I'm great at it.

Christmas Eve was a blur of visits to family and friends and attendance at Christmas Eve mass. We got home at nine, and I managed to get the children settled down and tucked into bed. That's when the fun began. I had some serious wrapping to do. By 4:30 that morning, my entire body was shaking with exhaustion, but everything was wrapped, assembled and ready for a joyful day.

My daughter Nicole was in my bedroom, one inch from my haggard face at 5:45 sharp. Bubbling over with excitement, she asked to open the family room door to see if Santa had arrived. I told her to wait for her sister, and then come and get me. At least it's what I said in my head—to this day I'm not sure what came from my lips, because at 7:00, I heard the sound of rustling paper coming from David's crib. I bolted out of bed to find him buried beneath a heap of Christmas wrap, chewing on an empty Barbie doll box.

I ran from his room to the family room to find every gift opened and strewn everywhere. Not even the stocking presents were left. Nicole looked at me sheepishly, knowing that she might have made a wrong move, and Amanda ran to me, dressed in her sister's oversized hat and mittens, holding a Tonka truck meant for David, joyfully exclaiming, "Look what Santa gave me!" The heat that rose from my feet to my head could have melted steel! I shrieked at my girls, sending them to their room to sit on their beds. They immediately began to cry as I stormed out of the room ranting and raving all the way downstairs. I had missed Christmas! The only part of all the traditions that I was looking forward to was seeing them open their gifts, and it was gone. Suddenly, I caught myself and realized what had really happened, and despair hit me like a boulder. I had ruined Christmas for my beautiful children.

I burst into uncontrollable tears and ran up the stairs to my daughters' bedroom. They were waiting, little angels with tears in their eyes, ready to offer apologies to me. I stopped them, hugging them close to me, sobbing. "This is not what Christmas is about. It's not the presents; it's the birth of baby Jesus!" I cried. "I need to ask you to forgive me." With smiles on their faces, Nicole and Amanda replied, "Okay, Mama! Let's go look at what Santa brought us."

Children are awesome with forgiveness. They forgive as God does, unconditionally. I felt so humbled by their love. I took them into David's room, and we pulled the papers from his fists and teeth, wiped the wrapper ink from his lips, redistributed the toys and played with their gifts.

I had tried so hard to keep everything the same with our family, but it wasn't the same. As a single mother, I was not capable of keeping up all our old traditions. In the frenzy that was the holiday season, I didn't see that the children never noticed the absence of our old rituals. They just wanted to be with me. I was now a single parent with limited time and energy, and that energy needed to be reserved for nurturing my babies. I let go of the traditions that were too much for me, kept the simple ones that meant so much and created new ones. Traditions are only important because they bring families closer. It is repetitive togetherness with a theme.

Nicole is now eleven, Amanda is nine and David is five. As a single mother, I've now learned to shop early. I wrap early. I go to bed early. I ask for help from my dear friends. The tree goes where it lands. When I feel that frenzy coming on and the pace gets hectic, I'm reminded to let go and be present to the meaning of Christmas. Our home is filled with family and friends, filled with laughs and love. We express our gratitude as a family. These are the traditions we'll never let go of.

~Suzanne Aiken
Chicken Soup for the Single Parent's Soul

60

One Christmas Card Coming Up

*E*very year in December we go through what is known as "picture time" at our house. It's sort of like World War Three but without rules.

The tradition started years ago when my wife and I thought it would be a good idea to have a Christmas card featuring our children and dog. It would be folksy, we agreed. And, since we didn't intend to be explicit about the children's faith, nobody could take religious offense.

However, there was one problem: we didn't have any children or a dog.

I was all for renting, but my wife figured it would be cheaper in the long run to have our own.

So I wound up having these three kids and a St. Bernard dog (my wife can do anything if she puts her mind to it) on my hands.

For 364 days in the year, they cost me money but on the 365th they have their one duty to perform: They pose for our Christmas card.

Well, yesterday was it.

For some unknown reason, we never get the same photographer twice. In fact, last year the one we had never even came back for his hat.

All we want is a simple picture of three sweet kids and a lovable 195-pound dog smiling in the Christmas spirit.

I can't think of anything easier than that.

But it never quite works out that way.

I assembled the cast and converged on the rec room only to find the floor littered with laundry.

"What are the sheets doing all over the bar stools?" I asked.

"They're supposed to be there," my wife replied.

"Why?"

"To look like snow," my wife explained. "Could you tell they're bar stools covered with sheets?"

"Never in a million years," I said. "It looks exactly like snow."

"Should we put the children on a toboggan and have it pulled by the dog?" my wife asked. "I could bend a coat hanger and make it look like a pair of antlers."

"Sounds swell," I encouraged.

"You don't think it looks a little phony, do you?" she wanted to know.

"Don't be silly. I would never guess that it's a dog pulling a toboggan across a rec room floor past some bar stools covered with white sheets," I said. "If I didn't know better, I'd swear I was looking in on a scene in the Laurentians."

My wife seemed pleased with that.

"Stephen!" she ordered. "Stop crossing your eyes." And then she added to me, "Do you think we should dress them like elves?"

I said it was fine by me. "Everything's fine, just as long as we hurry."

The photographer, meanwhile, was setting up his lights and trying to keep out of reach of the dog, who was going around smelling everybody's breath to see what they had enjoyed for dinner.

"Didn't you give the dog a tranquilizer?" I asked.

"No, I thought you had," my wife said.

"He's just a little excited," I explained to the photographer who was trying to get his camera bag out of the dog's mouth without much success. "C'mon, boy. Give us the bag."

"Jane! Stop punching your brother," my wife interrupted. "You'll make him blink for the picture."

We finally got the camera bag, the kids took their place and our "reindeer" gave a big yawn.

"Smile!" the photographer pleaded.

I made faces.

My wife waved toys.

It was swell except that nothing happened. One of the elves had pulled the floodlight cord from the wall socket and was trying to screw it into his sister's ear.

There's no point going into all of the details. Within ninety minutes or so, we had our picture and the photographer gratefully retrieved his camera bag and left. Next year, I think I'll handle it differently.

I'll mail out the kids and the dog directly and not bother with a photograph.

~Gary Lautens
Chicken Soup for the Soul Christmas Treasury

61

Make a Memory

What children need most are the essentials that grandparents provide in
abundance. They give unconditional love, kindness, patience, humor,
comfort, lessons in life. And, most importantly, cookies.
~Rudolph Giuliani

"Are you and the kids going to be home this weekend?" I asked my son. "I want to come up and see you guys." I live two thousand miles away from my grandchildren. Sometimes, the urge is so strong that I just have to see them.

"We'll be home. When can you get here?"

"I found a flight on the Internet that fits my budget. I'll be there in just three days."

"Cool. I'll tell the kids."

"I want to do something fun. Why don't we make Christmas cookies—the kind we used to make when you were a kid. The cut-out ones that you bake and then decorate with icing and colored sugars."

"Yeah. I like those. And the boys will, too."

It would be a messy, fun, memory-filled day. And since every moment I spend with my grandchildren is precious, I didn't want to waste time going to the grocery store, and I didn't want to bend over a mixing bowl when I could be holding a child in my arms. So I made the dough and the frosting ahead of time, using all the ingredients in my own home. After mixing up the dough, I placed it in an airtight

Tupperware container. Then I made a butter frosting, licking the bowl and the beaters afterwards, just like I did when I was a young mom, raising two sons. Oh, what memories!

After pouring the frosting into another Tupperware container, and putting both in the fridge, I was ready to gather the colored sugars for decorating. Of course we'd have to have green and red, but how about blue, yellow, pink and purple? We used to add chocolate sprinkles (they're called jimmies where I come from) and it was a tradition when my boys were small, to have red hots for the tips of the trees and the noses of the reindeer. Everything was gathered and ready.

I rolled two suitcases into the airport terminal that Friday morning. The biggest one held all the presents to put under the tree and the other held the rolling pin, cutout forms, and the dough and frosting containers nestled in ice packs for the trip. I even squeezed in a change of clothes for me.

Saturday morning found a house full of kids gathered around the kitchen table. My brother and his children joined us for the festivities.

"Grandma, can I roll out the dough?" asked 9-year-old Nick.

"I want to make a reindeer," said little 5-year-old Cole.

The first few rolls of the dough produced Santas that stuck to the floured table and reindeer with only two legs. We kept on going, though, and finally got the hang of it. Some of the kids wanted to throw back the cookies that were misshapen and less than perfect, but we kept every one. It was fun to look back after they were baked to see the elongated star and the funny looking stocking. After all, it's part of Christmas to accept things just the way they are.

We rolled out the dough numerous times, and cut out stockings, trees, Santas, reindeer, stars, and bells. We put the first two trays of cookies into the oven while we cut out more, and finished baking the last one two hours later. We had over four dozen cookies to frost and decorate.

Out came the box from my suitcase with sugars in all shades of the rainbow. The colors went into separate bowls, which were then lined up on one side of the table. The adults frosted the cookies and handed them to a waiting child, who would walk along the row of colors and sprinkle a little bit of red, a touch of yellow, and maybe a dash of green.

"I want a stocking, Grandma!" little Cole yelled out.

"I want a star," Amanda demanded. And on it went, the adults barely keeping up with the eager children.

As tray after tray became filled with brightly colored cookies, we oohhhed and aaaahhhed over each one. "Look at mine, grandma!" shouted Nick. "I put extra frosting on it, see the hump?"

"Look at my bell, daddy," said Kayla. "It has a red hot right at the top."

I thought about the memories we had all just made as I watched my son and his uncle wipe off the table, put all the colored sugar away, then grab the vacuum to clean up the floor. Happy memories. Loving memories. Fun times shared with laughter and joy.

"Who made the star with all the different colored points?" "Who made this one with the pretty stripes down the side?" "Nick, is this one yours with the extra frosting on it?" "Can I eat it?"

The afternoon wore on into the day, and cookie after cookie disappeared from the trays. Little hands would reach up and choose just the colors they were looking for. It was a happy day. But the best part came as music to my ears when I heard, "Grandma, can we do this again next year?"

~B. J. Taylor
Chicken Soup for the Soul Celebrates Grandmothers

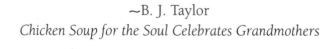

62

Charlie Brown Meets Baby Jesus

or years I had carefully placed the little plastic nativity under the Christmas tree. It had been purchased along with our other meager decorations the first Christmas we were married back in 1962. My husband was finishing his fourth and last year at college and money was tight. Each year as Christmas approached, I looked longingly at the beautiful wood and ceramic crèches wondering when there would be enough extra money to purchase one.

Finally the day arrived. Our sons were eleven and fourteen and we had recently moved into our newly built house. I watched the after Christmas sales and there it was, nothing elaborate, not a large crèche, but it was wood and ceramic with 50% off the original price. We made our way to the local department store with all the other after Christmas bargain shoppers, purchased the crèche and carefully packed it away until the following Christmas.

Several weeks before the next Christmas, we brought the box from the basement and arranged the crèche in a place of honor in the center hall where, as I went from one part of the house to another, I could enjoy my treasured gift. An angel on the top watched over Mary, Joseph, and the baby Jesus. Jesus lay in the manger with outstretched arms, surrounded by wise men, shepherds, and animals.

One day as I hurried by the crèche, something caught my eye. I stopped to look and there beside the manager, looking down at the baby Jesus was a rubber figure of Charlie Brown. Charlie Brown! Charlie Brown from the beloved Peanut cartoon series.

I was quick, much too quick, to question the boys and say, "Get that thing out of my crèche." I knew instantly our youngest son, Mark, had been the culprit as he looked at me with his boyish grin.

Charlie Brown disappeared. Christmas was over and the wooden stable and ceramic figures were lovingly packed away.

As Christmas approached the following year, the crèche was again displayed in its place of honor. It was the first thing holiday guests saw as they entered the front door. It was the last thing we saw each night as we turned off the lights and headed up the stairs to bed.

Several days before Christmas as I passed the crèche, I was again surprised. There gazing down at the baby Jesus was not only Charlie Brown but on the other side of the manager stood another little rubber figure. Linus! Linus, blanket and all, stood looking into the outstretched arms of baby Jesus.

For some strange reason as I beheld this, I was not upset as I had been the previous year. Maybe the crèche didn't belong to me alone. Maybe Mark with his childish prank was showing he loved it as much as I did. Maybe a young boy was mature beyond his years, knowing the baby with his outstretched arms was for everyone.

That afternoon as I watched my children get off the school bus and head for the house, my heart overflowed with love for them. I smiled when I mentioned that Charlie Brown had once again mysteriously appeared in the crèche and now Linus had joined him.

As the years went by, I never knew when Charlie Brown and Linus would make their mysterious arrival, but Christmas after Christmas they showed up, looking down into the outstretched arms of baby Jesus.

Mark left for college, but each Christmas Charlie Brown and Linus came home for Christmas break, too.

Then came marriage and the move away from home. Still Charlie

Brown and Linus continued to find their way into our crèche each Christmas.

Last Christmas I stood back with tears in my eyes as Mark bent over the crèche with his little daughter, Savannah, helping her quietly and carefully place Charlie Brown and Linus beside the baby Jesus when they thought I wasn't looking.

As the crèche was carefully packed away in its now-torn tissue paper and aging box, I smiled to myself, secure in the thought that the tradition of Charlie Brown and Linus would continue. And secure in the knowledge that those outstretched arms of the Christ child welcome us all to the manger.

~Jean C. Myers
Chicken Soup for the Christian Soul 2

63

The Christmas Star

*T*his was my grandmother's first Christmas without Grandfather, and we had promised him before he passed away that we would make this her best Christmas ever. When my mom, dad, three sisters and I arrived at her little house in the Blue Ridge Mountains of North Carolina, we found she had waited up all night for us to arrive from Texas. After we exchanged hugs, Donna, Karen, Kristi and I ran into the house. It did seem a little empty without Grandfather, and we knew it was up to us to make this Christmas special for her.

Grandfather had always said that the Christmas tree was the most important decoration of all. So we immediately set to work assembling the beautiful artificial tree that was stored in Grandfather's closet. Although artificial, it was the most genuine-looking Douglas fir I had ever seen. Tucked away in the closet with the tree was a spectacular array of ornaments, many of which had been my father's when he was a little boy. As we unwrapped each one, Grandmother had a story to go along with it. My mother strung the tree with bright white lights and a red button garland; my sisters and I carefully placed the ornaments on the tree; and finally, Father was given the honor of lighting the tree.

We stepped back to admire our handiwork. To us, it looked magnificent, as beautiful as the tree in Rockefeller Center. But something was missing.

"Where's your star?" I asked.

The star was my grandmother's favorite part of the tree.

"Why, it must be here somewhere," she said, starting to sort through the boxes again. "Your grandfather always packed everything so carefully when he took the tree down."

As we emptied box after box and found no star, my grandmother's eyes filled with tears. This was no ordinary ornament, but an elaborate golden star covered with colored jewels and blue lights that blinked on and off. Moreover, Grandfather had given it to Grandmother some fifty years ago, on their first Christmas together. Now, on her first Christmas without him, the star was gone, too.

"Don't worry, Grandmother," I reassured her. "We'll find it for you."

My sisters and I formed a search party.

"Let's start in the closet where the ornaments were," Donna said. "Maybe the box just fell down."

That sounded logical, so we climbed on a chair and began to search that tall closet of Grandfather's. We found Father's old year-books and photographs of relatives, Christmas cards from years gone by, and party dresses and jewelry boxes, but no star.

We searched under beds and over shelves, inside and outside, until we had exhausted every possibility. We could see Grandmother was disappointed, although she tried not to show it.

"We could buy a new star," Kristi offered.

"I'll make you one from construction paper," Karen chimed in.

"No," Grandmother said. "This year, we won't have a star."

By now, it was dark outside, and time for bed, as Santa would soon be here. We lay in bed, snowflakes falling quietly outside.

The next morning, my sisters and I woke up early, as was our habit on Christmas day — first, to see what Santa had left under the tree, and second, to look for the Christmas star in the sky. After a traditional breakfast of apple pancakes, the family sat down together to open presents. Santa had brought me the Easy-Bake Oven I wanted, and Donna a Chatty-Cathy doll. Karen was thrilled to get the doll buggy she had asked for, and Kristi to get the china tea set. Father was in charge of passing out the presents, so that everyone would have something to open at the same time.

"The last gift is to Grandmother from Grandfather," he said, in a puzzled voice.

"From who?" There was surprise in my grandmother's voice.

"I found that gift in Grandfather's closet when we got the tree down," Mother explained. "It was already wrapped so I put it under the tree. I thought it was one of yours."

"Hurry and open it," Karen urged excitedly.

My grandmother shakily opened the box. Her face lit up with joy when she unfolded the tissue paper and pulled out a glorious golden star. There was a note attached. Her voice trembled as she read it aloud:

Don't be angry with me, dear. I broke your star while putting away the decorations, and I couldn't bear to tell you. Thought it was time for a new one. I hope it brings you as much joy as the first one. Merry Christmas.

Love,
Bryant

So Grandmother's tree had a star after all, a star that expressed my grandparents' everlasting love for one another. It brought my grandfather home for Christmas in each of our hearts and made it our best Christmas ever.

~Susan Adair
A Second Chicken Soup for the Woman's Soul

Chapter
7

Christmas Cheer

The Santa Files

At Christmas play, and make good cheer,
for Christmas comes but once a year.

~Thomas Tusser

64

The Christmas Train

In 1963, I was a ten-year-old girl living with my parents and four-year-old brother in Madrid, Spain. We were poor Cuban refugees who had left our country just a few months before.

Our stay in Spain would be brief as we waited for our U.S. residency to be approved. My maternal grandfather and uncle had sacrificed their little savings—they were recently arrived refugees to New York—to send us a meager monthly stipend for our humble lodgings. Our only meals came from a soup kitchen where we lined up in the late morning along with dozens of other Cubans.

That particular winter was bitterly cold in Madrid. Our hospice room was freezing during the day, so we would spend our time walking Madrid's magnificent boulevards. We marveled at the architecture and the large plazas and the snow! We missed our homeland, but the promise of a fresh beginning beckoned, and la madre patria was a magnificent start for a new life.

The Christmas season arrived. Overnight, Madrid lit up. Every corner was awash in sparkling holiday lights, los madrileños were busy bustling about buying gifts and looking forward to la noche buena, and el día de los reyes.

Every storefront was a winter wonderland full of dolls, trolleys and every imaginable toy. The storefront at the Corte Inglés department store had a fabulous Christmas village full of enchanting chalets, snow-covered peaks and a shiny red train that circled the town, hooting its horn at every turn.

My younger brother, Santiago, was born during the first year of the Cuban Revolution, and he had never seen such a wondrous toy. Toys were considered a luxury then and were very hard to obtain.

My brother fell in love with that train. Every day he would push his nose against the glass in the window and ask: "Do you think los reyes magos will bring me that train? Do you? Do you?" My parents' pain was apparent as they looked at their son's hopeful face. They knew that no matter how hard their son wished for that train, his wish would not be granted.

Looking at my parents, I just wished Santiago would stop asking. But I also didn't want to destroy the innocence of a hopeful four-year-old. So the next time Santiago ran up to the storefront window and asked the question, I pulled him aside.

"Santiago, you know that we left our country and we are in a strange land," I said. "The three wise men are pretty smart, but since we are only here in Madrid for a little while, they probably don't have our address. I don't think we'll be getting any toys this year."

I also told him that once we were settled in the United States, the three wise men would find us once again. To my utter surprise, he accepted my explanation without question, and our excursions up and down the main boulevard continued without any major interruptions.

A year later, we were settled in Union City, New Jersey, the town we had moved to upon entry into the United States. Both my parents—a teacher and an engineer—were working at factory jobs. Santiago and I were adapting to a new school and quickly learning English.

That Christmas was modest, but my parents bought a silver-colored Christmas tree, and we put tiny, sparkling lights on it. They also bought the traditional pork and turrones for the Noche Buena meal.

On Christmas Day, I woke up early, and to my surprise and delight found several presents underneath the tree with my name on them. But even better than that was watching my brother's face as he opened a square box with a large red bow and his name on it.

Inside was a shiny, brand-new train! The locomotive and caboose resembled the one that had so enthralled my brother a year before. Santiago's face lit up like the Christmas tree. He looked at my parents and me, and his eyes shined with happiness and surprise.

"Babby, you were right!" my brother told me eagerly. "The three wise men found our address, and they gave it to Santa Claus!"

~Barbara Gutiérrez
Chicken Soup for the Latino Soul

65

Chicken Soup for the Soul

A Christmas Memory

The snow fell softly, its delicate lace-patterned snowflakes lingering on my woolen poncho. I half-carried, half-dragged my cumbersome load—a large garbage sack loaded with gifts—across the whitening street. It was almost midnight on Christmas Eve, but I was in no hurry to get home. Tears blurred the kaleidoscope of multicolored lights that blinked cheerily from our neighbor's houses. More subdued candles dimly lit every window at our house in their halfhearted attempt to feign cheer. Suddenly I stopped and stared. A white-bearded, red-clad, overstuffed figure was tapping gently at our front door and muttering "Ho! Ho! Ho!"

"What is he doing here?" I thought bitterly.

Christmas wasn't coming to No. 5 Jodi Lane this year. I feared it might never come again. My mind raced back to that day in November, the day our joy seemed to disappear forever.

The fall weather was just turning crisp, and my husband Jack and I and our three children squeezed into the car to head out for the Junior Midgets Sunday afternoon football game. Our two older children, Tara, four, and Sean, eighteen months, ran up and down the bleachers while I tended the baby, Christopher, who was three months old. He was snuggled up warmly in his carriage, napping on his stomach, oblivious to the noise and chill in the air.

"I haven't seen your newest addition yet," one of our friends, Tony, called, coming to my side. He smiled and peeked into the buggy.

Always eager to show off the baby, I lifted him out, his face turned toward Tony. The smile faded from Tony's face, and horror filled his eyes. What was wrong? I turned Christopher to me. His beautiful, perfect little face was a contorted, grayish-blue. I screamed.

Another parent—a New York City policeman—leapt from the bleachers, grabbed Christopher from my arms and began applying CPR before the screams had died from my lips. An ambulance was on standby for the football game, and the policeman ran toward it with our lifeless baby cradled in his arms. Jack ran behind them. By the time they pulled away, I had collapsed, and a second ambulance was called to take me to the hospital.

When I arrived minutes later, the policeman who had carried Christopher away opened the door of my ambulance. His name was John, and his brown eyes were kind as he jumped up and sat by me in the ambulance. I didn't like what I saw in his eyes. He reached out one of his massive hands—hands that had tried to save my baby   and held mine.

"Let's pray for a moment before we go inside," he said gently.

"Is he alive?" I pleaded.

I didn't want to pray—not then, not for a long time afterwards. John led me into the hospital to Jack, and we stood together as we heard the medical explanation: SIDS (sudden infant death syndrome). Our son was another infant who had simply died in his sleep. No one knew why or how. There had been little anyone could do at the hospital. Christopher was dead when I lifted him from the carriage. He had died sometime during his warm, safe naptime.

We had set out that morning—a family with three happy, healthy children. Jack and I returned that evening huddled and bewildered in the backseat of John's car. Tara and Sean were at a friend's house. And Christopher, our baby, was dead.

John and his family lived about three blocks from us. A twenty-year veteran of the NYPD, John was experienced in dealing with death, but he was neither hardened nor immune to it. It was his patience and compassion that carried us through the worst hours of our lives.

The weeks that followed encompassed the two most joyous

family holidays of the year—Thanksgiving and Christmas—but for us, they were a pain-filled blur. Jack and I were so overwhelmed with grief, we cut ourselves off from everyone and each other.

By the beginning of December, if I could have stopped Christmas from coming for the entire world, I would have done it. Christmas has no right coming this year, I thought angrily.

But now, close to midnight on Christmas Eve, Santa Claus was intruding at my front door. If ever I had entertained a belief in the existence of Santa Claus, this was certainly the moment of stark reality—the time I knew he didn't, never did and never would exist.

Angry and exhausted, I set down the load of packages I'd bought for the children weeks ago. I had donated Christopher's presents to Birth Right shortly after his death. Tara's and Sean's gifts had been hidden safely from their spying eyes at a neighbor's house until this evening. I felt a pang of guilt. Jack and I probably hadn't done a very good job of preparing for Christmas this year; we had numbly gone through the motions of selecting and decorating a tree with Tara and Sean.

By the time I reached the front steps, Jack had opened the door and was looking blankly at the bulky figure. His eyes landed on me, behind the Santa; he probably thought I had dragged the guy home in a feeble attempt to revive some Christmas spirit. I shrugged my shoulders, indicating I was just as bewildered as he, and entered the house behind the red-suited man.

Santa ignored us. He merrily bounced up the stairs and made a beeline to the children's bedrooms. He woke Tara first, gently calling her by name. She sat straight up and smiled. Of course Santa was standing by her bed! What else could you expect on Christmas Eve, her four-year-old mind reasoned, and she immediately launched into a recital of her wish list. "A Barbie doll with lots of clothes, a tea set, Candyland and a doll that really wets," she finished happily. Santa hugged her and made her promise she would go right back to sleep. "Don't forget, I've been a very good girl," she called after him.

Santa walked into Sean's room. Sean wasn't so enthusiastic about waking up (he never was), and he was a bit skeptical, but he remembered getting a reindeer lollipop at the mall from some guy who looked like this and decided to let him stay. Santa lifted him out of his crib. Sean smiled sleepily and gave Santa a hug.

I looked at the big strong hands that gently held my son and, lifting my eyes to Santa's face, saw kindly brown eyes gazing at me over the folds of his fluffy white beard. I remembered those strong hands and the warmth of those eyes.

"Oh, John!" I cried and burst into tears. Santa reached out to Jack and me and held us close. "Thought you might all need a little Christmas tonight," he said softly.

Soon Santa left, and we watched him walk out into the snow-covered street toward the warmth of his own home and family. Jack and I wordlessly placed our packages under the tree and stepped back to see their bright paper glow under the Christmas tree lights. Santa had come to No. 5 Jodi Lane. And so had Christmas.

~Lenore Gavigan
Chicken Soup for the Mother's Soul 2

66

A Gift of Love

Love is what's in the room with you at Christmas
if you stop opening presents and listen.
~Author unknown, attributed to a 7-year-old named Bobby

"It's time," my sister whispered, and I was instantly awake, my heart pounding frantically in my chest. It was 4:00 A.M., and I wondered how I could have ever slept so late. After all, it was Christmas morning. I should have been awake hours ago.

We crept down the hall as quickly as we could. In the back of the house, our parents slept peacefully. I had been waiting for this day all year, marking off the days on my calendar as they passed, one by one. I had watched every Christmas special on TV, from Charlie Brown to Rudolph, and now that Christmas morning was finally here, I could hardly contain myself. I wanted to laugh, I wanted to play and, perhaps most of all, I wanted to rip open my presents.

As we approached the den, my sister put a single finger to her lips and whispered, "Santa might still be here." I nodded in complete understanding. At six, I knew all about Santa and his magic. At eleven, my sister was trying to give me my dream.

When we finally walked into the den, my first instinct was to rush toward the presents that were stacked oh-so-carefully around the room, but something made me hesitate. Instead of rushing forward, I stared in wonder at the room, wanting this single moment to last as long as it could. My sister stood quietly beside me, and we stared at the beautiful tree that we had decorated together weeks before. The lights shimmered, the ornaments sparkled, and our golden angel sat just slightly off-center on the top of the tree. It was the most perfect sight I'd ever seen.

On a nearby table, the cookies that we'd left for Santa were gone, and a small note read, "Thank you. Merry Christmas!"

My eyes widened in amazement at the note, for I was sure that I had finally found real proof of the jolly man's existence. Yet before I could truly marvel over the letter, my sister was handing me a small package. "It's from me," she whispered with a shy smile.

With trembling fingers, I slowly opened the package, carefully preserving the green bow. Inside, I found my sister's favorite necklace. It was a small heart on a golden chain. She had received the present from our grandfather two years before. My eyes filled at the sight. Santa's note was forgotten.

She put her arm around me. "He was going to give you one this year, but…" She stopped, and carefully wiped her eyes. "He just did not get a chance." He had died on Easter morning—the heart attack had been a harsh shock to our family. Our mother still cried quietly when she thought no one was watching. My sister squared her slender shoulders with a brave air. "So, I thought you might like to have mine."

I held the necklace as if it were made of the finest gold in the world. It seemed to shine even brighter than the lights on our tree.

"Let me help you," she said as she moved to put the necklace around my neck.

The small heart felt warm against my skin, almost like it was alive. In my mind, I could see my grandfather. He'd loved Christmas, and he had always given each of us a special surprise on Christmas day.

"Consider this his surprise," my sister told me as if she'd read my mind.

I grabbed her hand and held onto her with all of the strength that I possessed.

When our parents finally made their way into the den two hours later, they saw a beautiful Christmas tree, a dozen unopened gifts, and two sisters holding each other tight.

~Cindy Beck
Chicken Soup for the Sister's Soul

Santa Claus

his was our first Colorado winter and we were excited about our first Christmas in our new home. We had just moved from the desert, and my daughters, who were six and nine, had only seen a real winter once before in their lives. They were so little then, they didn't even remember it.

It was Christmas Eve. The girls and I were out and about, running holiday errands. We delivered treats to some of our friends and made a last minute trip to Kmart. My younger daughter, Megan, was distracted by a simple jewelry box. You've probably seen them — the little square box with a dancer inside that twirls around when you open the box while sweet ballerina music plays. Megan and her big sister, Elizabeth, were enchanted. They each wanted to take one home. I just smiled and said, "Not tonight. Tomorrow is Christmas; let's see what Santa Claus will bring."

I, like thousands of other parents over the years, had given my children the gift of believing in Santa Claus. I'd spent hours of their young lives telling them the stories, wrapping "Santa's gifts" in different colored paper and leaving milk and cookies. Among my favorite childhood memories that I shared with them were those annual movies, *Rudolph, the Red-Nosed Reindeer* and *Santa Claus Is Comin' to Town*. I still love them!

I would really have liked to have sneaked those gifts into the shopping cart that Christmas Eve. The jewelry boxes weren't very expensive, but with our move to a new home that year, we were on a budget, and Christmas spending was done. Though I yearned for the day when we could afford such simple gifts, I was thankful to God for how far we had come. You see, there were Christmases past when the girls and I relied on the kindness of others. When Megan was born, we were living on public assistance, in an old trailer in a very small town on the prairies of the Midwest. We had struggled to make our lives better since then, and in answer to my prayers, my husband, Randy, came into our lives when the girls were four and seven years old. Yes, though times were frugal, life had become so much richer for us. There was a great deal to be thankful for.

We left the store that night without the jewelry boxes. Our errands were just about done. One last stop for gas on the way home, and then it would be time to tuck the girls in for the night, while Randy and I played Santa Claus. It was dark at the gas station at about 8:30. As I got out of the car to begin fueling, I was careful to be aware of my surroundings. You can imagine how nervous I was as a beat-up old truck pulled into the gas station right up next to my car and a gruff-looking man rolled down his window and beckoned me over. With a glance at the girls to make sure they were snug in the car with windows rolled up, I cautiously approached the truck. The man looked like he had been working hard in filthy conditions all day and had not had a chance to bathe. I expected a question about where to find a hot meal or a warm bed and was prepared to direct him to our church or the police station. Imagine my surprise as the man held up two jewelry boxes almost exactly like the ones we had seen at the store!

"Ma'am, I won these two jewelry boxes at the movie theater," he said, "and I noticed you had two little girls. I don't have anyone to give them to and was wondering if your girls might like them."

I was speechless as I stood there, face-to-face with Santa Claus. Somehow I stuttered my way through thanks and gratitude, and assured him that the girls would be delighted to have the gifts he offered. I watched as he disappeared into the night—Santa Claus in an old, beat-up truck.

It has been four years since that night, and it still brings a tear to my eye as I tell the story. Who was that man? I don't know. I've never seen him again, but I do believe that God used him that night to answer my simple prayer. He opened my eyes to the true Santa Claus—the love of Christ shining through us to the whole world.

~Kimberly Henrie
Chicken Soup for the Christian Woman's Soul

68

The Right Touch

Christmas waves a magic wand over this world, and behold,
everything is softer and more beautiful.
~Norman Vincent Peale

*I*t was four days before Christmas and the town sat still, as if Old Man Winter had forgotten the snow everyone was wishing for.

Grandpa and I worked at the department store where he asked kids what they wanted for Christmas while I distributed candy canes and small presents. Grandpa's beard was real, bushy and full. Some of the kids who tugged it were quite surprised. And when he ho ho-ed, his stomach shook. Grandpa was Santa Claus, no question.

Most of the lap-sitters were under ten. They were pretty much alike, asking for bikes, dolls, radios and games. But one little girl was different. Her mother led her up, and Grandpa hoisted her onto his lap. Her name was Tina. She was blind.

"What do you want for Christmas, Tina?" Grandpa asked.

"Snow," she answered shyly.

Grandpa smiled. His eyes twinkled. "Well, I'll see what I can do about that. But how about something just for you? Something special?"

Tina hesitated and whispered in Grandpa's ear. I saw a smile creep over his face.

"Sure, Tina," was all he said.

He took her hands in his and placed them on his cheeks. His

eyes drifted shut, and he sat there smiling as the girl began to sculpt his face with her fingers. She paused here and there to linger, paying close attention to every wrinkle and whisker. Her fingers seemed to be memorizing the laugh lines under Grandpa's eyes and at the corners of his mouth. She stroked his beard and rolled its wiry ringlets between her thumbs and forefingers. When she finished, she paused to rest her palms on Grandpa's shoulders.

He opened his eyes. They were twinkling.

Suddenly her arms flew out, encircling Grandpa's neck in a crushing hug. "Oh, Santa," she cried. "You look just like I knew you did. You're perfect, just perfect."

As Tina's mother lifted her down from his lap, Grandpa smiled, then blinked, and a tear rolled down his cheek.

That night when my grandmother came to pick us up, I watched her help Grandpa transfer into his wheelchair and position his limp legs on the footrests. "So, Santa," she winked, "how was your day?"

He looked up at me and pressed his lips together. Then he looked at Grandma, cleared his throat, and said with a tiny smile, "Sweetheart, it was perfect, just perfect."

Outside it began to snow.

~Steve Burt
Chicken Soup for the Soul The Book of Christmas Virtues

69

A Doll from Santa

At Christmas, we are all of us, little children again.
~Author Unknown

Alice's mother died when she was five years old. Although her nine brother and sisters were loving and caring, they were no replacement for a mother's love.

The year was 1925, and life was hard. Alice, who grew up to be my mother, told me that her family was too poor to even afford to give her a doll.

In the aftermath of her loss, Alice vowed to care for others. First, her father, then her husband, later her three children and then her grandchildren were the main focus of her life. She felt that she could make up for her sad childhood through her dedication to her own family, but an unfilled void seemed to remain.

In December 1982, I had a job at a local bank. One afternoon, we were decorating the tree in the bank lobby and singing carols, getting ready for the Christmas season. One of my customers approached me with a sample of her handiwork: beautiful handmade dolls. She was taking orders for Christmas. I decided to get one for my daughter, Katie, who was almost five years old. Then I had an idea. I asked my customer if she could make me a special doll for my mother—one with gray hair and spectacles: a grandmother doll.

The doll maker felt that this idea was certainly unique and took it on as a creative challenge. So I placed my Christmas order: two dolls, one blond and one gray-haired for Christmas morning!

Things really started to fall into place when a friend had told me that his dad—who played Santa Claus at various charitable functions in my area—would be willing to make a visit on Christmas morning to our home to deliver my Katie her presents! Knowing that my parents would be there as well, I began to get ready for what would turn out to be one of the most memorable days of my mother's life.

Christmas Day arrived and at the planned time, so did Santa Claus. I had prepared the presents for Santa to deliver, along with one for my mother tucked into the bottom of Santa's bag. Katie was surprised and elated that Santa had come to see her at her own house, the happiest I had ever seen her in her young life.

My mother was enjoying watching her granddaughter's reaction to the visit from this special guest. As Santa turned to leave he looked once more into his knapsack and retrieved one more gift. As he asked who Alice was, my mother, taken aback by her name being called, indicated that she in fact was Alice. Santa handed her the gift, which was accompanied by a message card that read:

For Alice:

I was cleaning out my sleigh before my trip this year and came across this package that was supposed to be delivered on December 25, 1925. The present inside has aged, but I felt that you might still wish to have it. Many apologies for the lateness of the gift.

Love,
Santa Claus

My mother's reaction was one of the most profound and deeply emotional scenes I have ever witnessed. She couldn't speak but only clasped the doll she had waited fifty-seven years to receive as tears of joy coursed down her cheeks. That doll, given by "Santa," made my mother the happiest "child" alive.

~Alice Ferguson
Chicken Soup for the Mother's Soul 2

Santa Redeemed

*T*ypically, young kids start out believing in Santa Claus, then learn later that the Santa who visited them was just their grandpa dressed in a red suit. Me, I was onto the truth pretty quickly. As a savvy seven-year-old, I knew that the Santa Clauses I met were just another adult scam. Anyone could see that. The problem was that as the two oldest grandchildren, my sister and I were expected to help convince the younger grandchildren that Santa was real. I went along with this farce reluctantly. "You ask for what you want, and Santa brings it to you," I would say, dutifully.

But how could I, or anyone else for that matter—young or old—be expected to believe it? Life just wasn't like that. You didn't get what you wanted. You got what you didn't want. Look at us. We had recently lost our dad, and now, after thirteen years of staying at home, Mom had to go out and look for a job. This was tough. Mom had few qualifications for the world of work. She had been raised during the Great Depression, and had dropped out of school at an early age to help support the family. Not only had she little education, she had limited experience and no special training.

For months, she searched unsuccessfully for work as we sank further and further into poverty. Mom was unable to hold on to the home that Dad had built, and a relative in another town allowed us to live in a back room of her home for a while. The family car disappeared into the night as the repo man performed his duties.

Thus Mother's options were further limited to jobs that were within walking distance.

In our new town, there were a number of bars that could be reached on foot, but Mother believed that her working in a bar would not be good for her children. So she continued the search.

As Christmas approached, Mother planned to take my sister and me to the school festival. Admission was free, and we could walk there. After we had spent some time looking around, Mother asked us to get in line to talk to Santa, which was the only activity you could do for nothing. I got in line, just to please her.

After Santa lifted me onto his lap, he asked what my Christmas wish was. It didn't really matter what I told him, because I thought Santa was just somebody's grandpa dressed in a red suit. Naming a toy would only sadden my mother because she couldn't afford any toys. I decided to tell the truth. "My wish is that my mother would get a job so we can buy groceries," I said in a bold voice.

"And where is your mother?" Santa asked. I pointed her out. "Ho, ho, ho," said Santa, "I'll see what I can do."

Why do they always say ho, ho, ho? I thought.

A few days after Christmas, the phone rang and Mother picked it up. There was a brief conversation. "Yes... yes... oh, I would love to, yes.... All right... Goodbye."

She turned to my sister and me with a smile that I hadn't seen in a while.

"I've been offered a job in the school," she said, her voice rising with excitement. "In the lunch room. Now we're going to be all right." She hugged us both. Then she added, "I wonder how they knew I needed a job?"

Later I found out that Santa Claus, whether he is your grandpa in a red suit or the school superintendent doing his bit at the Christmas festival, is not such a scam after all.

And the following Christmas I told the younger kids that if they didn't believe in him they were really missing out.

~Jean Bronaugh
Chicken Soup for the Single's Soul

My Love
Is Like a Mountain

You know when you have found your prince because you not only have a
smile on your face but in your heart as well.
~Author Unknown

The fog was so thick I couldn't see the mountain. But I knew it was there and my fiancé and his best man were somewhere on it. Not knowing exactly where filled me with a fear that was almost unbearable. It was our wedding day.

The mountains were in our blood. Living at the foot of the Adirondacks as we did, how could they not be? During our growing-up years, our families lived near the tallest of the Adirondacks — Whiteface Mountain — a few miles from Lake Placid, New York.

Bob and I loved hiking and one day decided to climb Whiteface to the top. Looking at the world below in all its peace was a surreal moment.

"This is the perfect place to share our vows," Bob suggested.

Not wanting the typical wedding with a church, gown, tuxedo and four-tier cake, we agreed on a nontraditional ceremony at a place where our hearts lived — on top of the world.

Our excitement grew as we planned for a September wedding. The fall colors, that no florist could ever match, would be in bloom; and no church could compare to God's mountains.

We found a justice of the peace in the small town at the foot of Whiteface and reserved cabins for excited friends and family. Everybody met at the local restaurant for dinner and celebrating the night before the wedding. Everybody except the groom.

Bob's testimony of his love for me was unlike any other. He had a plan to climb Whiteface in honor of his commitment to me. He and his best man would climb halfway that night, camp out and then finish the climb to the top the next morning, the day of our wedding. All in time to meet me at the top by one o'clock.

With camping gear on his back, Bob kissed me goodbye. My heart in my throat, I was worried and excited at the same time. I couldn't believe this man was climbing a mountain to show his love for me.

When morning came, I looked out the window and there it was—surrounding me like a large white blanket—fog. Although I knew the mountain was there, I couldn't see it. And Bob and Kirk were somewhere on it.

Frightening thoughts went through my mind. What if they're lost? What if they're hurt? What if they ran into a bear? The mountains were full of them.

I was so upset I couldn't think straight. Finally my maid of honor took me by my shoulders.

"God takes care of the pure of heart," she assured me. And that was Bob, for sure. Holding on to that thought, I calmed down—until I was faced with even more bad news. The state ranger closed the mountain to the public due to the thick fog.

"Closed to the public?" I screamed. "They can't do that! I have to meet Bob in three hours at the top. He's on his way and I'm stuck at the bottom with no way of letting him know. What do I do now?"

The park ranger was alerted that there were two men on the mountain climbing to the top. He told me they would be all right; there was a ranger at the top who would notify us of their arrival.

Gathered at the restaurant, the rest of us worried as hours passed with no word. By now I was a total wreck and didn't know how much more waiting I could take.

It was three o'clock and I should have been on my honeymoon. The ranger called: Bob and his best man had reached the castle at the top. While everyone else was cheering, I was tearing. A heavy weight lifted from my heart.

I asked if the ranger was driving them back, but to my surprise the answer was no! It was against the law. So after climbing all day in thick fog, the poor guys had to walk another two hours down. But I thanked God they were safe.

After I calmed down, a thought came to me. The wedding! Where will we have the wedding? If not on top of Whiteface, where?

Someone suggested Santa's Workshop, a tourist spot known as The North Pole, located at the base of the mountain. The village had a small chapel, too. Our wedding day went from "on top of the world" to "Santa's world" in one day.

To my surprise, I didn't even need to tell the villagers my story. They already knew and graciously opened the tourist attraction and the chapel to us at no cost. Now all that was missing was... the groom and his best man.

Five hours late to his own wedding, Bob finally made it—dirty, sweaty, bleeding, hips chafed from his backpack, toes raw and bleeding. This sight for sore eyes was my sight for complete joy. My knight in shining armor had returned and, to my amazement, in his backpack were flowers he had picked for me.

"All I could think of was you and our wedding," he told me.

The town was abuzz—a wedding at the North Pole! Santa's helpers embroidered bride and groom on red hats and the "elves" were all in attendance. A sight to behold, for sure.

We exchanged vows, but to my surprise Bob had his own. "My love for you is like a mountain: strong, forthright and everlasting." My eyes filled with tears as his words echoed in my mind and heart.

After the ceremony we were whisked off to see Santa. Pictures were taken, jokes were made and Santa gave us a beautiful wedding candle. But our most prized gift was our wedding certificate. It reads, "Married at the North Pole. Witnessed by Santa Claus!"

We may have gotten off to a rocky start, but after almost thirty years of marriage, our love for each other is more like the mountain every day. Strong. Forthright. Everlasting.

~Eileen Chase
Chicken Soup for the Bride's Soul

Chapter
8

Christmas Cheer

Lessons from
Christmas Past

*I will honor Christmas in my heart,
and try to keep it all the year.*

~Charles Dickens

I'm Not Poor at All

Dear Lord, I'm feeling down today,
The bills are stacked up high;
With Christmas just two weeks away,
Our bank account's run dry.
The kids have all presented lists
Of things they want to see;
I hope and pray there's nothing missed
Beneath our Christmas tree.
But I don't have the money for
Expensive clothes and toys;
My credit card can't take much more,
Lord, where's my Christmas joy?
Perhaps it's wrapped up in that hug
My daughter gave this morn;
Or stacked with wood my son did lug
To keep us nice and warm.
Perhaps it's in my oldest's eyes
When he comes home on break,
And sees I've baked those pumpkin pies
He wanted me to make.
Perhaps it's in the tired lines
Around my husband's eyes;
Perhaps in love that's grown with time
I've found the greater prize.

A friend who gives a hearty smile,
And cupboards that aren't bare;
And, even if they aren't in style,
I've got some clothes to wear.
A family who believes in me
In all things great and small;
Dear God, I think I finally see --
I am not poor at all!

~Michele T. Huey
Chicken Soup for the Christian Family Soul

The Humbug Holidays

Isn't it funny that at Christmas something in you gets so lonely for—
I don't know what exactly,
but it's something that you don't mind so much not having at other times.
~Kate L. Bosher

I was going through the motions, everything a good mom is supposed to do before Christmas. I lugged out the boxes of holiday decorations. I baked my every-year-the-same two kinds of cookies. I even bought a real Christmas tree, for a change. I was going through the motions, but my heart was bogged down with a dull ache. I wasn't looking forward to Christmas one bit. My divorce had been finalized the past April, and my husband was already remarried. My oldest daughter, Jeanne, was in Yugoslavia for the year as a foreign-exchange student and wouldn't be home for the holidays—the first time ever that all four of my children wouldn't be with me for Christmas. Plus, the annual New Year's Eve get-together at my folks' house in Illinois had been canceled.

I was tired and grumpy. My job writing radio commercials at Milwaukee's biggest radio station was getting more hectic every day. Nearly every business in town wanted to advertise during the holiday season, and that meant longer and longer hours at work. Then there was the real nemesis: holiday shopping, a chore I kept putting off. I was supposed to be planning and buying, not only for my annual neighborhood holiday party, but also for two of my children's birthdays—Andrew would be eight on December 27th; Julia, seventeen on January 4th. How would I get through it all when "bah humbug" was constantly on the tip of my tongue?

During the night of December 15th, a snowstorm ripped through Wisconsin, dumping twelve inches of snow on the ground. Even though Milwaukee is usually prepared for the worst, this blizzard finished its onslaught just before rush-hour traffic, bringing the highways to a standstill. The next day, all the schools and most businesses were closed. Even the radio station where I worked, eighteen miles from my home, was urging early-morning risers to stay in bed because the roads were definitely not passable.

After viewing the picture-postcard scene outdoors, I grabbed Andrew, and forgetting my down-in-the-dumps attitude, said, "Come on, buddy, let's make a snowman." Andrew and I scooped up big handfuls of wet, perfect packing snow and built a base fit for a kingpin. Andrew rolled a ball of snow for the next level into such a huge mass that I had to get down on my hands and knees to shove it toward our mighty base. When I hoisted Andrew's third boulder onto this Amazonian snowperson, I felt like Wonder Woman bench pressing a hundred pounds.

As our snowman reached a solid seven feet tall, with the help of a stool, I carefully placed Andrew's bowling-ball-sized snow head on top.

"He needs a great face, Mom." While I smoothed the snow and pounded arms and a waistline into our giant snowman, Andrew ran inside and returned with a silly beach hat with built-in sunglasses for eyes and his Superman cape that we plastered on the front of the giant. Andrew and I stepped back to admire our noble snowman. Straight and tall. Ruler of the yard. When I took their picture, Andrew's head barely reached the snowman's middle.

It was warmer the next morning, and when I looked out the kitchen window, I noticed that Super Snowman seemed to be leaning forward a little. I hoped he wouldn't fall over before Andrew got home from school that day.

Late that afternoon when I returned home after a hectic, make-up-all-the-work-from-yesterday day at the radio station, I saw that our snowman hadn't fallen over, but he was leaning forward at a very precarious forty-five-degree angle. His posture reminded me of the way I felt: tired and crabby, with the weight of the world on my shoulders.

The next morning, Super Snowman was leaning so far forward as to seem physically impossible. I had to walk out into the yard to see him up close. What on Earth is holding him up? I wondered, absolutely amazed. The Superman cape, instead of being on his front, now dangled freely in the wind as old Frosty's bent chest, shoulders and head were almost parallel to the ground.

My own shoulders sagged beneath the weight of my own depression as I remembered that Christmas was almost here. A letter from Jeanne arrived saying that since Christmas wasn't a national holiday in Yugoslavia, she'd have to go to school on December 25th. I missed Jeanne's smile, her wacky sense of humor and her contagious holiday spirit.

The fourth day after we built the snowman was Saturday the 19th, the day I'd promised to take Andrew to Chicago on the train. Andrew loved the adventures of his first train and taxi rides, the trip to the top of the world's tallest building, the visit to the Shedd Aquarium and the toy departments of every major store on State Street. But I was depressed by the fact that it rained all day, that the visibility at the top of the Sears Tower was zero and that the all-day adventure left me totally exhausted.

Late that night, after the two-hour train ride back to Milwaukee, Andrew and I arrived home only to be greeted by the snowman, who by this time, after a warm day of drizzling rain, was now totally bent over from its base and perfectly parallel to the ground... and yet still balanced six inches above the slushy snow.

That's me out there, I said to myself. About to fall facedown into a snowbank. But why didn't our snowman fall? Nothing, absolutely nothing, was supporting the weight of that seven-foot-tall giant. Just like there isn't anything or anybody supporting me during this awful holiday season, I blubbered mentally, wondering what had supported the snowman in such a precarious position. Was it God in his almighty power? A freak of nature? A combination of ice, wind, rain and snow that had bonded to the mighty Super Snowman? I had a feeling there was a lesson to be learned from watching his decline. Sure enough, the lesson came to me gradually during the next two weeks.

On Christmas Eve, at the children's insistence, we attended family services at our parish church and afterward dined on our traditional oyster stew. Then, Andrew brought out the Bible for the yearly reading of the Christmas story before we opened our gifts. Later, we attended a midnight candle service with friends at their church. Finally, a phone call from Jeanne in Yugoslavia brimmed with good news of an impromptu Christmas celebration her host mother had planned.

The next day, some friends offered to cohost my big neighborhood party, which turned out to be a smashing success. On December 27th, Andrew was delighted with his three-person birthday party. The next weekend, my out-of-town family got together for a long New Year's Eve weekend at my house, filling our home with the madcap merriment of ten houseguests, all of whom pitched in to help. And when Julia simplified another dilemma by saying that all she wanted for her birthday was a watch and "lunch out with Mom," I smiled all day.

I learned that no matter how depressed, overwhelmed, saddened, lonely or stressed out we get, there's always someone or something to help us find or recapture our own inner strength, just like there was for the falling-down, stoop-shouldered Super Snowman. During his four-day life span, he showed me an amazing strength from within—a strength that came to me gradually, bit by bit, as each person in my life stepped up to boost my faith and my spirits to heavenly skies.

It was indeed a holiday season to cherish.

~Patricia Lorenz
Chicken Soup for the Single Parent's Soul

A Timeless Gift

Pleasure is spread through the earth
In stray gifts to be claimed by whoever shall find.
~William Wordsworth

Shopping for a Christmas gift can be the most nerve wracking event of the year. Shopping for my wife can be a special challenge. Vacuum cleaners are too impersonal, football tickets are too impractical, and kitchen gadgets are downright impossible. I was at a loss, with Christmas fast approaching. In desperation, I asked my secretary, Sally, to help me pick out a present.

We walked side by side in a fast-paced walk, two blocks to the jewelry store. Working in the downtown business district had its advantages; being close to a lot of shopping places was one of them. However, there were disadvantages as well. On the way, our path crossed a couple of homeless men, huddled together by a vent from one of the nearby buildings.

I started to cross the street to avoid them, but traffic was too thick. Just before we approached, I switched sides with Sally to keep them from confronting her. They were surely going to beg for money, pretending to buy food, but any donation would surely end up as beer or wine.

As we got closer, I could see that one was probably in his mid-thirties and the other was a boy of school age — around thirteen or fourteen. Both were dressed shabbily, the older with a too-tight sport coat ripped at the sleeve, while the boy was without a coat at all, only a tattered shirt separating him from the blowing wind. A quarter or two and they'll leave us alone, I thought. "I'll handle this," I said with my best male bravado.

But Sally seemed undisturbed by the sight of the two beggars. In fact, she seemed comfortable in their presence. Before they asked, she offered.

"Is there anything I can do for you?" she directed her question to the two homeless men. I was in shock, waiting to pull Sally away from a dangerous situation, but she stood firm.

The two men looked at her with surprise until the older one spoke up. "Yes, ma'am. We do need something."

Here it comes—the hook, the gouge, I thought. The two panhandlers are looking for a handout, an easy mark. As I watched, I could tell the younger boy was shivering in the winter breeze, but what could I do?

"Could you tell us the time?" asked the older man. Sally glanced at her watch and replied, "Twelve-fifteen." He nodded his thanks and didn't say another word. We continued on our way to the jewelry store, and I had to ask Sally about the encounter.

"Why did you ask if you could help that man?"

"He was cold and in need, that's why," she replied in a matter-of-fact tone.

"But he's a bum. He could have tried to rob you or something."

"I take care of myself. But sometimes you have to take a chance on someone."

We arrived at the jewelry store, and Sally quickly found the perfect gift for my wife—a pair of diamond earrings. While she was there, she bought a man's watch, not an expensive one, but she was always thrifty. Probably a gift for her husband, I thought.

As we walked back to our building, the two vagabonds were still hovering around the sidewalk grate. Once again, I tried to come between Sally and the two, but she wouldn't let me. To my surprise, when we got next to them, she pulled the watch out of the bag and handed it to the older man.

"Here, I'm sure you know how to use it."

He was as shocked as I was. "Thank you, much obliged, ma'am," he said, trying the watch on his wrist. As we walked away, Sally had a gleam in her eyes, proud of what she had done.

"Why on Earth did you do that?"

Sally shrugged and said, "God has been so good to me, and I decided to do something good for him."

"But he didn't deserve it."

"Even the poor want something special, and besides, God's done things for me that I don't deserve—but He did them anyway."

"He's probably going to buy beer with that watch."

Sally just smiled at me and said, "Well, so what if he does? That's not my concern. I did something for good and that's all that matters. What he does with the watch is his challenge."

We arrived back at our building and went into our separate offices. I wondered about the encounter, and I thought about the two men. Surely they were at the pawnshop, getting ready for a hot time at Sally's expense.

The next day, I was going to lunch alone at a hamburger stand outside our building. As I walked down the street,

I noticed the same two men that Sally and I had encountered. They were both still hovering around the heater vent. The older man recognized me and said, "Excuse me, sir. Could you give me the time?"

Aha! I had caught him. Sally's watch was nowhere to be found. Exactly what I thought.

"Where is the watch my secretary gave you yesterday?" I asked, hoping to stir his heart.

He hung his head down and admitted his guilt. "Sir, I'm sorry but I had to do something." It was then I noticed the new parka around the shoulders of his young companion. "Wouldn't you do something for one of your own?"

Speechless, I handed him a quarter and continued on my way. As I walked, I started thinking about the incident. He had sold the watch all right, but he bought a coat, not beer, with the money. Sally's act of kindness did have meaning. So did her words: The challenge was answered.

As I arrived at the hamburger stand, I suddenly lost my appetite. I turned around and headed back to the office. The two men were still by the grate. I tapped the older man on the shoulder and he looked up at me, obviously freezing. I took my long, gray overcoat off and draped it over his shoulders without saying a word. As I walked away, I knew that my own challenge had been met. The few steps back to my office made my teeth chatter. But, you know... it was one of the warmest trips I have ever made in my life.

~Harrison Kelly
Chicken Soup for the Soul Christmas Treasury for Kids

Remember
with Courage

C hristmas is a special time of year. And while pretty packages and twinkling lights are the window dressing for this exciting festivity, it is the warmth and love of family that make the holiday season so memorable. However, it can be a painful time for those experiencing the recent loss of a loved one.

Twelve years ago, my husband died suddenly. Although it was only the end of October, department stores glittered with decorations and staff worked eagerly to jump-start sales. When purchasing outfits for my ten- and twelve-year-old daughters to wear to their father's funeral, the salesclerk innocently asked if I was getting an early start on my Christmas shopping. I shall never forget the piercing pain in my heart as I stumbled for an answer.

I drove home in tears, realizing just how out of sync I was with the outside world. The holiday momentum was building, and I felt as though I was being swallowed by a huge black hole. I wanted to scream. I wanted the world to stop spinning. I wanted to run away... find some place that wasn't dripping with tinsel and holiday cheer. But more than anything, I wanted my family back.

The following weeks passed, and December 25th approached quickly. I struggled with wanting to dismiss Christmas and yet, at the same time, to embrace the childhood excitement my daughters were beginning to brim with. While it was easy for me to sustain resentment toward the outside world, it was impossible to resist them. They made their annual wish list and insisted on decorating the house. Through their actions, it became abundantly clear that Christmas was going to happen whether I wanted it to or not.

My girls taught me more about grieving than I could have ever taught them. They missed their dad terribly. Yet they were able to perceive the enchantment of Christmas as they had in years prior, albeit in a different way. It was obvious they'd made a choice to participate in the ardor of Christmas. Being children, they may not have been aware of the implications of this choice. Perhaps that was the saving grace. By making an unconscious choice they were relieved of any damning self-judgment that would cite disrespect to their father's memory. They instinctively knew their lives had to go on, and they showed me that mine had to as well.

Christmas did go on for us that year. And yes, it was very different. The three of us pulled together as a family and developed new traditions to help face the day. For instance, we hung a picture of my husband in the Christmas tree, declaring him our "Christmas Star." We also dedicated Christmas Eve as the day to honor him by making a visit to the cemetery. It was there that I presented each daughter with one of our wedding bands as a gift from both their father and me. We returned home for a quiet evening to reminisce about our favorite family times together. The tears flowed, at times uncontrollably, but in a very healing way.

Surprisingly, Christmas Day was quite pleasant. It was not filled with the heavy sadness or feelings of sorrow that I'd anticipated. Instead, it was filled with love and compassion. We invited our extended family and close friends to spend the day with us. During dinner, we exchanged stories of years gone by, many of them bringing smiles and laughter to everyone.

In reflection, I am thankful we found the courage to embrace Christmas that year. In doing so, we renewed our strength and courage to go on and live our lives as we were meant to. Two years later, my daughters and I were blessed to receive a new family, complete with a dad and three more children.

Today, we embrace Christmas as a way of celebrating not only those we are fortunate to have in our lives, but to also remember those we hold so dearly in our hearts.

If you are facing Christmas alone for the first time, I encourage you to reach out to someone you trust and share your feelings with them. Devote a time and place prior to Christmas Day in which you can openly honor your loved one and acknowledge your feelings. Finally, on Christmas Day, intentionally set your focus on family and friends who not only share in your loss, but who bring precious gifts of love and support to aid you in your healing journey.

You are not alone, although you may feel this way. Many people have been where you are, and we care deeply.

-Janelle M. Breese Biagioni
Chicken Soup for the Grieving Soul

76

Chicken Soup for the Soul

The Gift of Understanding

Kindness, like a boomerang, always returns.
~Author Unknown

For many years, I have been a nurse. I have tended to the needs of my community members, friends, neighbors, relatives and strangers. I have loved and hated my job, sometimes within the same shift. Nursing can be exhilarating and uplifting. It can also be stressful and exhausting. Most of all, it can be lonely. The shift work, the work on holidays, the need for confidentiality, all of these can contribute to a sense of isolation, especially for a single person.

Holidays are the hardest time. I don't think that I could count, nor would I want to, the number of times that a coworker or supervisor has asked me to work a holiday for another, because, "You don't have a family." So I work Thanksgivings so that families can serve the holiday dinner in their home. I work Christmas Eves so that mothers can see their children in the Christmas pageant at church. I work the nights before Christmas so that fathers can assemble toys. I work Christmas Days so that parents can see the wonder in their children's eyes on Christmas morning.

These are difficult shifts to work. Many of the patients hospitalized during this time will not see another holiday. They are there because they are too ill to go home. There are not many elective procedures scheduled during these times, and anyone who is able will hastily be discharged in time for the festivities. So nurses are usually left with the sickest and the saddest of patients. It is a time to minister to both the physical and emotional needs of your fellow man; it can be a time of great communion. After the shift is over, it can also be a time of great loneliness.

Going home to an empty house on Christmas morning can be a desolate thing.

This is what I faced the year that I received my most beloved Christmas gift. I was scheduled to work night shift on Christmas Eve, from 7:00 P.M. to 7:00 A.M. My family of origin lived several hours away and would be going to church, opening their gifts, having Christmas dinner. I would be working during most of these events and sleeping during the remainder. Eventually, when the celebration was nearly over, and I had attained some much-needed sleep, I would make the trip home.

It was a bitterly cold winter night when I arrived for work. The wind bit through my uniform and whipped at my face. The parking lot was nearly empty, as the hospital was down to a skeleton crew. I made my way through the lot, the corridors and to the elevator that would deliver me to my floor. Cursory glances at those around me revealed a subdued mood. But when the elevator doors opened on my floor, I could sense excitement. I thought maybe there were carolers on the unit, or that a favorite patient was going home to be with his family for one final Christmas. All of the nurses, coming on shift and going off shift, were milling around the desk at the nurses' station. This was rather unusual, because change of shift tends to be a very busy event, with not much time for idleness.

After I clocked in, I made my way to the nurses' station to find out what was going on. When I rounded the corner, all of my coworkers were waiting for me with big smiles. Anticipation was hanging in the air, as heavy as the big red garland hanging from the pillars of the station. I knew something big was up, and that they were waiting for me to be a part of it. Just then, one of my coworkers stepped forward, and I realized that I was not just a part of it... I was it.

This kind and gentle person, whom I had not felt especially close to before that moment, had done a most amazing thing. She had celebrated an early Christmas Eve with her daughter so that I could have the shift off, and go home to be with my family. Another coworker had taken her shift, and two more had split that person's shift. My coworkers, my friends, my family; the line of demarcation was shifting irrevocably and the definitions were melding together at that moment. Happy tears filled my eyes as I was escorted back to the elevator and offered best wishes. By the time I reached the parking lot, I was crying in earnest. The tears froze to my cheeks as I reached the car.

There was hardly any traffic as I sped along the deserted roads toward home that night. Most anyone who was going somewhere was already there. The stars twinkled in the black sky, and I sang along in hearty voice to the Christmas carols playing on the radio. The air was frigid, and I was alone on long stretches of highway. But I was not alone in my heart, for it was filled with gratitude and wonder. My coworkers had given me the greatest Christmas gift I had ever received—their gift of friendship, understanding and insight into my world. Because of that gift, and the sweet memories of that night, I would never be alone on Christmas again.

~Susan Stava
Chicken Soup for the Working Woman's Soul

77

Christmas –
Military-Family Style

*I*was a child of the Great Depression and all its deprivation. World War II soon followed, which brought rationing. Food was rationed, especially sweets and sugars, fats and oils. Red meat was nonexistent, although fish and fowl were occasionally available. Shoes were rationed (two pairs per year), as was gasoline. Many "luxury" items were scarce. Car manufacturing had ceased.

In 1944, my husband was stationed at Peterson Field, Colorado, as a four-engine plane instructor. Each day, he walked through the commissary and PX, looking for Chux (the first disposable diapers), baby furniture or anything that we might use for our crawling ten-month-old. On one of these forays, just before Christmas, he bought a twenty-three-pound frozen turkey and a white enamel combinet (diaper pail) with a lid, to be used later when the baby outgrew the disposables.

Just as my husband hunted for bargains, I economized with food, and everything else, by following the admonition of the ladies' society at church: Use it up, wear it out; make it do, or do without. I knew that everyone was experiencing similar circumstances, but that didn't calm my panic. My mother-in-law was coming for Christmas dinner, and to see her first and only grandchild. I had only seen my husband's immediate family three times since our wedding.

Now, twenty months and seven moves into our marriage, his mother, father and younger brother were coming for Christmas—and would be sampling my cooking!

The only winterized summer cabin at Green Mountain Falls served as our living quarters. From our front picture window, we could see the twin-engine mail plane flying against the incredibly beautiful winter snow and icescape each morning and night. But I had to forget the beauty for the moment and focus on Christmas dinner!

Our cabin had a coal furnace in the basement, a huge six-burner coal stove in the kitchen and a two-burner kerosene burner, which is what I used to heat water and for the small amount of cooking I did. There were several small saucepans and a teakettle—no large pots or kettles. No roasting pan. No dishes.

My husband found several things at the post stores. He bought sturdy paper plates and cups. We had eight place settings of sterling flatware, plus a few serving spoons. There were a few pieces of my early American crystal still intact after all the moves, that could possibly be used for service vehicles—a punch bowl, a smaller bowl, a few salad plates.

The family arrived on Christmas Eve. We drove down to the Antlers Hotel and ate lunch there. We went sightseeing at the Garden of the Gods. We visited the new Broadmoor Hotel ice-skating arena, and treated our guests to an evening meal there.

Back at the cabin, I went to sleep still nervous and wondering how on earth I would feed them the next day. I would learn quickly.

The next morning, while I was still bathing and dressing the baby, my mother-in-law spied the as-yet-unused combinet and latched on to it, hauling it off to the kitchen, where she ordered Dad to fire up the monstrous coal range. Mom scalded the pail and its lid at least six times. She disjointed the turkey and managed to fit it all in, along with salt, pepper, onion, basil, sage, poultry seasoning and goodness knows what else—anything she could find. Soon our cabin had the most delightful aroma of Christmas dinner. She made use of the cabin's percolator by adding cinnamon and other spices to mull some apple cider. Grinning, Dad kept reminding us frequently to "Keep close check on that slop jar; that slop smells good and I would hate for it to scorch." We sat down to what seemed like the most delicious of feasts.

What a great lesson in improvising and making do I learned from my mother-in-law, not only on Christmas day but throughout that wonderful weeklong visit. Dad taught me the value of pleasantness and humor throughout a testy situation. That will always be my most memorable Christmas, when far from home, we turned war and rationing into a holiday of food, fun and family unity.

~Marjorie H. Lewis
Chicken Soup for the Military Wife's Soul

A Tale of Two Christmases

And the Grinch, with his Grinch-feet ice cold in the snow, stood puzzling and puzzling, how could it be so? It came without ribbons. It came without tags. It came without packages, boxes or bags. And he puzzled and puzzled 'till his puzzler was sore. Then the Grinch thought of something he hadn't before. What if Christmas, he thought, doesn't come from a store. What if Christmas, perhaps, means a little bit more.
~Dr. Seuss

I have many happy memories of Christmas when I was a child, but there are two in particular that stand out from the others. The first took place when I was in the sixth grade; the second a year later.

Dad would line up five kitchen chairs in the living room (one for each of us kids) after we had gone to bed on Christmas Eve. Out of coat hangers, he had made hooks that fit over the backs of each chair; on each, he hung the large red and green Christmas stockings my mother had made for each of us. Presents too big to fit into our stockings were placed on and under the chairs.

On this particular Christmas morning, Mom and Dad were sitting on the couch at one end of the living room watching us hastily tear into the packages. Excited yells of "Look what I got—look what I got!" added to the din we made as we played with each toy briefly before discarding it and ripping into another present.

I don't remember what gifts I received, but it wasn't the presents that made that Christmas memorable.

We had finished opening the last of the packages when my younger brother John and I happened to glance over at our parents, who were still sitting on the couch. Both of their faces were lit with beaming smiles.

"Mom and Dad," asked my brother, puzzled, "why are you smiling? You didn't get anything."

At the time, I didn't give much thought to my brother's question—or to my parents' actions. After all, I had gotten what I wanted. All was well with the world, and I expected that future Christmases—because of the presents I would receive—would bring me even greater feelings of joy.

The next holiday season began like all the others. My friends and I reminded each other on a daily basis of how much time remained until Christmas. Weeks turned into days, until finally, Christmas Eve arrived. It was the day before "the Big One."

I went to bed that night as excited as I had ever been. Thoughts of all the wealth I would soon inherit filled my head. It was rough, but somehow I managed to drift off to sleep.

Finally, Christmas morning arrived. Being the oldest, I felt that it was my solemn duty to lead the stampede to the presents—and so I did. The ripping of paper was punctuated with the usual excited squeals of happiness and the shouts of "Look what I got!" as my brothers and sisters noisily showed off each newly opened gift.

I was tearing the wrapping from my second present when I noticed that something was wrong. Pausing to take a quick inventory of my emotions, I realized that my feverish excitement of the night before was gone. Well, no need to panic yet, I thought. After all, the first present had been the usual can of Planters peanuts from my dad, so maybe the present I was now opening would restore my excitement to its proper level. Encouraged by that thought, I finished opening the package. Inside was a plastic rocket. It could be partially filled with water, pressurized with the included plastic pump, then launched about 30 feet into the air. My younger brother

John was practically drooling all over it with envy. And I... didn't even want it.

A third and final present proved to be equally unexciting, so, bored, I picked up my toys and carried them to the dining room table.

Mom and Dad noticed my let-down look.

"Terry," my dad said above the laughter of the other children, "you missed a present. It's under your chair."

Unexcitedly, I opened a small, white, two-inch-square box. Inside was a Westclox brand pocket watch. I had never owned any watch before, and while I decided that this present was definitely the most practical one of an otherwise sorry lot, I was still very disappointed. The Spirit of Christmas, it seems, had left me.

Vanished.

Poof!

Gone.

I was trying to come to grips with this unexplained emptiness when suddenly I remembered my brother's question to my parents the previous Christmas when he had asked: "How come you're smiling? You didn't get anything."

Something happened inside me then. I looked over at my mother and father, who were sitting in their usual positions on the couch. The same beaming smile as before was on their faces. Maybe, I thought, they knew something I didn't, so I walked over to the couch and sat down beside them.

And I watched.

A different kind of Christmas began for me then. I found myself smiling broadly at the delight a brother or sister would display upon opening a present. I felt particularly pleased when a small gift I had bought for one of them was given more appreciation than it really deserved. I felt pride when one of them would come to me requesting my help in putting together a toy or a game.

That year, just like Dr. Seuss's Grinch, I found out that Christmas doesn't always come in a box. That year, Christmas — for me — came in the shining eyes and joyous smiles of my younger brothers and sisters. My one regret was that they couldn't see what I was seeing from my position on the couch.

They just didn't know how much fun they were missing!

~Terry Tippets
Chicken Soup for the Latter-day Saint Soul

Christmas Joy

Christmas, children, is not a date. It is a state of mind.
~Mary Ellen Chase

*I*n one terrible September, both my mother and sister were killed in a tragic car accident. That December, I couldn't imagine celebrating Christmas.

Christmas? How would I ever crawl through this holiday? Joy to the world? How could I rejoice and be merry when my heart was splintered apart? I, who had always gloried in the joys and wonders of Christmas, wanted to wipe the day off the calendar. But having two small daughters, I numbly moved through all the usual preparations.

As the days moved closer to Christmas, my sorrow deepened and I found myself immersed in the quicksand of self-pity. Wasn't it enough that I had a helpless and handicapped child, and hardly any financial resources? Add the crushing blow of both my mother and sister being killed, and it was more heartache than I could carry.

On the twenty-third of December, I was so deep into the pit of tears, I could hardly function. That evening, my heart aching, I despondently started out for a walk. The magic of Christmas was everywhere: fresh snow, star-sprinkled skies, lighted trees in the windows, wreaths on the doors and candles shining.

As I dragged along, I imagined that everyone was happy except for me. Passing the house of a neighbor, it began to seep into my memory that her husband had died, and this would be her first Christmas alone. I looked at the next house: They were having horrendous problems with their teenager. In the next home, behind those lighted windows, were sorrowing parents, for they had lost a child in the spring.

Silently I walked through our little town, and as I passed each home, for the first time in months, I began to remember other people's suffering instead of my own, and to realize I was not the only person life had punched in the solar plexus. There was hardly a household that didn't have sorrow or tragedy. Did not everyone bear their own burdens and cry their own tears?

Back home, standing at the window, I glanced down the hill at the house on the corner. Within those walls lived a mother, her four children and their grandmother. There were no twinkling lights or wrapped packages under that roof. Everyone in town was aware of their plight and struggles, and although my financial resources might be slim, theirs were downright precarious. What type of Christmas would they be having? Would the little girl, who was my youngest daughter's age, receive a doll or any toy? What would they have for Christmas dinner?

Empathy began to awaken me and nudge the edges of my grief. It dawned on me that I had found the key to unlock myself from misery, for there—right under my nose—was someone worse off than myself. If I could gather my strength and forget about me, I could make a difference in a family's Christmas.

December twenty-fourth was a flurry of activity. I called people and they called others, resulting in a steady stream of cheerful givers crossing my threshold. By afternoon, an amazing assortment of toys, clothing and food was piled high on my dining room table.

Heather, my five-year-old daughter, helped me, while Audrey, my handicapped daughter, looked on. Together we wrapped packages, fixed a box with the makings of a complete dinner and shared the excitement.

Night came, and we were at last finished. Leaving Audrey with her father, Heather and I loaded the overflowing boxes in the car and coasted down the hill. It was exhilarating to creep from car to porch, sliding the boxes across the wooden boards, all the while tiptoeing and whispering "Sh-h-h-h." When everything was deposited, we knocked on the door and ran like rabbits. We tumbled into the ditch and peered out from behind a bush.

The porch light blazed on. The little girl who was Heather's age opened the door, stood in the glow of light looking at boxes with wrapped gifts spilling out and began jumping up and down, shouting, "Christmas has come! Christmas has come!"

The family crowded onto the little porch, laughing and shouting, the children taking out packages and calling out the names on the tags, the light from within and without shining over them. Then, with merriment, they took everything inside, closed the door, flicked off the porch light and everything was silent.

There in the darkness and stillness of the night, peace poured into my soul, wrapping its sweet warmth around my heart. The warmth didn't extinguish sorrow... but made it bearable. It didn't wipe out memories... but softened them, so I could once more welcome happiness.

Heather and I scrambled up from the ditch, and I hugged my daughter close while we softly laughed. I had found the secret: In reaching out to others, we heal ourselves; in giving happiness, we receive our peace; and in rising above our sorrows, we find our joy. My soul was filled, for there on that lovely winter's eve, Christmas came into my heart!

~Phyllis Volkens
Chicken Soup for the Mother's Soul 2

80

A Jewish Christmas Story

*E*very year, after Thanksgiving, I long for the first signs of Christmas. I delight in the appearance of the green twigs, red ribbons and silver balls, sprinkled with artificial snow. The fat Santa amusing children in department stores and the big tree at Rockefeller Center fill me with excitement. Yet, I am Jewish, and in my own home Hanukkah is celebrated. So why does Christmas mean so much to me? I would like to tell you my own "Jewish" Christmas story.

It is Christmas Eve, 1942. I am eleven years old. I live in Poland, a predominantly Catholic country where Christmas is widely celebrated. I am fascinated by the Christmas atmosphere. I am also cold, hungry, tired and very much afraid.

For the entire month of December, German soldiers have searched the Jewish quarter of our small town, looking for children and old people. Since they cannot work or bring any benefit to the Third Reich, they are to be "eliminated." The victims are rounded up, assembled in an old courthouse and taken to be killed in a small forest at the outskirts of town. Most of my friends are not here anymore.

I have been hiding with my mother, who is not old but whose hair turned prematurely gray at the beginning of the war. We have changed our hiding place several times. Once, we were caught and then miraculously set free. We have hidden in cellars, attics, barns and other improbable places. We do not bathe or eat hot meals. We live like hunted animals, just escaping our predators, always on the run. We have finally run out of hiding places and returned to the ghetto.

My parents know that my chances of surviving are nil, so as a last resort they contact Frania, the woman who worked for us as a housekeeper before the war. She is a deeply religious Catholic woman and was with our family since before I was born.

Frania comes to our small, shabby apartment on Christmas Eve. She figures that on that night, the guards at the entrance of the ghetto will be drunk and more lenient. Her estimation proves to be correct. She has no trouble entering the forbidden area. She is appalled by our living conditions. She remembers our affluent, prewar lifestyle.

She does not take long to make up her mind. She has nothing to gain and everything to lose. If she is caught hiding me, she will be tortured and hanged in the middle of town, as a warning to others. We have all witnessed such scenes. Yet without hesitation, she tells me to get ready. She promises my parents that she will take good care of me and after the war raise me as her own daughter. There is almost no chance that my parents will survive. Frania is a plain woman. She never went to school and she cannot read or write. She is not a woman of big words, but her heart is very big—made of gold.

It takes me no time to prepare. I am always ready to run. In the preceding four weeks, I have never taken off my clothing. I wear my entire wardrobe: two dresses, a sweater, some underwear and an old coat that belonged to my late brother. Because I am skinny, I fit easily into all these clothes. By wearing everything I own, I stay warmer and nothing can be stolen. Frania covers my black hair with a woolen cap. My pale, starved face is bundled with a big scarf. I am protected against the cold and my non-Slavic looks are camouflaged. I realize that I will never see my family again, yet I do not cry. I do not know how to cry. I hug my parents. Frania takes my hand and tells me not to be afraid. She calls me by my old pet name and we go.

Nobody stops us as we leave the ghetto. We are accompanied by the stars shining in the dark sky as the white snow crunches under our feet. We meet people going to the midnight Mass. We greet them with "Merry Christmas" and Frania starts singing carols. After a while, I join her in singing, and suddenly I am one of the many people in the street singing.

We reach Frania's small apartment. During the day, she works and I hide under a bed. I miss my mother, and I am very sad, yet I do not complain. After several months, Frania realizes that she cannot take the place of my mother and my older sister, so they come, too. We all hide under beds. I do not know how we manage. All the while, Frania's deep faith helps us survive.

We remain with Frania through two more Christmases. Each of them is filled with careful preparations. We make Christmas decorations from scraps of paper, small gifts from old boxes and pieces of fabric. We sit at a festive table and try to bake and cook. The cakes are made of inferior black flour and artificial sweetener. They look sad and lie flat like mud pies.

After two and a half years, the Russians liberate our town and we are freed. Eventually, we are reunited with my father, who returns from a concentration camp. In December 1949, we leave Poland for good. With heavy hearts, we part from Frania. We believe we will never see her again. As the train leaves the station, the last thing I see is her face full of tears. It is heartbreaking, and I have begun to cry again.

Twenty-five years later, I was fortunate enough to see Frania again. She came to visit us in the United States. I did not recognize her at the airport. She was very worn. Her face looked like plowed earth. When we both got over the initial shock — after all, she last saw me as an eighteen-year-old — we resumed our loving relationship. She was the same person I remembered: generous and full of common sense. She spent several weeks with us, cooking my favorite dishes and spoiling my children. She remained modest and never considered herself a hero. According to her, everything happened on Christmas Eve, when people are supposed to love each other and she only did what she had to do.

~Irene Frisch
Chicken Soup for the Jewish Soul

81

Christmas in the Silver Egg

*M*y husband Dave and I have always believed you're never really poor as long as you have hope. And hope was about the only thing we had in the winter of 1948, when we packed up our little boys and left our family and friends in Oklahoma for the "boom town" of Houston, Texas, where we'd been told the streets were paved with jobs.

Knowing that better days were on the way, we cheerfully moved into a trailer court because it was the cheapest place we could find, and we rented the cheapest trailer in the court. It cost thirty dollars a month — inexpensive even by the standards of the times — and we christened it "the Egg" because it was shaped like a silver egg. At times, it didn't seem much bigger than an egg, either, especially with two active toddlers — Mike, age two, and Tony, three and a half. That made four of us trying to live in a teensy trailer not big enough to swing a cat in.

There was only one room in the Egg, and that room served as dining room, kitchen and bedroom; the bathroom was as large as a broom closet. The bed was the size of a train bunk... maybe. David and I had to sleep in each other's arms every night, even if we were mad. But we didn't get mad too often — you can't cuddle up to someone like that without feeling loving, so I figured it was good for our marriage.

Because the boys were so little, we could all four squeeze into the breakfast nook—two seats facing each other, with a table between—if we really scrunched together. At night, that little table collapsed, and the boys slept on top of it.

A full-sized adult could reach from wall to wall if he stood with his arms outstretched. No one did, though, because the Egg wasn't grounded very well, and any time you touched a wall you were in for a shock. Literally. We all learned to walk around leaning inward.

Still, we managed to have a pretty good time. The trailer court was full of nice people and some of them were eccentric enough to delight me. One woman, who became one of my best friends, worked as a hula dancer in a carnival. She tacked her old grass skirts up at her window, parted them in the middle, tied them back, and presto—curtains!

"Isn't that a cute idea?" she asked proudly. I nodded, not daring to trust my voice because I was so full of the giggles.

So it was sort of fun, usually. Then Christmas drew near.

Houston Decembers aren't your snowy, Christmas-card kind of Decembers, but they can be very nice—delightfully warm with brilliant sunshine and even flowers and green grass. Or they can be miserable—chilly rain, gray skies and gloom. That's the kind of Christmas we had that year.

My background is Cherokee, and never before had I so missed my loving, extended family. Our Christmases in Oklahoma might not have been opulent, but they were rich in love, laughter, savory smells of cooking and the earthy aroma of pine filling the house.

The trailer court was a sea of mud that clung to our shoes and came off on the floor the minute we stepped inside. Everything was damp, moldy and cold. Christmas seemed a million years away, but it was only a few days away—and there wasn't any money.

Oh, there was a wee bit. David had a job in a car lot—not selling, just washing the cars and shifting them around the lot. We didn't miss any meals, though the menu was mostly macaroni and cheese.

But when David and I sat down four days before Christmas, we found that, even though we'd saved like crazy, we had less than ten dollars to provide Christmas dinner and gifts for two little boys.

"I guess there isn't going to be any Christmas this year, hon," David said, and for once, his brown eyes weren't sparkling. "No toys for the kids or anything."

Or anything. No grandparents, aunts, uncles and cousins bustling around, laughing and telling tales. No turkey on the carving board or special desserts mounded on the table.

No Christmas tree. In a way, that was the hardest thing for me. The Christmas tree had always been for me the very symbol of Christmas, of love and prosperity. Of hope.

Not that a tree could fit in the Egg anyway.

I clung to David a second longer than usual when he started off to work. My smile was very stiff, for it was rigidly holding back a sob.

That afternoon, the misting rain let up for the first time in days, so I took the kids for a walk. It was rough keeping a couple of little widgets cooped up in something like the Egg.

The wind was raw. We slogged through the mud, frosty hands clasped in each other's. My heart felt as mired as my feet—but Tony and Mike were having a wonderful time. After being shut inside for a couple of days, the outdoors was newly wonderful—especially because Christmas decorations were up all over! The boys splashed through the puddles and laughed with glee as they pointed out wreaths, plastic Santas and Christmas trees in windows.

Suddenly, Tony pointed at the far end of the trailer court. "Look, Mommy, look! A million Christmas trees. Come on, Mommy!"

Mike caught the excitement, and he and Tony towed me along like a couple of tug boats towing a shabby scow.

There weren't a million trees. It was actually a modest little lot, but the trees had been stuck into the ground so they looked like a small forest. The kids and I walked between them. Fir and pine, smelling wet and cold and fresh-smelling like Christmas! The earthy aroma took me back to my childhood Christmases, and my own excitement started building.

Then Tony whispered urgently, "Buy one, Mommy. Buy one now!"

And reality crashed down. There would be no tree for us. It just wasn't fair! They weren't so terribly expensive, but even the cheapest was beyond me. And all around, people were happily picking out this one or that. They were even fussy because the trees weren't absolutely perfect, so they'd ask the lot owner to trim off branches to make them look more symmetrical. How spoiled they were to ask that precious branches be cut off and just thrown away, when I longed so much for just....

My mouth dropped open "... for just one big, beautiful branch," I whispered. Yes, a big branch with a lot of little limbs would look almost like a miniature Christmas tree. In fact, even the smallest tree would be too big for the Egg, but a branch would be just right! Surely I could afford a branch!

I went over and pulled on the owner's sleeve. "How much would a branch cost?" I asked, feeling shy but fierce.

The man, chilled and seeing his trees like a little forest of dollar signs—he probably didn't have much money himself—snarled at me. "Lady, I don't sell branches. You want a tree, buy one. I ain't gonna cut one up just so you can have a branch."

My feelings weren't even hurt. "No, no!" I cried. "I don't want you to cut a branch from a tree. I want one of those." I pointed to the sizable pile of trimmed-off branches.

"Oh, sure," he grunted. "Them. Help yourself."

"How much for a big one?"

"Lady, I told you, I don't sell branches. Take all you want free."

I could hardly believe it! Joy overtook us as the boys and I hunkered down, selecting a branch with all the care that others were taking to pick out a full tree. When we were certain we'd found the most beautiful branch of all, we proudly carried it home, Mike holding the top, Tony holding the bottom, and me supporting the middle.

While my friend with the hula skirt babysat, I ran five blocks to the five-and-ten-cent store. I hid my packages when I got home. Then I retrieved the kids, and we anchored the branch firmly in one corner of the trailer, where it fit exactly. In the Egg, it looked as big as a real Christmas tree.

When David got home, we all decorated it together with a big package of tinsel I'd found for ten cents and some little balls really meant to decorate packages that had cost another dime. When we were done, it was—well, beautiful, that's all. David made a star out of the tinfoil from a found cigarette pack, and we perched it right up at the top. There weren't any lights, but it gleamed and glistened all by itself.

On Christmas Eve, David came home with a fat boiling hen he'd managed to buy for a dollar. She was cheap because she was tough, but no matter. I would boil her and boil her until she became tender, and David would make German dumplings to drop in the rich broth, just like his mother had taught him. He was a wonderful cook.

As that old hen boiled merrily away on the hot plate and the kids were cuddled down asleep on their table-bed, we put toys under the branch—two cars, two trucks, a fire engine and a red and yellow train. All plastic, all less than a quarter, but they looked wonderful. The trailer looked wonderful.

I reached up and kissed David's cheek. Although he was so tall, it was easy to reach him, for of course in the Egg, he was a little bent over. "There once were four people who lived in an Egg," I said.

"Oh, hon, hon!" He put his arm around me and pulled me close. His eyes were twinkling again like dark brown stars, and we stood together in the shadow of our tree, which smelled of Christmas and of magic, of the memory of childhood and of the promise of the future. Of hope.

And we knew we were one of the richest families on earth.

~Mechi Garza
A Second Chicken Soup for the Woman's Soul

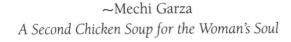

82

A Light in the Darkness

A Christmas candle is a lovely thing;
It makes no noise at all,
But softly gives itself away.
~Eva Logue

Shortly after our fifteen-year-old son, Adam, died, I wanted to do something as a public remembrance of him. I needed to let the outside world know that we were grieving thoroughly for the loss of all that Adam was and all that he would have been. I especially didn't want others to forget my son. Our house is nestled in a clearing in the woods and accessible only by a very long driveway. Passersby cannot see our house from the road. And so, on a blustery November day barely a month after he died, I tied a large white bow for our Adam on a tree by the side of the road at the end of our driveway. It was a sign of love, of hope, of sorrow beyond all comprehension. Throughout the past year, as the bow became tattered and worn, I replaced it several times and have even managed to grow a few white flowers at the base of the tree beneath that white bow. Little else that I have done for my son since he died has held as much significance to me as this white bow, which has come to symbolize Adam's life, death and our grief.

Just prior to leaving for a family gathering at my mother's house on a Christmas day, I was feeling, as I regularly do, that I wanted to do something special for Adam. I made a luminaria with a gold angel on it; my husband, surviving son and I placed the luminaria under the white bow in the small flower garden. There, in the brilliance of a cold, clear Christmas afternoon, we lit a candle for our Adam. We added a second luminaria to burn in remembrance of all the children who have died. No one else could see the candles burning on that bright, sunlit day, but knowing they were there gave me a sense of peace. Last year, our first Christmas without Adam, the day had been unbearable; Adam's absence had been so pervasive. This year, all afternoon while I was at my mother's house, I thought of those luminarias burning by the side of the road for our Adam and all of the children who have died. I was uplifted and embraced by a sense of warmth I had not previously experienced.

It became apparent that those luminarias had also been of great importance to my husband and surviving son, for that evening, as we were preparing to leave my mother's house, we each wondered aloud if the candles would still be burning. Throughout the day, our thoughts of those luminarias had allowed each of us to endure the unendurable, and it now seemed crucial that the candles would still be lit when we returned home. My husband, surviving son and I NEEDED to see that very small flicker of light glowing through the darkness.

The ride home from my mother's house on Christmas night had always been a time of supreme bliss for me; my two boys tucked safely into the backseat of the car, each of us filled with the joy and wonder of the day. I had savored this time and counted my blessings. Last year, our first Christmas without Adam, I wept. But this year, I was focused on those candles and all they represented. We drove home in silence, each of us lost in our own private memories of Adam; each of us wishing that somehow, some way the candles still burned.

As we anxiously approached our driveway, we strained to distinguish a glimmer of light in the darkness of that Christmas night. And YES, the candles remained burning and so much brighter than we had expected! When we reached our driveway, our hearts soared as we saw that there, under the white bow in the very small flower garden by the side of the road, a third candle now burned with our two.

The third candle had been placed by two very caring people who undoubtedly understood the very profound nature of their very compassionate deed. They are bereaved parents as well, who on a cold, dark Christmas night had come to our home to secretly fill our mailbox with small, meaningful gifts. All to be discovered on another day, at another time. What they left behind was a promise of light, perhaps just a small flicker at first, but a light nonetheless, always burning through the darkness of our grief.

~Nina A. Henry
Chicken Soup for the Grieving Soul

83

The Christmas I Was Rich

Poor and content is rich, and rich enough.
~William Shakespeare

There was a tree that Christmas. Not as big and full as some trees, but it hung with all the treasured ornaments and glowed with lights. There were presents, too. Gaily wrapped in red or green tissue paper, with colorful seals and bits of ribbon. But not as many as presents as usual. I had already noticed that my pile of gifts was very small.

We weren't poor. But times were hard, jobs scarce, money tight. My mother and I shared a house with my grandmother and my aunt and uncle. That Depression year, they all stretched meals, carried sandwiches to work and walked everywhere to save bus fares.

Years before the World War II slogan became famous, we, like many families, were living it: "Use it up, wear it out; make it do, or do without." There were few choices.

So I understood why my pile of presents was so small. I understood, but I still felt a guilty twinge of disappointment.

I knew there couldn't be any breathtaking surprises in those few gaily wrapped boxes. I knew one would be a book. Mom always managed a new book for me. But no new dress, or sweater or warm quilted robe. None of the hoped-for indulgences of Christmas.

But there was one box with my name on it. From my grandmother. I saved that box for last. Maybe it would be a new sweater, or even a dress — a blue dress. Grandmother and I both loved pretty dresses, and every shade of blue.

Dutifully ooh-ing and aah-ing over the fragrant bar of honeysuckle soap, the red mittens, the expected book (a new Nancy Drew!), I quickly reached that last package. I began to feel a spurt of Christmas excitement. It was a fairly big box. Ashamed of myself for being so greedy, for even hoping for a dress or sweater (but hoping anyway), I opened the box.

Socks!

Nothing but socks!

Anklets, knee-highs, even a pair of those awful long white cotton stockings that always sagged and wrinkled around my knees.

Hoping no one had noticed my disappointment, I picked up one of the four pairs and smiled my thanks to my grandmother. She was smiling, too. Not her polite, distracted, "Yes, dear," smile, but her sparkling, happy, "This is important woman-to-woman stuff, so pay attention!" smile.

Had I missed something? I looked back down at the box. Still socks — nothing but socks. But now I could see there was another pair under the pair I had picked up. Two layers of socks. And another. Three layers of socks!

Really smiling now, I began taking them out of the box. Pink socks, white socks, green socks, socks in every imaginable shade of blue. Everyone was watching now, laughing with me as I tossed socks in the air and counted. Twelve pairs of socks!

I got up and squeezed Grandmother so tight it hurt us both.

"Merry Christmas, Joan-girl," she said. "Every day now you'll have choices to make — an abundance of choices. You're rich, my dear."

And so I was. That Christmas and all year. Every morning, as I chose which pair of socks to wear from my elegant hosiery wardrobe, I felt rich. And I still do.

Later, my mother told me that Grandmother had been hiding

those socks away for almost a year—saving nickels and dimes, buying a pair at a time; once, seeing a lovely blue pair with hand embroidery on the cuff, she had actually asked the understanding salesclerk to take a deposit and hold it for her for three weeks.

A year of love had been wrapped in that box.

That was a Christmas I'll never forget.

My grandmother's gift, her extravagance of socks, showed me how wonderful and important little things can be.

And how enormously wealthy love makes us all.

~Joan Cinelli
Chicken Soup for Mother's Soul 2

84

The Last Gift

To give and then not feel that one has given
is the very best of all ways of giving.
~Max Beerbohm

On a bright June afternoon, my world turned upside down. Mom called to tell me she had malignant masses in her lungs and was scheduled for surgery the next day. Hundreds of miles away, I felt helpless, but I attempted to comfort my ailing mother. "It will be okay, Mom. I will be there for you." But something told me that it was not going to be okay. Silently, I complained, Why, God? Haven't we endured enough tragedies?

It was hard enough losing my father when I was sixteen. Five years later, a prison escapee murdered my brother.

As I packed hastily to be with Mom, the irony of the moment hit me: I was expecting our second child, while my mother just received a death sentence. What comfort could I bring her in her final weeks?

As I peered around the corner and into her hospital room, I found Mom puttering around as if she were perfectly well. A powerhouse of energy, faith and enthusiasm, this lady was going to hang tight for as long as she was able. Her defining attitude was one of simplicity and grace. As we hugged and talked, it became clear to me that she had put her things in order with no trace of fear or bitterness. I came away feeling small and unnecessary, as if nothing I did could impact her life.

After her surgery, I stayed to help Mom transition back to her home. She deteriorated rapidly. It became apparent that additional care was needed, so a hospice nurse joined our team.

My sister Jill came to give me a break, so I could return to my husband and eighteen-month-old son for a while. I struggled with the idea of leaving Mom, yet I knew she was in the very best hands.

Summer turned to fall and then to winter, then Jill called to tell me Mom's time was drawing close. I took the first flight out, hoping to share Mom's last hours with her. Mom recognized me and gave my hand a squeeze. She faded in and out of consciousness, but her lips moved constantly, as if she were talking to someone. As I drew closer to her bedside, I gasped realizing she was repeating the Lord's Prayer over and over.

On December 23rd, she called everyone to her side. "There's no Christmas present that I need; however, I want to make a request. Will you adopt a needy family as your Christmas gift to me? Buy them some groceries and Christmas presents, and please be as generous to them as you would to me," she whispered lovingly.

Suddenly, our mournful Christmas had a purpose! My brother, Bucky, scurried off to find a needy family through Mom's church. With names in hand, we were off shopping like there was no tomorrow! Each of us went our separate ways with individual grocery baskets, filling them to the brim with ham, turkey, yams, green beans and cranberry sauce. Then came the rolls, stuffing and butter, along with lots of lavish trimmings. The next stop was the toy store, for a doll, a ball, a bat, a jump rope and jacks.

Driving up to the tiny clapboard shack, we wondered who and what we would encounter inside. After knocking lightly on the door, it took a few moments for someone to answer. Finally, a little face with wide eyes peered around the door at us.

"Hello," Bucky cautiously greeted the little boy with the tousled blond hair. "We have some Christmas gifts for you. Is your mother home?"

The door slammed shut. We didn't know whether to run or wait. In an instant, a young girl opened the door. Her mother stood behind her. "Please, come in," they chimed. As we brought in the baskets and boxes, the children's faces wore looks of astonishment. They smiled and chattered among themselves, "Now we'll have a real Christmas!"

A warm feeling of heavenly accomplishment filled our souls. We felt blessed. For months, I had wondered what I could do to comfort my dying mother. Now it had been done with her simplicity and grace. Our Christmas gift to Mom was also her last gift to us.

~Janice Jackson O'Neal
Chicken Soup for the Caregiver's Soul

85

Happy Holidays

*I*n prison, holidays are the worst. Birthdays, anniversaries, Thanksgiving, Christmas, even Valentine's Day can be a "bummer." It's difficult and painful to be away from those we love—to be left out of the celebrations and the memory making. Many times, we feel a little forgotten or overlooked.

Birthdays in prison come and go without the comfort of cake with candles and the magic of blowing them out. Christmas mornings are without a fancy tree or presents. Thanksgivings are hard to feel thankful for, with dinner served on a cold, metal cafeteria tray.

My first Thanksgiving in prison, I refused to eat. My first birthday, I spent alternating between rage and feeling more sorry for myself than ever before. On Christmas, I wouldn't even get out of bed. I stayed under the covers to hide the tears I cried all day.

So holidays in here are the worst—at least I thought they were until I realized a few things. Once I stripped away all the commercialism and hype, I saw what holidays were all about. They're elaborate excuses we use to take a look at our lives, our successes and failures, and to spend quality time with our loved ones.

In here or out there, we can still take stock of ourselves and make plans, dream dreams, examine our behavior to see what we like and don't like. Even in here, we have the power to change what falls short of our ideal self-image.

Not being able to spend quality time with those we love is a little tougher—until we realize that the people we care for are always with us—in our hearts and minds. And just as they're with us, we are with them in spirit.

The days we can't spend together physically, we can still take time to remember them fondly... making phone calls, sending cards or letters helps both us and our loved ones.

Other people don't make us happy. Special places and people might help the mood, but the celebration and love comes from within. The challenge is to find it there—a state of mind, a positive attitude. It's easy to use a holiday as an excuse to be sad or edgy. I've been there. Our challenge is to celebrate every day as special. Life is a precious gift, whether we're in jail or not.

I'm planning a celebration every day this year—a celebration of life. You're invited. Happy Holidays! RSVP.

~Daryl D. Foley
Chicken Soup for the Prisoner's Soul

Chapter 9

Christmas Cheer

The Love of Family

A happy family is but an earlier heaven.
~Sir John Bowring

Red, White and Blue Christmas

Honey, you're gone, you're so far away!
And you know that I miss you each and every day!
Things are so much harder this special time of year.
Because you are my gift, and I wish you were here.
Now don't get me wrong, I'm so very proud,
And I'll be the first to say it out loud.
Although I am lonely, I'll get through each night,
Knowing you're out there to fight for what's right.
Baby, I love you and think you're so brave,
And this Christmas I thank you that my flag proudly waves!

~Roxanne Chase
Chicken Soup for the Military Wife's Soul

87

Chicken Soup for the Soul

A Christmas for Toby

Happiness is a warm puppy.
~Charles Schulz

On Christmas morning, 1950, my parents gave my sister, Alyce, my brother, Chuck and me a black Lab puppy named Toby. I was seven and the youngest.

Toby, just two months old but large for his age, bounded out of his carrying cage, a red ribbon around his neck. Excited, he wagged his mighty tail wildly, and before we knew it, he had knocked over the Christmas tree. Ornaments went flying in every direction. Then Toby's tail got wrapped in the wiring. He dragged the tree across the floor and proudly presented it to my mother.

Mom stood stock-still, squinted her eyes and opened her mouth wide, but no sound came from her. She just stared at Toby through half-opened eyes as his tail continued a vigorous thumping against the wood floor. With every thump, more ornaments fell from the ravaged limbs of the tree, landing in shattered, colorful piles. Finally, Mom opened her eyes wide and yelled, "The tree is ruined!"

"No, Mom. We'll fix it. It'll be like new, but with fewer ornaments," I said soothingly, fearing she would banish Toby from the family. Mom stood motionless as Alyce, Chuck and I untangled Toby's tail from the wiring. I held the squirming pup while my brother and sister reassembled the tree and propped it up against the wall in the corner of the living room.

Dad tilted his head from side to side. "Doesn't look too bad," he said as he rubbed his chin. "It's really not leaning all that much. Could have been worse. Toby's just excited, Mother."

We all studied the tree, forgetting about Toby, whom I had lowered to the floor.

"What's that sound?" Mom asked as we surveyed the room.

"Toby's in the packages!" Chuck shouted. He pointed to the stack of wrapped Christmas presents. "He's tearing the ribbons."

I grabbed Toby again and took him outside to save him from himself—and the need to look for a new home.

A year passed. We all survived the loss of at least one shoe to Toby's teething. Despite his mischief-making, Toby became a beloved member of our family. He grew to be the biggest black Lab anyone in our town had ever seen.

A few days before Christmas, Toby became ill and we rushed him to the animal hospital. The veterinarian thought someone had poisoned Toby during one of his unauthorized outings.

I began to cry. "Can we see Toby for just a few minutes?" I sniffled. "He'll be so lonely without us, and it's almost Christmas."

"Sure," he said. "But be careful not to excite him."

We stood around Toby's kennel. He looked much smaller than the mighty dog we so often caught gliding over the fence. His eyes were sad. His breathing was loud and unsteady.

Dad stuck his large hand through the cage's meshing so he could touch Toby. Tears filled all our eyes when Dad said, "You'll be all right, boy."

Toby lifted his head for a moment, and then dropped it back with a heavy thump against the floor. I heard that thump all the way home as we rode in silence.

The next day, when the bell rang signaling the end of class at Park Hill Elementary, my third-grade schoolmates rushed from the building into the cold December air, eager to start the Christmas holiday. I trudged in silence behind, neither feeling the joy of the season nor wanting to talk to anyone.

My walk home was filled with thoughts of happier moments

when Toby would run to meet me at the end of the driveway each day after school. He'd jump up to lick my face, forcing me to the ground as he tugged at my coat sleeve. Toby only released his grip so he could carry my book bag between his powerful jaws as he marched to the door. He never asked me about my grades or if I had been chosen for the school play. And he never cared if I wore the latest clothing craze.

When I entered the house, I found everyone sitting around the kitchen table. No one was talking. Their heads were bent, their eyes directed at the center of the empty surface.

I dropped my book bag. My eyes stung. "What's the matter? Has something happened to Toby?"

Mom stood and walked to me. "No, dear." She circled her arms around me in a comforting hug. "Toby's alive. But we have another problem. It'll take a family decision. Take off your coat and come sit with us."

I did as Mom instructed, but worry didn't subside. "What's the problem, then? I mean, what could matter if Toby's okay?" A sour liquid rose into my throat.

Dad took my hand. "The vet says that Toby will need to stay in the hospital for another few days."

"That's not so bad. Why's everyone so unhappy? Will he be home for Christmas?"

"Slow down." Dad raised his hand. "Let me finish." He got up from the table to get a cup of coffee from the pot simmering on the old gas stove. He took a sip and turned to us. "The vet isn't positive Toby will recuperate. If we decide to leave Toby in the hospital, we'll have to pay a large bill. There'll be no Christmas presents." He took another sip of the hot brew before he added, "We can't afford both."

This news didn't come as a surprise. "I knew that. But, I still don't see what the problem is." I looked at Alyce and Chuck, who had said nothing. "You two can't want presents instead of Toby. It wouldn't be Christmas without him. We've got to try."

Alyce wrapped her leg around the chair leg. Chuck rubbed the worn spot on the tabletop and spoke first. "I was hoping for a new bike... but, it wouldn't be any fun riding it if Toby wasn't following, barking to make me go faster."

Alyce kept her head lowered toward the empty table. "I really can't think of anything I would want more than Toby," she said.

I jumped from the table. "It's settled then. Tell the vet we'll do whatever it takes to give Toby a chance."

The next two days crawled by. Then the day before Christmas, the vet called to tell us that Toby was going to be okay and was ready to come home.

"Hooray!" I whooped. "We get Toby—again—for Christmas."

For the first time in nearly a week, everyone laughed. Then we all piled into the family Ford. Unlike the silent trip when we left Toby at the hospital, we chattered all the way there, each sharing a favorite Toby story. A few of the more memorable tales brought a scowl to Mom's face, especially the one about last year's smashed Christmas tree.

Though the ride to the hospital seemed interminable, the minutes before Toby's arrival in the waiting room seemed even longer. Finally, the door swung open and out walked Toby, wearing a red ribbon around his neck. He was slower than he had been last Christmas, but he had the same mischievous glint in his eyes.

We all rushed to Toby, hugging and kissing him. His mighty tail thumped in happy response. Mom leaned over, and holding Toby's face between her hands, whispered, "Merry Christmas, Toby."

~Tekla Dennison Miller
Chicken Soup for the Dog Lover's Soul

88

Majestic Moms

Being a full-time mother is one of the highest salaried jobs in my field,
since the payment is pure love.
~Mildred B. Vermont

I was nursing my newborn when my middle son Matthew came in from the thawing front yard. We had had the Texas version of snow—an ice storm—the night before.

"I got all the ice off your car, Mommy!" he chirped.

"Thank you so much, sweetie! How did you do that?" I asked.

"With a bat!"

Just another day in a house full of boys.

I should know—my husband and I have been blessed with three sons, ages three, eight and twelve. I've always had an inkling that there is something pretty special about being the only source of estrogen in a household. One night, during book time, my gut feeling was proven beyond the shadow of a doubt.

We were reading *The Chronicles of Narnia* when one line jumped out at me. The Snow Queen was ordering a minion about, when he replied, "I hear and I obey, my queen!" Well, I just stopped story time right there. "What did he say?"

"I hear and I obey, my queen." My chaotic chorus replied.

"What was it again?"

"I hear and I obey, my queen."

"Oh, just one more time because it makes me happy!"

"I HEAR AND I OBEY, MY QUEEN!" they shouted, dissolving into giggles.

That became our battle cry. I heard it when they were being sweet. I heard it said through clenched teeth when they were annoyed because I stopped the fun to remind them about their chores. I heard it when they knew I was having a bad day and needed a smile.

That year on Christmas morning, the boys presented me with my very own tiara. Made of plastic, it had big purple gems, complete with matching earrings. I tried it on; it fit perfectly, and I declared myself queen of the household.

As my reign went on, I felt the need to share my newfound status with other moms of boys. I broadened my queendom, if you will, and re-coronated myself as Her Royal Highness, The Queen of Lakewood, after the lovely neighborhood we live in.

In April 2002, I held a brunch and invited the eighteen women I could name off the top of my head who were also drowning in testosterone. I hired my boys and some of their friends to be my pages for the brunch. As the moms came up the red-carpeted walk, the boys offered them their arms.

"May I escort you to the festivities, your majesty?"

As the queens entered my castle, they were announced. "Presenting Her Royal Majesty Queen Deb!" the boys shouted in the entryway. I then crowned the queens by placing a tiara on their heads and a glass of champagne in their hands and then sent them off to join the fun.

During brunch, I listened as the moms traded war stories and got advice from each other. One mom, who was our pediatrician, asked for hints on dealing with her middle son, who was more emotional than the other two. "Wow!" I said to myself. "If she has boy-raising questions and is getting ideas and answers from other moms, I may be onto something here." And the wheels started to turn. "What is our common goal?" I asked my reigning queens. Amassed from that conversation, a quest for queens came to me: Take over the world by raising smart, responsible, spiritual, mom-loving boys and have a lot of fun in the process.

In February 2003, I took my mission to the Internet and launched www.itsgoodtobethequeen.com. It started small—just a funny story about my boys posted once a week on the site—then a sign-up to get The Queen of Lakewood's Weekly Address via e-mail. After a profile in a national women's magazine, the queendom grew by leaps and bounds. We have official chapters now, my favorite being in Queensland, Australia.

I added a message board feature and sat back to watch the queens chat. Sometimes it's about favorite TV shows, party ideas or money-saving tips. Sometimes it's about handling temper tantrums and potty training. And sometimes it's about the yearning for a daughter or the overwhelming grief of losing a pregnancy. I am so proud of the fact that a mom can be all alone in the middle of the night with a feverish baby and help is just a mouse-click away. These moms are family, to me and to each other. On this journey through momhood that is the most unexpected blessing.

Recently, a mom, Queen Bethany, e-mailed me:

My husband puts his arm around me and says to our three-year-old, Cole, "This is my wife." Cole's response is always, "No, Dad. She's my life!"

Mission accomplished.

~Linda Marie Ford
Chicken Soup for the Mother and Son Soul

89

My Christmas Wish

Home is a shelter from storms — all sorts of storms.
~William J. Bennett

It became a very sad Christmas for us when we found out why Grandpa had been so sick lately. The doctors called my family to tell us that Grandpa had cancer. If that wasn't bad enough news, we learned that we wouldn't be able to have Christmas at home with him because he would be in the hospital getting treatment. We went to visit him on Christmas Day, but he was too weak to really enjoy celebrating with us.

Over the next nine months, he was admitted to many hospitals and was continually moved from room to room: from ICU to private room, etc. I could hardly keep up with where he was.

One day, while Grandpa was watching TV in the hospital, he saw a commercial with a Jack Russell Terrier that was shown flying through the air to the slogan, "Life's a journey — enjoy the ride." Grandpa fell in love. When my Uncle Shane went to visit him, Grandpa wouldn't stop talking about "that cute little dog on the commercial." To humor him, Uncle Shane found a picture of a Jack Russell Terrier just like the one in the commercial. He brought it to the hospital and hung it on the wall of my grandfather's room. Whenever Grandpa moved to another room, he brought the picture with him.

By September, Grandpa wasn't improving like the doctors expected he would, so they told him he should see a special doctor in Dallas. Everyone agreed, and Grandpa was flown by air ambulance to another hospital in Texas.

One day, as we were chatting with him on the phone, Grandpa told us, "I want a Jack Russell Terrier, and I am going to get one when I get well." We realized then that the thought of getting a little terrier was encouraging him to keep going and was giving him hope.

Months passed and Grandpa had several surgeries to help him beat the cancer. He was still very weak, so I wondered if he would be home for Christmas. As December arrived, having Grandpa home with us on Christmas became the only thing I wished for. Every night, I prayed that my wish would come true.

Then right before Christmas, the doctors said he could go home. With some help from Uncle Shane, my grandpa would be able to leave the hospital and begin his journey back home.

My whole family was excited to get the news. It had been a long, hard year for all of us. Since Grandpa would be coming home on Christmas Eve, everyone wanted to do something extra special for him this year. As soon as a Jack Russell Terrier was mentioned, we knew that it was the surprise that would really make Grandpa happy. It was the kind of dog that Grandpa had looked at every day on his hospital wall, the dog that kept my grandpa hoping to get well. So, for days, my mom, uncles and aunts searched the ads in the papers looking for a real Jack Russell Terrier puppy to give to Grandpa.

Finally, the day before Christmas Eve, we found a home that had Jack Russell Terrier puppies for sale. I helped pick out just the right one that I knew would make my grandpa very happy.

The following evening, as we were sitting by the fire playing with the puppy, we got a phone call from Uncle Shane saying that he and Grandpa were stuck in New York City because of a storm. They wouldn't be making it home that night. We were all so disappointed. Before I fell asleep, I prayed once again that Grandpa would make it home for Christmas. He was so close!

I woke up Christmas morning to wonderful presents under the tree. But even though they were all things that I liked, they didn't make up for not having Grandpa home. Throughout the day, my family waited anxiously to hear from Uncle Shane again. Finally, we couldn't take it anymore and decided to just go over to Grandpa's house and wait there. We played games, did jigsaw puzzles and tried to enjoy the day, but by late in the afternoon, we were getting sadder by the minute.

Then suddenly, we heard someone coming up the front stairs. I peeked out the front door to see my uncle holding my grandpa in his arms. He had to carry him because he was so weak from the long trip.

We all screamed when they came through the door. They were finally home! Suddenly, the puppy began barking from all of the excitement. You should have seen the look on my grandpa's face. I can't remember seeing him smile that big in my life. He was so happy! All night long, the puppy, which he named Tara, and Grandpa, snuggled together in Grandpa's favorite chair.

Before Christmas day had ended, the only thing I had wished for had come true.

Grandpa was home.

~Megan McKeown
Chicken Soup for the Soul Christmas Treasury for Kids

90

Stolen Christmas

He is a wise man who does not grieve for the things which he has not,
but rejoices for those which he has.
~Epictetus

When I was a child, our Christmas Eve rituals never varied. First, we sat down to an all-fish dinner—which I absolutely dreaded—followed by a talent show run by my bossy older cousin. At midnight, we attended Mass and then, in the wee hours of Christmas morning, we opened some of our presents at Grandma's house.

The year I was seven, my mother, three brothers and I made the long drive home from Grandma's house. Finally, Mom eased the car slowly into our driveway. As she got out of the car, she told us later, she had a strange feeling in the pit of her stomach.

Leaving us safely sleeping in the car, my mother entered the house. But as soon as she opened the door, she realized we had been robbed. She immediately took a short inventory of the house, to make sure that the robbers were gone and to see exactly what had been stolen.

As she surveyed our small home she discovered that food from our freezer—mostly chopped meats and frozen vegetables—and her meager life savings, the nickels, dimes and pennies that she saved in a container hidden in her underwear drawer, were missing. It wasn't much, but to a single mother living on a limited income, the loss was devastating.

Then to her horror, she saw that the robbers had also taken our Christmas tree, the presents, even the stockings—leaving only a few name tags and a roll of wrapping paper. While other parents were putting the finishing touches on bicycles and dollhouses, she stood gazing at the spot where the Christmas tree had been, too heartsick to cry. It was two in the morning. How was she going to fix this? But fix it she would. Her children were still going to have a Christmas. She would see to that.

Carrying us in one by one, my mother put us to bed. Then she stayed up for what was left of the night and, using buttons, cloth, ribbon and yarn, made handmade gifts of finger puppets and shoelaces.

As she sat and stitched, she remembered the Christmas tree lot around the corner, certainly abandoned for the season by then. Just before dawn, she slipped out and came back with a small broken tree, the best one she could find.

My brothers and I woke up early that morning excited to see what Santa had brought us for Christmas. Our house was filled with the wonderful smell of blueberry muffins and hot chocolate. We hurried to the living room and stopped in the doorway, confused by the strange magic that had turned our beautiful Christmas spruce, glittering with decorations, into a small, bare, pear-shaped tree leaning against the wall.

When my little brother asked my mother what had happened to our tree and stockings, she hugged him tight and told us that someone really poor had needed them. She told us not to worry because we were very lucky; we had the most important gift of all—God's love and one another.

As she filled our cups with the steaming hot chocolate, we opened our gifts. After breakfast we made Christmas ornaments from old egg cartons and cereal boxes. Together we laughed, sang carols and decorated our new tree.

It is an odd thing: Although I do not remember now what I got for Christmas when I was five, ten or even thirteen years old, I have never forgotten anything about that strange and wonderful Christmas the year I was seven. The year someone stole our Christmas and gave us the unexpected gift of joyous togetherness and love.

~Christina Chanes Nystrom
Chicken Soup for the Mother's Soul 2

91

Keeping the Connection

The hardest arithmetic to master
is that which enables us to count our blessings.
~Eric Hoffer, Reflections On The Human Condition

As a mother grieving the loss of a child, the road ahead stretches long and difficult. Not having had the opportunity to complete your child's life to adulthood breaks a mother's heart over and over again. You wonder every day what he is doing. Is he okay? You pray that he is happy.

My first Christmas without my son, Justin, was a painful struggle. I just couldn't find the strength to decorate a tree with all the beautiful ornaments Justin and my daughter, Stephanie, had made over the years. Instead, I decorated my elderly mother's tree and my family shared Christmas with her. It helped us survive the first year.

The next year, I summoned the courage to put up the Christmas tree with lights, but once again Justin and Stephanie's precious ornaments remained packed away. That's as far as I got, but it was a major step.

Justin had loved Christmas, and for the sixteen years of his life he had always helped put up the tree. In fact, since Stephanie had been away at college, he'd taken charge of the decorating. He always assembled the nativity scene under the Christmas tree, a job he especially enjoyed. My father had made the manger using barn boards from my grandfather's barn, and I had painted the figures in a ceramics class, so it had a very special meaning to our family.

By our third Christmas, I felt stronger. I needed a connection to the Christmas times past when Justin had been alive. This time I put up the tree and lovingly decorated it with the children's ornaments. Then I went to get the box containing the nativity manger and ceramic figures, which had not been touched for three years.

As I looked inside the barn board manger, I discovered a tiny little Christmas card. The front of the card showed a picture of a little boy carrying lots of Christmas cards to be delivered. I opened the card and read the inside verse:

If I could just pick up and leave
I'd start this minute, I believe
To be with you on Christmas Eve.

At that moment, I knew I'd make it—not only through the holidays, but also through the long journey ahead of me without Justin. I never found out how the card got into the manger, but I viewed its presence there as a gift from my son. In my heart, I knew the tiny card with its message of wanting to be together for Christmas Eve was my much-needed connection to Justin. It would see me through that third Christmas, and ever after.

~Patricia Chasse
A 5th Portion of Chicken Soup for the Soul

92

Christmas Lights

Before my dad died, Christmas was a bright, enchanted time in the long, dark winters of Bathurst, New Brunswick. The cold, blizzardy days would sometimes start as early as late September. Finally, the lights of Christmas would start to go up, and the anticipation would build. By Christmas Eve, the ordinary evergreen tree that my father dragged in the door ten days earlier took on a magical, sparkling life of its own. With its marvelous brilliance, it single-handedly pushed back the darkness of winter.

Late on Christmas Eve, we would bundle up and go to Midnight Mass. The sound of the choir sent chills through my body, and when my older sister, a soloist, sang "Silent Night," my cheeks flushed with pride.

On Christmas morning I was always the first one up. I'd stumble out of bed and walk down the hall toward the glow from the living room. My eyes filled with sleep, I'd softly bounce off the walls a couple of times trying to keep a straight line. I'd round the corner and come face-to-face with the brilliance of Christmas. My unfocused, sleep-filled eyes created a halo around each light, amplifying and warming it. After a moment or two I'd rub my eyes and an endless expanse of ribbons and bows and a free-for-all of bright presents would come into focus.

I'll never forget the feeling of that first glimpse on Christmas morning. After a few minutes alone with the magic, I'd get my younger brother and sister, and we'd wake my parents.

One November night, about a month before Christmas, I was sitting at the dining room table playing solitaire. My mother was busy in the kitchen, but was drawn from time to time into the living room by one of her favourite radio shows. It was dark and cold outside, but warm inside. My father had promised that tonight we would play crazy eights, but he had not yet returned from work and it was getting near my bedtime.

When I heard him at the kitchen door, I jumped up and brushed past my mother to meet him. He looked oddly preoccupied, staring past me at my mother. Still, when I ran up to him, he enfolded me in his arms. Hugging my father on a winter night was great. His cold winter coat pressed against my cheek and the smell of frost mingled with the smell of wool.

But this time was different. After the first few seconds of the familiar hug, his grip tightened. One arm pressed my shoulder while the hand on my head gripped my hair so tightly it was starting to hurt. I was a little frightened at the strangeness of this and relieved when my mother pried me out of his arms. I didn't know it at the time, but my dad was suffering a fatal heart attack.

Someone told me to take my younger brother and sister to play down in the recreation room. From the foot of the stairs, I saw the doctor and the priest arrive. I saw an ambulance crew enter and then leave with someone on a stretcher, covered in a red blanket. I didn't cry the night my father died, or even at his funeral. I wasn't holding back the tears; they just weren't there.

On Christmas morning, as usual, I was the first one up. But this year, something was different. Already, there was a hint of dawn in the sky. More rested and awake than usual, I walked down the hall toward the living room. There was definitely something wrong, but I didn't know what until I rounded the corner. Then, instead of being blinded by the warm lights, I could see everything in the dull room. Without my dad to make sure the lights on the tree were glowing, I could see the tree. I could see the presents. I could even see a little bit of the outside world through the window. The magic of my child-hood Christmas dream was shattered.

The years passed. As a young man, I always volunteered to work the Christmas shifts. Christmas Day wasn't good, it wasn't bad; it was just another gray day in winter, and I could always get great overtime pay for working.

Eventually, I fell in love and married, and our son's first Christmas was the best one I'd had in twenty years. As he got older, Christmas got even better. By the time his sister arrived, we had a few family traditions of our own. With two kids, Christmas became a great time of year. It was fun getting ready for it, fun watching the children's excitement and most especially, fun spending Christmas day with my family.

On Christmas Eve, I continued the tradition started by my dad and left the tree lights on for that one night, so that in the morning, my kids could have that wonderful experience.

When my son was nine years old, the same age I was when my father died, I fell asleep Christmas Eve in the recliner watching Midnight Mass on TV. The choir was singing beautifully, and the last thing I remember was wishing to hear my sister sing "Silent Night" again. I awoke in the early morning to the sound of my son bouncing off the walls as he came down the hallway toward the living room. He stopped and stared at the tree, his jaw slack.

Seeing him like that reminded me of myself so many years ago, and I knew. I knew how much my father must have loved me in exactly the same complete way I loved my son. I knew he had felt the same mixture of pride, joy and limitless love for me. And in that moment, I knew how angry I had been with my father for dying, and I knew how much love I had withheld throughout my life because of that anger.

In every way, I felt like a little boy. Tears threatened to spill out and no words could express my immense sorrow and irrepressible joy. I rubbed my eyes with the back of my hands to clear them. Eyes moist and vision blurred, I looked at my son, who was now standing by the tree. Oh my, the glorious tree! It was the Christmas tree of my childhood!

Through my tears the tree lights radiated a brilliant, warm glow. Soft, shimmering yellows, greens, reds and blues enveloped my son and me. My father's death had stolen the lights and life from Christmas. By loving my own son as much as my father had loved me, I could once more see the lights of Christmas. From that day forward, all the magic and joy of Christmas was mine again.

~Michael Hogan
Chicken Soup for the Canadian Soul

The Unwrapped Gift

Gratitude is the memory of the heart.
~Jean Baptiste Massieu

"**M**om," came the frantic call from my teenage daughter's bedroom, "Come here quick!"

I opened one eye, still tired from the last-minute details of Christmas Eve, and was on my feet just as Jennifer cried out again. Waves of dizziness struck me, almost knocking me back into bed. What was going on?

I managed to make it to my daughter and saw her sitting up, pale-faced and holding her stomach. She looked like I felt.

"What's the matter, Jennifer?" I asked.

"Mom, I've got the stomach flu, and it's Christmas!"

"Well, if it's any consolation, I don't feel so great myself." And, with that, I ran to the bathroom. I lay on the cold tile and thought, *Oh, God, why today of all days? Not today, Lord, not today.*

By now, my husband, hearing all the commotion, was up preparing breakfast. He assumed our noisy hoopla was the excitement of Christmas morning. Popping his head into the bathroom he said, "Bacon and eggs are on when you're ready." A closer look and he discovered his faux pas and slipped quietly back out of the room.

Our other two children went to church with him while Jennifer and I moaned encouragement to each other across the hall. After an hour of this, I thought, "This is silly... we certainly can't catch anything from each other, so why not bunk together?"

Jennifer came and got in our king-size bed with me. We spent the day talking, sucking ice chips and sleeping. When we were awake, we talked about boys, life at her new high school and friends she had made when she had changed schools midyear.

I told her how hard it was to be a working mother and still stay on top of all the family activities. I confessed that I had missed sharing with her lately, and we made a pact to spend more time together. We told each other secrets, giggled and laughed at our predicament. We became closer that day than we had been in a long time.

Many years have passed, and my daughter is grown with a husband and two children of her own. Yet not a Christmas goes by that one of us doesn't say, "Remember the Christmas when...?" We both laugh, knowing we received a gift that year better than any we found under the tree.

~Sallie Rodman
Chicken Soup for the Mother & Daughter Soul

The Healing Power of Love

We dreaded Christmas that year. It was 1944, and the war would never be over for our family.

The telegram had arrived in August. Bob's few personal possessions, the flag from his coffin, the plan of his burial site in the Philippine Islands, and a Distinguished Flying Cross had arrived one by one, adding to our agonizing grief.

Born on a Midwest prairie, my brother rode horseback to school but wanted to fly an airplane from the first day he saw one. By the time he was twenty-one, we were living in Seattle, Washington. When World War II broke out, Bob headed for the nearest Air Force recruitment office. Slightly built, skinny like his father, he was ten pounds underweight.

Undaunted, he persuaded Mother to cook every fattening food she could think of. He ate before meals, between meals and after meals. We laughed and called him "lardo."

At the Navy Cadet Office he stepped on the scale—still three pounds to go. He was desperate. His friends were leaving one after the other; his best buddy was already in the Marine Air Corps. The next morning, he ate a pound of greasy bacon, six eggs and five bananas, drank two gallons of milk, and, bloated like a pig, staggered back on their scales. He passed the weigh-in with eight ounces to spare.

When he was nominated Hot Pilot of primary training school in Pasco, Washington, and involuntarily joined the "Caterpillar Club" (engine failure causing the bailout) at St. Mary's, California, we shook our heads and worried. Mother prayed. He was born fearless, and she knew it. Before graduating from Corpus Christi, he applied for transfer to the Marine Air Corps at Pensacola, Florida. He trained in torpedo bombers before being sent overseas.

They said Bob died under enemy fire over New Guinea in the plane he wanted so desperately to fly.

I never wept for Bob. In my mind's eye, I pictured my debonair big brother wing-tapping through the clouds, doing what he loved best, his blue eyes sparkling with love of life. But I wept for the sadness that never left my parents' eyes.

Mother's faith sustained her, but my father aged before our eyes. He listened politely whenever the minister came to call, but we knew Daddy was bitter. He dragged himself to work every day but lost interest in everything else, including his beloved Masonic Club. He very much wanted a Masonic ring, and at Mother's insistence he had started saving for the ring. Of course, after Bob died, that too ceased.

I dreaded the approach of Christmas. Bob loved Christmas. His enthusiasm excited us long before reason took over. His surprises were legendary: a dollhouse made at school, a puppy hidden in mysterious places for little brother, an expensive dress for Mother bought with the very first money he ever earned. Everything had to be a surprise.

What would Christmas be without Bob? Not much. Aunts, uncles and Grandmother were coming, so we went through the motions as much for memory as anything, but our hearts weren't in it. Dad sat for longer and longer periods, staring silently out the window, and Mother's heart was heavy with worry....

On December 23rd, another official-looking package arrived. My father watched stone-faced as Mother unpacked Bob's dress blues. After all this time, why oh why did they—the nameless they—send his dress uniform, I thought bitterly. Silence hung heavy. As she refolded the uniform to put it away, a mother's practicality surfaced, and she went through the pockets almost by rote, aching with grief.

In a small, inside jacket pocket was a neatly folded fifty-dollar bill with a tiny note in Bob's familiar handwriting: "For Dad's Masonic ring."

If I live to be a hundred, I will never forget the look on my father's face. Some kind of beautiful transformation took place—a touch of wonder, a hint of joy, a quiet serenity that was glorious to behold. Oh, the healing power of love! He stood transfixed, staring at the note and the trimly folded fifty-dollar bill in his hand for what seemed an eternity; then he walked to Bob's picture hanging prominently on the wall and solemnly saluted.

"Merry Christmas, Son," he murmured, and turned to welcome Christmas.

~Mary Sherman Hilbert
A 6th Bowl of Chicken Soup for the Soul

95

Big Red

The first time we set eyes on "Big Red," father, mother and I were trudging through the freshly fallen snow on our way to Hubble's Hardware store on Main Street in Huntsville, Ontario. We planned to enter our name in the annual Christmas drawing for a chance to win a hamper filled with fancy tinned cookies, tea, fruit and candy. As we passed the Eaton's department store window, we stopped as usual to gaze and do a bit of dreaming.

The gaily decorated window display held the best toys ever. I had an instant hankering for a huge green wagon. It was big enough to haul three armloads of firewood, two buckets of swill or a whole summer's worth of pop bottles picked from along the highway. There were skates that would make Millar's Pond well worth shovelling and dolls much too pretty to play with. And they were all nestled snugly beneath the breathtakingly flounced skirt of Big Red.

Mother's eyes were glued to the massive flare of red shimmering satin, dotted with twinkling sequin-centred black velvet stars. "My goodness," she managed to say in trancelike wonder. "Would you just look at that dress!" Then, totally out of character, mother twirled one spin of a waltz on the slippery sidewalk. Beneath the heavy, wooden-buttoned, gray wool coat she had worn every winter for as long as I could remember, mother lost her balance and tumbled. Father quickly caught her.

Her cheeks redder than usual, mother swatted dad for laughing.

"Oh, stop that!" she ordered, shooing his fluttering hands as he swept the snow from her coat. "What a silly dress to be perched up there in the window of Eaton's!" She shook her head in disgust. "Who on earth would want such a splashy dress?"

As we continued down the street, mother turned back for one more look. "My goodness! You'd think they'd display something a person could use!"

Christmas was nearing, and the red dress was soon forgotten. Mother, of all people, was not one to wish for, or spend money on, items that were not practical. "There are things we need more than this," she'd always say, or, "There are things we need more than that."

Father, on the other hand, liked to indulge whenever the budget allowed. Of course, he'd get a scolding for his occasional splurging, but it was all done with the best intention.

Like the time he brought home the electric range. In our old Muskoka farmhouse on Oxtongue Lake, Mother was still cooking year round on a wood stove. In the summer, the kitchen would be so hot even the houseflies wouldn't come inside. Yet, there would be Mother—roasting—right along with the pork and turnips.

One day, Dad surprised her with a fancy new electric range. She protested, of course, saying that the wood stove cooked just dandy, that the electric stove was too dear and that it would cost too much hydro to run it. All the while, however, she was polishing its already shiny chrome knobs. In spite of her objections, Dad and I knew that she cherished that new stove.

There were many other modern things that old farm needed, like indoor plumbing and a clothes dryer, but Mom insisted that those things would have to wait until we could afford them. Mom was forever doing chores—washing laundry by hand, tending the pigs and working in our huge garden—so she always wore mended, cotton-print housedresses and an apron to protect the front. She did have one or two "special" dresses saved for church on Sundays. And with everything else she did, she still managed to make almost all of our clothes. They weren't fancy, but they did wear well.

That Christmas I bought Dad a handful of fishing lures from the

Five to a Dollar store, and wrapped them individually in matchboxes so he'd have plenty of gifts to open from me. Choosing something for Mother was much harder. When Dad and I asked, she thought carefully, then hinted modestly for some tea towels, face cloths or a new dishpan.

On our last trip to town before Christmas, we were driving up Main Street when Mother suddenly exclaimed in surprise: "Would you just look at that!" She pointed excitedly as Dad drove past Eaton's.

"That big red dress is gone," she said in disbelief. "It's actually gone."

"Well... I'll be!" Dad chuckled. "By golly, it is!"

"Who'd be fool enough to buy such a frivolous dress?" Mother questioned, shaking her head. I quickly stole a glance at Dad. His blue eyes were twinkling as he nudged me with his elbow. Mother craned her neck for another glimpse out the rear window as we rode on up the street. "It's gone..." she whispered. I was almost certain that I detected a trace of yearning in her voice.

I'll never forget that Christmas morning. I watched as Mother peeled the tissue paper off a large box that read "Eaton's Finest Enamel Dishpan" on its lid.

"Oh Frank," she praised, "just what I wanted!" Dad was sitting in his rocker, a huge grin on his face.

"Only a fool wouldn't give a priceless wife like mine exactly what she wants for Christmas," he laughed. "Go ahead, open it up and make sure there are no chips." Dad winked at me, confirming his secret, and my heart filled with more love for my father than I thought it could hold!

Mother opened the box to find a big white enamel dish-pan—overflowing with crimson satin that spilled out across her lap. With trembling hands she touched the elegant material of Big Red.

"Oh my goodness!" she managed to utter, her eyes filled with tears. "Oh Frank...." Her face was as bright as the star that twinkled on our tree in the corner of the small room. "You shouldn't have..." came her faint attempt at scolding.

"Oh now, never mind that!" Dad said. "Let's see if it fits," he laughed, helping her slip the marvellous dress over her shoulders.

As the shimmering red satin fell around her, it gracefully hid the patched and faded floral housedress underneath.

I watched, my mouth agape, captivated by a radiance in my parents I had never noticed before. As they waltzed around the room, Big Red swirled its magic deep into my heart.

"You look beautiful," my dad whispered to my mom — and she surely did!

~Linda Gabris
Chicken Soup for the Canadian Soul

96

How Much Love Can You Fit in a Shoebox?

Feeling gratitude and not expressing it
is like wrapping a present and not giving it.
~William A. Ward

On a cold and rainy February morning, my mom, four brothers and I cleaned out Dad's apartment. There were a thousand places we would have rather been, but we were together and the rest of the world seemed distant. With Dad's funeral scheduled for the next day, it was all I could do to take my mind off the reality of his heart attack. Everything he owned was in his apartment. He wasn't materialistic, yet every belonging seemed priceless. His countless drawings filled every room. His notepads of sketches he drew in the hospital had a flavor of who he really was. His deteriorating car and torn furniture didn't begin to describe what made him successful in my eyes.

He took life one day at a time, never taking anything too seriously. It was his best quality... and his worst. I was thirty-seven years old and had grown up much like him, putting tremendous value on the little things in life.

I moped around from room to room, gathering souvenirs and

throwing out the garbage he never had the chance to. As I turned the corner and entered his bedroom, I quickly spotted his prized possession. It was a letter from my eight-year-old nephew declaring his unconditional love for his grampa—how much he loved him, loved fishing with him and how he hoped he would never die. Dad's heart melted and eyes watered whenever he spoke of the letter. It touched him deeply. He proudly displayed it to anyone and everyone. I gathered the cleanup crew to read it one last time. We all seemed to realize where this letter belonged—with Dad, forever.

My mind wandered back to the time I wanted to write a similar message to Dad. It was less than a year ago when I sat down to write. My heart wanted to fill the page with the traits and values I had grown to respect. Before a single word was written, my head took over and I realized Dad could never keep such a letter to himself. Even if he promised never to show it to my brothers, I somehow knew his good intentions would eventually be overtaken by his heartfelt pride. I'd be too embarrassed expressing such feelings at this point in my life. Besides, my actions had always spoken louder than words, so I didn't write it. Knowing Dad was indestructible, I always figured there'd be time.

As the years rolled on, it bothered me that I never wrote that letter. My mom wasn't getting any younger, and thoughts of not having thanked her for all the things she had done for me started creeping in. Now, instead of feeling embarrassed, I wanted to include my brothers in this project. Christmas was only a month away, and what a great present this could be for all of us to write about something we'd never thanked her for. We all had to write something because if one of us declined I knew she'd put more weight on why one didn't write anything.

It would not be an easy task to get my brothers to write. I needed a plan.

I was committed to the point of listing my brothers' names in order from who I imagined was the easiest to convince to the hardest. I determined Bob would be the easiest. He always got along with Mom. Gary would be second. He usually mailed a Mother's Day card. Mark was next. He hadn't spoken to her for six months. Even worse, he had four kids who weren't seeing their gramma, and I knew Gramma missed the kids. Rick lived in Rochester and, except for the occasional ninety-minute obligatory trips to Buffalo to see her, he had limited contact with Mom.

We all crafted our reasons for not staying in contact with Mom. My brothers and I didn't intentionally alienate her, but we didn't seem to go out of our way to stay in touch either. She seemed the perpetual martyr, and her words and tone of voice left us upset to the point where the frustration her words created overpowered our understanding of her hurt.

I sat by the phone, frozen in my thoughts. This would either happen or it would be the most embarrassing idea I ever shared with my brothers.

So there I was... nervous... shaking... feeling all the insecurities that kept me from writing Dad. By now, the "what ifs" were coming faster than my hands were moving toward the phone. But this time, I was determined to succeed or be humiliated.

So I picked up the phone and called Bob. I explained what I wanted to do, why I wanted to do it and what my plan was. To me, Bob was a given, no problem, just a matter of explaining the game plan. When I got done with my two-minute speech, there was a pause at the other end. "Well, it would have been a lot easier if we had written one for Dad!" he said with deadpan reasoning.

Yikes! What kind of an answer was that? I thought. This brother was the "for sure." Under other circumstances, I may have crumbled and agreed with him, but this was not the direction I had committed to take. So I restated, "Putting that aside, can you think of something you've never thanked Mom for?"

"Sure," he said.

"Well, could you write a letter and have it ready to hand me on Christmas Eve when the family gets together at Mom's house?"

"All right, I'll do it!" he stated without further hesitation. I hung up the phone, and my first thought was, Good, I have one in the bank. I could use that to enroll brothers number two, three and four.

It was a plan. I hadn't expected Bob to give me any resistance, so I knew the job wasn't going to get any easier.

Gary was next. He replied in the sensitive, caring fashion I had anticipated. "How long does it have to be, and what do we have to say?"

Mark was next. I was nervous before I called him. Not only hadn't he spoken to Mom in months, I knew he was mad at her. I started my conversation by explaining the idea and that Bob and Gary had already agreed. I was expecting my hardest time with Mark.

I'll never forget what happened next.

As I finished, he started right into a story. "I remember when I was in junior high school and got suspended for something I didn't do. I got sent home, and Mom asked me, 'Did you do it?' I said, 'No!' She took me back to school to face Mr. Schaefer, the most feared disciplinary teacher any student ever encountered. We marched into his office, and before I knew it, Mom was screaming at him, saying, 'If my son said he didn't do it, he didn't do it.' When she was done with him, he was somewhere under the desk apologizing for his obvious mistake."

Mark's story rolled off his lips as if it happened yesterday. I was shocked because not only had I never heard that story, but he recalled it so vividly.

Rick was next. He had a similar story to Mark's from back in high school. Besides Bob, Gary and Mark had already agreed, and my work actually seemed to get easier. It was like my brothers' stroll down memory lane rekindled a different message and memory they had of Mom. I hopefully put them back to a time when she was always there, as if she had never left. Four in the bank, at least verbally.

Two days before Christmas Eve, I called all four brothers, and each had finished his letter. My final instructions to them were to bring the letters to Mom's, and I was going to put all five into a shoebox I had wrapped to give to her.

Christmas Eve arrived. I handed the box to Mom and said, "This present is from all of us. Do not open it until tomorrow." She looked puzzled, wondering what we were up to, but agreed and said, "Thank you."

Christmas Eve was always fun at Mom's, but this year it was special for me. I knew I pulled off something I couldn't have imagined. As my brothers and their families gathered to open presents, this year was different. Closer... nicer... warmer.

I drove home that night with the greatest feeling of accomplishment. I recalled Mom talking to the grandkids and laughing all night long. Maybe the night was special for everyone. We all seemed a lot closer to her that night, or maybe it was just me hoping it was all this way again.

Christmas morning the phone rang. It was Mom. She told me how she couldn't wait until morning to open the shoebox. She read all the letters three times and cried herself to sleep. She said, "I knew you were the one responsible for doing this, and it was wonderful." I told her we were all responsible for doing this, and it was long overdue.

I never knew what my brothers wrote in their letters, not completely. As for me, I included a story of when I was ten years old and wanted to go to a sports competition. I can't remember the exact words, but it went something like this: "No one seemed to feel it was a big deal, but you saw the disappointment in my face and said, 'I'll take you.' You sat in the rain for over an hour as I tried my best to win a prize. I don't think I ever thanked you, but it meant a lot to me."

I also told her how hard it must have been for her to raise five boys with all of us being a little closer to Dad. "We knew he got the easy job of playing good guy while you were forced to be the one who disciplined us when we were bad. You were the one who taught us right from wrong, fair and unfair, and to apologize when we were wrong. You did that, and I thank you."

Mom had longed to hear such words for years. It was always in our hearts but never got translated to her. I always saw her cry after cooking Thanksgiving dinner. She would prepare all day, while Dad, my brothers and I gobbled it up and proceeded to the living room to tend to our own priorities.

I see a lot of Mom and Dad in me, and I couldn't be happier. I started out wanting to do something for Mom to show her how we felt. We got to revisit our appreciation for her and how she had always been there for us.

In hindsight, I really did it for Bob, Gary, Mark, Rick and me.

I hung up the phone that snowy Christmas morning, reclined on the couch and looked up to imagine Dad wiping a tear from his eye.

Seems everyone got something special out of this Christmas.

~Jim Schneegold
A 6th Bowl of Chicken Soup for the Soul

97

Nickled and Dimed

*Don't let the fear of the time it will take to accomplish something
stand in the way of your doing it. The time will pass anyway;
we might just as well put that passing time to the best possible use.*
~Earl Nightingale

I was sitting at my desk involved in paperwork one sunny May afternoon when the door opened, and a young boy, about nine or ten, came into the store.

He walked confidently toward me and said he wanted to purchase a gift for his father. His serious countenance made it obvious: This was a mission of importance.

As we wound through the furniture division of Loy's Office Supplies, he expressed dismay at the cost of each chair and lamp. Finally, I suggested a desk-pad set. With eyes glowing, he thoughtfully chose a maroon faux leather unit with matching pencil cup, memo holder and letter opener. His joy nearly matched my own—the whole process ate two hours of my time—and we headed toward my desk to finalize the sale.

"Okay, I'll be in every week to pay on this for my dad," said young Michael Murphy.

"And you'll pick it up just before Father's Day?" I asked.

"Oh, no, ma'am. This is for Christmas."

My mouth gaped as wide as my eyes when he handed me his

first payment: a nickel and two dimes. But that day changed all of our lives at Loy's.

As the months passed, neither rain nor snow kept Michael away. Week after week, he arrived promptly at four o'clock every Friday to make his payment. His mother stood outside during each recorded transaction, and one day I asked to meet her.

From her, I learned that Michael's father was out of work. She took in laundry and ironing to eke out a living for the family of seven. I felt badly, but I respected their pride and refusal of help. But with the approach of winter, all of us at Loy's noticed Michael wore only a thin sweater, no matter how deep the snow. We concocted a story about a stray coat left at the store—that just happened to be his size. It worked.

One day Michael ran in to announce he had a job—bringing in the newspaper and sweeping the front steps for an old lady down the street every day after school. The ten cents she paid each week would bring him closer to his purchase.

As the holiday season drew near, I feared Michael would not have enough money to pay off the gift, but my boss advised me not to worry.

Two days before Christmas, a dejected Michael came into the store. He hadn't earned enough money to make his final payment.

"Could I please take the present for my dad so he'll have it for Christmas?" His eyes bored straight into my own. "I promise I'll be in after Christmas to finish paying it off."

Before I could answer, my boss looked up.

"Why, young man, there's a sale on desk sets today." He glanced at a paper in his hand. "I think it's only fair that you get the sale price, too."

That meant his dad's gift was paid for!

Michael raced outside to tell his mother. Amid teary hugs and broken thank-yous, we sent them on their way, with Michael clasping the precious, gift-wrapped present to his chest. All of us were proud of Michael's commitment to his project and his devotion to the dad he loved so much.

A few weeks after Christmas, a shabbily dressed man came into Loy's and limped directly to my desk.

"Are you the lady my son Michael talks about?" His voice was gruff and as oversized as the man himself.

When I nodded, Mr. Murphy paused. He cleared his throat.

"I've just come to thank you for all your help and patience. We don't have much," he picked at his worn glove, "and I still can't believe that youngster would do this for his old dad. I'm awful proud of him."

Rising from my chair, I walked around the desk to give him a hug. "We think Michael is pretty special, too. As we watched him pay off that desk set, it was clear he loves you very much."

Mr. Murphy smiled in agreement and walked away. But as he approached the door, his head swiveled my way and he blinked back the tears.

"And you know what? I don't even own a desk!"

~Binkie Dussault
Chicken Soup for the Soul The Book of Christmas Virtues

98

The Puzzle

I grew up on a farm in Iowa, the youngest of four boys. My dad had made it through the eighth grade and then started working. My mom was the valedictorian of her small high school class, but started working on the family farm rather than going to college. Even though neither had gone to college, education was very important in our house. My parents said that they didn't care if we read comic books, so long as we were reading. I later realized that they were two of the more intelligent people I would ever meet, but when I was in high school, I thought they were incredibly dumb. I am not sure if my brothers felt the same, but I could not wait to get away from home and go to college.

I first saw the Rockwell picture during the Christmas season of my sophomore year at college. It hit me with a lot of emotions I didn't know I had inside me. I was walking with my girlfriend (who eventually became my wife) down an aisle of jigsaw puzzles, utterly bored. Puzzles had never been part of my family, but they were very popular in hers. The picture caught my eye because it had been made into a puzzle. I took one look at it and went to pieces.

The son could have been me: anxious to go to school, looking beyond the father, not considering what he might be thinking. I was the son who went to college and never wrote home. The father represented what I thought of my father: a hard-working farmer wondering about his son, but not able to express his thoughts or his feelings.

The final straw was the collie. When I was growing up, we had a beautiful collie named Lassie.

I immediately started crying and bolted from the store. My girlfriend finally found me, standing outside with tears running down my cheeks. I took her back inside and showed her the puzzle and started crying again. She gave me the strangest look. Emotional outbursts were not something Iowa farm boys did.

I bought the puzzle and wrapped it up for Christmas for Dad. I added a note: "Dad, I got this present, not because it was a jigsaw puzzle, but because of the picture on it. Somehow, it really struck home when I saw it." I had some concern about giving it because it was an emotional gift. Emotions were not something easily shared among the males in our house.

Christmas morning came, and I kept a close eye on Dad when he picked up my gift to open. I really did not know what to expect — whether to be excited or embarrassed. Dad took off the paper and looked at the box, his expression never changing. It was clear to me that he did not think much of the present. Just as well — we never did puzzles in our house. He put the box down and without a word left the room. After about a minute, Mom noticed he was gone. She went out to the kitchen and found Dad crying. She could not understand what had happened.

When Mom brought Dad back into the family room and I saw Dad crying, I started crying and laughing at the same time. I had never seen my dad cry before. Dad showed Mom the picture. He explained that when he saw that the father had a tobacco bag just like the one he used to roll cigarettes, the emotions became too much. Like any good farmer, he did not think it was right to cry in front of his family, so he had left the room. My older brother somehow missed the magic of the moment and looked at us both as if we were losing it.

I have often wondered how Norman Rockwell drew a picture with details that fit our family so perfectly: the eager son, the weathered father, the collie and the tobacco bag. If we had paid him to paint a picture summarizing the first eighteen years of my life, he could not have done better. We put the puzzle together and Mom glued it to a board so they could hang it in their bedroom.

Dad is now eighty-four and slowed by Parkinson's disease. I live in Minneapolis and visit him several times a year. A few years ago, Dad decided to give us a hug when we were leaving. He said he did not want to die without hugging his boys. It has taken years to get used to a hug from him.

Every time I drive back to Iowa to see my parents, I think of the picture hanging in their bedroom. It still reflects what I think of my dad. How he worked so hard to get us through college, something he really did not understand, but knew was important. How he never really told us how much he thought of us. And I am still ashamed by how it embodies me at that time. How I went to college never thinking how my parents might feel about me, just ready to get away. I still get tears in my eyes when I think of that picture.

Several years ago, I decided I would talk about this picture when the time came for my father's funeral, and how this picture was able to say things to my dad on that special Christmas that I was not able to say myself. But then I thought, "Why am I going to wait? Let me write it down now so Dad can read about it while he is still alive." So I have. Only one more thing to say: "I love you, Dad."

~Jerry Gale
A 5th Portion of Chicken Soup for the Soul

Father of Fortune

Son, you outgrew my lap, but never my heart.
~Author Unknown

Once again, the Christmas season was upon us. And once again, my daughter Tania was asking, "What do you want for Christmas, Dad?"

"The usual," I replied. After twenty-three years, she knew that this meant boxer shorts and some happy socks, the kind that help that tender old bunion. These were Christmas rituals for me.

In the small town of Peterborough, Ontario, where we lived, life had a certain rhythm, and the festive season was full of ritual. After living in Calgary for many years, I had returned to my hometown to be near my own aging dad, and life took on a fairly predictable sort of rhythm. But this particular year, my daughter, Tania, and her young husband, Barry, changed all that.

Every day for two weeks prior to Christmas, unable to contain her excitement, she repeatedly said, "You'll never guess, but you're going to love what we got you for Christmas!" The girl was relentless in her teasing and her quest for my reaction. She was determined that I should be impressed.

Now, I'm no Scrooge, so please don't get me wrong. I'm simply one of those individuals who's been around for some time and who's gotten a bit cynical and hard to impress. I must admit, however, that it was fun to watch and listen to her excitement and enthusiastic teasing day after day. Her joy and anticipation of my reaction to this special gift was contagious. By the morning of Christmas Eve, I had become more than a little curious.

At 11:00 A.M. on the 24th, my wife and I were asked to join the kids for some last-minute shopping. We elected to opt out. My wife wanted to finish up her own festive preparations, and old Dad, well, I just wanted a cold beer and a snooze. Four hours later, the kids were back at the door, shopping mission completed.

"We have your gift out in the car, Dad," Tania exclaimed, "and it's getting cold!"

We were then not asked, but ordered to vacate the premises. No, not just to another room, but upstairs and out of sight with an emphatic, "No peeking!" command. Heck, my old army sergeant was gentler. "Get out! Get out!" Tania ordered.

So, obediently, we retreated upstairs.

The minutes passed in that odd kind of anxious, wondering, quiet anticipation that makes butterflies in your stomach. We strained our ears but couldn't hear anything.

"Big deal," I grumped to myself. "I'm still not impressed, but I'll play their silly game."

Then we heard them hollering, "Okay, you can come down now!"

Descending the stairs, we were directed into the front room where the surprise Christmas gift was waiting to be opened. Immediately, my excited daughter said, "No waiting until Christmas morning. Open it now!"

"Okay," I said. "This is highly irregular, this is breaking the ritual... but what the heck is it?" I wondered out loud. The three-foot-square, irregularly shaped lump over by the tree was smothered under blankets. Out came Tania's camera, and the guessing game started in earnest.

"Maybe it's a pinball machine," my wife offered.

"No, no," I said. "It's gotta be something perishable, otherwise they wouldn't have been so anxious to bring it in out of the cold. Maybe it's a crate of Florida oranges, or maybe it's a puppy!"

By now, my daughter was about to explode with excitement, and I, too, had passed the stage of mildly curious, feeling somewhere between inquisitive and demanding.

"What on earth can it be?" I asked as I felt the lumpy object, looking for a clue. My daughter sharply rapped my knuckles with a classic, "Da-ad!"

Finally, we arrived at the unveiling. "Okay," Tania instructed us, "on the count of three both of you grab a corner of the blanket." She stood by with the camera, and even though I was trying my best to remain unimpressed, I'd by now reached an emotional state ranging from paranoia to frustration. My heartbeat sped. My wife and I lifted the blanket in one fell swoop, and the gift was exposed.

The next few minutes were a blur. My heart pounded. The blood rushed to my head. My stomach contracted. My mind jumbled. Overwhelmed with astonishment, I thought, I can't believe my eyes! Perhaps I am delusional! This is just not possible!

The flash of my daughter's camera went off when, rising up out of that heap of blankets and wrapping me in an enormous bear hug was none other than my six-foot-two, one hundred and seventy-five pound first-born son Greg, home for Christmas for the first time in nineteen years!

~Ted Bosley
Chicken Soup for the Father & Daughter Soul

The Gift of Giving

G ram and Gramps lived on the other side of the country, and although we called and wrote often, it had been twenty years since I'd seen them in person. Their health was failing, and age kept them close to home. My responsibilities at home with a husband, two young children and a part-time job, kept me from visiting.

I did make a point of going in March one year. I'd spoken to Gram and realized that, in their eighties now, they weren't going to be around forever—as much as I would like them to be. I made the arrangements and flew there for a week.

The moment I walked in the door, I was home again. The memories from a childhood long past immediately returned. The cookies baking in the warm oven, watching Gram ice the fairy-tale cake and letting me dig in the bowl of icing when she was done. The beautiful clothes she'd sewed, smocked dresses and shorts with pop-tops to match.

As she often did in her letters, she told stories of what I was like as a little girl and how she'd given me Muriel as my middle name. I never told her how much I was teased as a child because of that name—suddenly, it was prettier somehow and its very uniqueness was so like Gram.

Gramps talked of the two wars he lived through, and I told him how proud I was to know he'd served his country so well. He made me laugh, and I believe I made him feel young again, if only for awhile. In turn, he made me cry. He told me that he and Gram had given up on celebrating Christmas about ten years back. They were just too old.

How can one let Christmas pass by unnoticed? I remembered best the Christmas as a child when they lived with us. They loved the season and always went to Midnight Mass. Gramps took my brothers, sisters and me to cut down the tree, while Gram baked every Christmas cookie imaginable, then decorated the tree just so. Our house had been filled with the love and togetherness I had always associated with Christmas. I couldn't believe they had stopped celebrating it.

Gramps explained that they were too old to bother with a tree and their friends too old to travel to see it. Even shopping, now, was too difficult, and they had all of the necessities delivered. I wanted to cry for the joy they'd once had—and lost.

That week remains one of the most joyous of my life. Knowing that it might be the last time I saw either of them saddened me, but I was determined to make it a happy visit. I took the two of them out to dinner—something they hadn't done in well over two years, since Gram had her hip surgery. I know they had a good time.

Saying goodbye was difficult. Gramps, the brave, strong hero of mine, cried and Gram did her best not to. She never succeeded. I cried on the plane all the way home.

As Christmas approached, I thought of them more than ever. I wanted to do something so they would know I was thinking of them. The idea came to give them back Christmas, and I set about to do just that.

First, I found a small artificial tree and decorated it with miniature bulbs and fine gold ribbon. With this, I added colorfully wrapped presents for each of them; slippers, chocolates, a hand-knit scarf for Gramps and a pretty bed jacket for Gram. I made up a box of cookies and bars; many of the recipes were from Gram's cookbooks. Then I filled stockings for each of them with toiletries wrapped and tied with ribbons.

In the card, I wrote that they had given me so many wonderful memories throughout the years that I wanted to give them some new ones. I asked both of them to promise to set the tree up in the living room and stack the gifts around it. My last instruction was, "Do not open 'til Christmas!"

I mailed the parcel, barely able to contain my excitement. Gram called as soon as it arrived. She was crying and, this time, not even attempting to hide it. We spoke for a long time, reminiscing about Christmas past, and when I knew for certain they had the tree up, I promised to call Christmas morning.

When my boys had opened every gift and were digging through their stockings, I made the long-awaited call. Gramps answered on the first ring. I thought he sounded strange, and we only spoke briefly, then Gram took the phone.

"We were like two kids," she told me. "Neither of us got any sleep last night. I even caught Harry in the living room, shaking one of the packages and had to make him go back to bed. Honey, this is the first time in years we've been so excited. Don't tell your grandfather, but after he went to bed, I just had to rattle a few of the gifts myself."

I laughed, imagining the two of them sneaking out to guess at the presents I'd sent. I wished there was more money to send more expensive gifts, and told Gram that maybe next year they would be better.

"Your grandfather can't talk right now because he's too busy crying. He keeps saying, 'That's one heck of a granddaughter we have there, Muriel.'"

~Hope Saxton
Chicken Soup for the Grandparent's Soul

Grandpa's Gift

Grandchildren are the dots that connect the lines
from generation to generation.
~Lois Wyse

Grandpa Louie was quite positively the most respected and well-known man my young eyes had seen. His knowledge of what seemed to be everyone in town was spectacular. Growing up, I watched him answer every question with references, intellect and backing and thrust his love upon each and every person without any need of the love being returned. His volunteer coaching career spanned nearly fifty years, and children were his passion. Loving others was certainly his calling.

But Grandpa Louie didn't do as he did for the return of love, and when he was given a gift, either in thanks or for any certain gift-giving occasion, he frequently had trouble accepting it. I remember it being nearly impossible to purchase anything for him.

One Christmas, while I was still very young, I decided that I wanted to be able to give each member of my family a gift. Being the age I was, I didn't have much money of my own. Most of my gifts were handmade. But Grandpa's I bought. It was a red glossy key chain that simply said "Grandpa." I do not recall how much or how little I spent on the silly little gift, but I was quite proud. One can only imagine how disappointed I was when Grandpa opened it with his characteristic half scowl, nodded at me and then set it aside.

This was just his way, but I was too young to understand how every present could not be means for celebration!

Years passed and somehow I never saw Grandpa's keys or the key chain. He kept them in his pocket, and I was too afraid to ask what had happened to the little red Christmas gift. But I always looked for glimpses when he would arrive at our house with a car full of groceries as a surprise. He brought fruits and vegetables for my mother, ice cream for me and licorice for my brothers. Each time I looked, though, his keys were in his pocket or somewhere out of my sight.

Grandpa grew older, and with time his health declined. His mind and ability to tell stories, however, refused to do the same. One day he seemed worse than ever before, and we quickly took him to the hospital. He had horrid cramps in his legs and had pneumonia. After being checked out, he returned to our family farm to recover. My father took me aside and asked if I would be able to help Grandpa regain his strength at the gym. By this point I was working at a local health club and had dedicated myself to bodybuilding. I gladly accepted the task.

The following weekend Grandpa still had not regained his health, but I visited him nonetheless to talk to him about our personal training sessions. Grandpa sat up in his chair with a tube in his nose, unshaven. I had never seen him unshaven or dressed in such shoddy clothing, since appearance always was important to him. Something wasn't right, but Grandpa smiled anyway. He told me that he heard I was going to be his personal trainer, a thought I beamed at. Then he proceeded to tell me that I would need to pick him up — me, who had just turned sixteen — since he could not drive, and that I should use his car. Then he offered his car to me when he died. I was emotionally torn. I could not imagine my life without Grandpa in it. He then reached into his pocket, brought forth his hand and advised me to go get acquainted with the vehicle. In his hand shined a set of car keys accompanied by an old gray key chain.

Grandpa went back to the hospital later that morning. He slipped into a coma he never came out of. Later that night he died.

The mourning quickly funneled through my family to all in the community. Hundreds upon hundreds showed up for the funeral.

And me? I drove to the funeral in an old, beat-up Mercury, courtesy of Grandpa. At the steering column dangled my own set of keys, with an old gray key chain attached firmly. If you looked closely enough you could still see the little red specks of paint that had clung on all of those years where the word "Grandpa" used to be.

It was the first present I ever gave Grandpa, and the last one he ever gave me.

~Cazzey Louis Cereghino
Chicken Soup for the Teenage Soul IV

Share with Us

We would like to know how these stories affected you and which ones were your favorites. Please e-mail us and let us know.

We also would like to share your stories with future readers. You may be able to help another reader, and become a published author at the same time. Please send us your own stories and poems for our future books. Some of our past contributors have launched writing and speaking careers from the publication of their stories in our books!

Your stories have the best chance of being used if you submit them through our web site, at:

www.chickensoup.com

If you do not have access to the Internet, you may submit your stories by mail or by facsimile. Please do not send us any book manuscripts, unless through a literary agent, as these will be automatically discarded.

Chicken Soup for the Soul
P.O. Box 700
Cos Cob, CT 06807-0700
Fax 203-861-7194

Chicken Soup for the Soul

Christmas Cheer

~More Chicken Soup~
~About the Authors~
~Acknowledgments~

A parent becomes a new person the day the first grandchild is born. Formerly serious adults become grandparents who dote on their grandchildren. This new book includes the best stories on being a grandparent from past Chicken soup books, representing a new reading experience for even the most devoted Chicken Soup fan. Everyone can understand the special ties between grandparents and grandchildren—the unlimited love, the mutual admiration and unqualified acceptance.

978-1-935096-09-2

Dating and courtship, romance, love, and marriage are favorite Chicken Soup topics. Women, and even men, love to read true stories about how it happened for other people. This book includes the 101 best stories on love and marriage chosen from a wide variety of past Chicken Soup books. These heartwarming stories will inspire and amuse readers, whether they are just starting to date, are newly wed, or are veterans of a long marriage.

978-1-935096-10-8

Christmas is... Celebrating

We are all crazy about our mysterious cats. Sometimes they are our best friends; sometimes they are aloof. They are fun to watch and often surprise us. These true stories, the best from Chicken Soup's library, will make readers appreciate their own cats and see them with a new eye. Readers will revel in the heartwarming, amusing, inspirational, and occasionally tearful stories about our best friends and faithful companions — our cats.

978-1-935096-08-5

We are all crazy about our dogs and can't read enough about them, whether they're misbehaving and giving us big, innocent looks, or loyally standing by us in times of need. This new book from Chicken Soup for the Soul contains the 101 best dog stories from the company's extensive library. Readers will revel in the heartwarming, amusing, inspirational, and occasionally tearful stories about our best friends and faithful companions — our dogs.

978-1-935096-05-4

More Christmas Books!

This is Chicken Soup for the Soul's first book written just for Catholics. From the once-a-year attendee at Christmas Mass, to the devout church volunteer and daily worshipper. 101 poignan, spirit-filled stories written by Catholics of all ages, this book cover the gamut, including fun stories about growing up Catholic to serious stories about sacraments and miracles. Whether the reader is a cradle Catholic, a convert, simply curious, or struggling, these stories bestow happiness, hope, and healing to everyone in all stages of life and faith.

978-1-935096-23-8

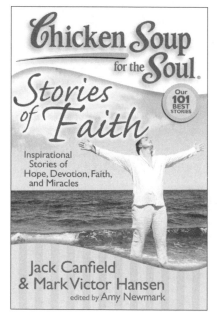

This is the first Chicken Soup book to focus specifically on stories of faith, including 101 of the best stories from Chicken Soup's library on faith, hope, miracles, and devotion. These true stories written by regular people tell of prayers answered miraculously, amazing coincidences, rediscovered faith, and the serenity that comes from believing in a greater power, appealing to Christians and those of other faiths, and everyone who seeks enlightenment and inspiration through a good story.

978-1-935096-14-6

*C*heck out our great books on

This is the first Chicken Soup book, with 101 great stories from Chicken Soup's library, created specifically for Christian parents to read themselves or to share with their children. All of the selected stories are appropriate for children and are about raising Christian kids twelve and under. Christian parents will enjoy reading these heartfelt, inspiring, and often humorous stories about the ups and downs of daily life in today's contemporary Christian families.

978-1-935096-13-9

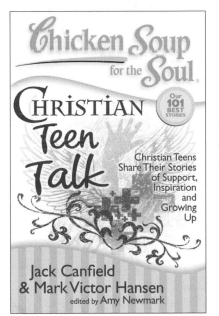

Devout Christian teens care about their connection and relationship with God, but they are also experiencing all the ups and downs of teenage life. This book provides support to teens who care about their faith but are trying to navigate their teenage years. This book includes 101 heartfelt, true stories about love, compassion, loss, forgiveness, friends, school, and faith. It also covers tough issues such as self destructive behavior, substance abuse, teen pregnancy, and divorce.

978-1-935096-12-2

Christian Faith

The Wisdom of Dads

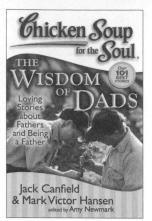

Children view their fathers with awe from the day they are born. Fathers are big and strong and seem to know everything, except for a few teenage years when fathers are perceived to know nothing! This book represents a new theme for Chicken Soup – 101 stories selected from 35 past books, all stories focusing on the wisdom of dads. Stories are written by sons and daughters about their fathers, and by fathers relating stories about their children.

Dads & Daughters

Whether she is ten years old or fifty – she will always be his little girl. And daughters take care of their dads too, whether it is a tea party for two at age five or loving care fifty years later. This wide-ranging exploration of the relationship between fathers and daughters provides an entirely new reading experience for Chicken Soup fans, with selections from forty past Chicken Soup books. Stories were written by fathers about their daughters and by daughters about their fathers, celebrating the special bond between fathers and daughters.

On Being a Parent

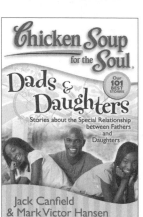

Parenting is the hardest and most rewarding job in the world. This upbeat and compelling new book includes the best selections on parenting from Chicken Soup's rich history, with 101 stories carefully selected to appeal to both mothers and fathers. This is a great book for couples to share, whether they are just embarking on their new adventure as parents or reflecting on their lifetime experience.

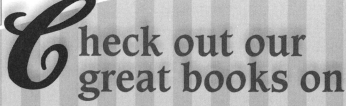

*C*heck out our great books on

Moms Know Best

"Mom will know where it is…what to say…how to fix it." This Chicken Soup book focuses on the pervasive wisdom of mothers everywhere, and includes the best 101 stories from Chicken Soup's library on our percep tive, understanding, and insightful mothers. These stories celebrate the special bond between mothers and children, our mothers' unerring wisdom about everything from the mundane to the life-changing, and the hard work that goes into being a mother every day.

Like Mother, Like Daughter

Fathers, brothers, and friends sometimes shake their head in wonder as girls "turn into their mothers." This new collection from Chicken Soup represents the best 101 stories from Chicken Soup's library on the special bond between mothers and daughters, and the magical, mysterious similarities between them. Mothers and daughters of all ages will laugh, cry, and find inspiration in these stories that remind them how much they appreciate each other.

Moms & Sons

There is a special bond between mothers and their sons and it never goes away. This new book contains the 101 best stories and poems from Chicken Soup's library honoring that lifelong relationship between mothers and their male offspring. These heartfelt and loving stories written by mothers, grandmothers, and sons, about each other, span generations and show how the mother-son bond transcends time.

Who Is
Jack Canfield?

Jack Canfield is the co-creator and editor of the *Chicken Soup for the Soul* series, which *Time* magazine has called "the publishing phenomenon of the decade." Jack is also the co-author of eight other bestselling books including *The Success Principles™: How to Get from Where You Are to Where You Want to Be, Dare to Win, The Aladdin Factor, You've Got to Read This Book,* and *The Power of Focus: How to Hit Your Business and Personal and Financial Targets with Absolute Certainty.*

Jack has recently developed a telephone coaching program and an online coaching program based on his most recent book *The Success Principles.* He also offers a seven-day *Breakthrough to Success* seminar every summer, which attracts 400 people from fifteen countries around the world.

Jack is the CEO of the Canfield Training Group in Santa Barbara, California, and founder of the Foundation for Self-Esteem in Culver City, California. He has conducted intensive personal and professional development seminars on the principles of success for over a million people in twenty-three countries. Jack is a dynamic keynote speaker and he has spoken to hundreds of thousands of others at more than 1,000 corporations, universities, professional conferences and conventions, and has been seen by millions more on national television shows such as *The Today Show, Fox and Friends, Inside Edition, Hard Copy, CNN's Talk Back Live, 20/20, Eye to Eye,* and the *NBC Nightly News* and the *CBS Evening News.*

Jack is the recipient of many awards and honors, including three honorary doctorates and a *Guinness World Records Certificate* for having seven books from the *Chicken Soup for the Soul* series appearing on the *New York Times* bestseller list on May 24, 1998.

To write to Jack or for inquiries about Jack as a speaker, his coaching programs, trainings or seminars, use the following contact information:

Jack Canfield
The Canfield Companies
P.O. Box 30880 • Santa Barbara, CA 93130
phone: 805-563-2935 • fax: 805-563-2945
E-mail: info@jackcanfield.com
www.jackcanfield.com

Who Is
Mark Victor Hansen?

Mark Victor Hansen is the co-founder of *Chicken Soup for the Soul*, along with Jack Canfield. He is also a sought-after keynote speaker, bestselling author, and marketing maven. For more than thirty years, Mark has focused solely on helping people from all walks of life reshape their personal vision of what's possible. His powerful messages of possibility, opportunity, and action have created powerful change in thousands of organizations and millions of individuals worldwide.

Mark's credentials include a lifetime of entrepreneurial success. He is a prolific writer with many bestselling books, such as *The One Minute Millionaire*, *Cracking the Millionaire Code*, *How to Make the Rest of Your Life the Best of Your Life*, *The Power of Focus*, *The Aladdin Factor*, and *Dare to Win*, in addition to the *Chicken Soup for the Soul* series. Mark has had a profound influence in the field of human potential through his library of audios, videos, and articles in the areas of big thinking, sales achievement, wealth building, publishing success, and personal and professional development.

Mark is the founder of the *MEGA Seminar Series*. *MEGA Book Marketing University* and *Building Your MEGA Speaking Empire* are annual conferences where Mark coaches and teaches new and aspiring authors, speakers, and experts on building lucrative publishing and speaking careers. Other MEGA events include *MEGA Info-Marketing* and *My MEGA Life*.

He has appeared on *Oprah*, *CNN*, and *The Today Show*. He has been quoted in *Time*, *U.S. News & World Report*, *USA Today*, *New York Times*, and *Entrepreneur* and has had countless radio interviews, assuring our planet's people that "You can easily create the life you deserve."

As a philanthropist and humanitarian, Mark works tirelessly for organizations such as Habitat for Humanity, American Red Cross, March of Dimes, Childhelp USA, and many others. He is the recipient of numerous awards that honor his entrepreneurial spirit, philanthropic heart, and business acumen. He is a lifetime member of the Horatio Alger Association of Distinguished Americans, an organization that honored Mark with the prestigious Horatio Alger Award for his extraordinary life achievements.

Mark Victor Hansen is an enthusiastic crusader of what's possible and is driven to make the world a better place.

Mark Victor Hansen & Associates, Inc.
P.O. Box 7665 • Newport Beach, CA 92658
phone: 949-764-2640 • fax: 949-722-6912
www.markvictorhansen.com

Who Is
Amy Newmark?

A my Newmark was recently named publisher of Chicken Soup for the Soul, after a thirty-year career as a writer, speaker, financial analyst, and business executive in the worlds of finance and telecommunications.

Amy is a graduate of Harvard College, where she majored in Portuguese, minored in French, and traveled extensively. She is also the mother of two children in college and has two grown stepchildren.

After a long career writing books on telecommunications, voluminous financial reports, business plans, and corporate press releases, Chicken Soup for the Soul is a breath of fresh air for Amy. She has fallen in love with Chicken Soup for the Soul and its life-changing books, and found it a true pleasure to conceptualize, compile, and edit the "101 Best Stories" books for our readers.

The best way to contact Chicken Soup for the Soul is through our web site, at www.chickensoup.com. This will always get the fastest attention.

If you do not have access to the Internet, please contact us by mail or by facsimile.

Chicken Soup for the Soul
P.O. Box 700
Cos Cob, CT 06807-0700
Fax 203-861-7194

Chicken Soup
for the Soul

Thank You!

Our first thanks go to our loyal readers who have inspired the entire Chicken Soup team for the past fifteen years. Your appreciative letters and emails have reminded us why we work so hard on these books.

We owe huge thanks to all of our contributors as well. We know that you pour your hearts and souls into the stories and poems that you share with us, and ultimately with each other. We appreciate your willingness to open up your lives to other Chicken Soup readers.

We can only publish a small percentage of the stories that are submitted, but we read every single one and even the ones that do not appear in a book have an influence on us and on the final manuscripts.

As always, we would like to thank the entire staff of Chicken Soup for the Soul for their help on this project and the 101 Best series in general.

Among our California staff, we would especially like to single out the following people:

- D'ette Corona, our Assistant Publisher, who is the heart and soul of the Chicken Soup publishing operation, and who put together the first draft of this manuscript

- Barbara LoMonaco, our Webmaster and Chicken Soup for

the Soul Editor, for invaluable assistance in obtaining the fabulous quotations that add depth and meaning to this book

- Patty Hansen for her extra special help with the permissions for these fabulous stories and for her amazing knowledge of the Chicken Soup library and

- Patti Clement for her help with permissions and other organizational matters.

In our Connecticut office, we would like to thank our able editors, Valerie Howlett and Madeline Clapps, for their assistance in setting up our new offices, editing, and helping us put together the best possible books.

We would also like to thank our master of design, Creative Director and book producer, Brian Taylor at Pneuma Books, for his brilliant vision for our covers and interiors.

Finally, none of this would be possible without the business and creative leadership of our CEO, Bill Rouhana, and our president, Bob Jacobs.